KU-438-629

A Guide to the Buddhist Path

Sangharakshita

A Guide to the Buddhist Path

Windhorse Publications

Published by Windhorse Publications
Unit 1-316 The Custard Factory
Gibb Street, Birmingham, B9 4AA

First published 1990
Reprinted 1994
Second edition 1996

Design Dhammarati

Illustrations Aloka

Printed by The Lavenham Press, Water Street
Lavenham, Sudbury, Suffolk, CO10 9RN

The cover shows scenes from the life of the Buddha
Courtesy of the London Buddhist Centre

British Library Cataloguing in Publication data
A catalogue record for this book is available from the British Library
ISBN 1 899579 04 4
(First edition 0 904766 35 7)

Also by Sangharakshita:
A Survey of Buddhism
The Three Jewels
Mind – Reactive and Creative
The Essence of Zen
Peace is a Fire
The Thousand-Petalled Lotus *(memoirs)*
Human Enlightenment
The Religion of Art
The Ten Pillars of Buddhism
The Eternal Legacy
Travel Letters
Going for Refuge
Alternative Traditions
Who is the Buddha?
The Meaning of Orthodoxy in Buddhism
Ambedkar and Buddhism
Crossing The Stream
The History of My Going for Refuge
The Taste of Freedom
Vision and Transformation
Learning to Walk *(memoirs)*
New Currents in Western Buddhism
My Relation to the Order
The Buddha's Victory
Facing Mount Kanchenjunga *(memoirs)*
Buddhism and the West
The Priceless Jewel
The Drama of Cosmic Enlightenment
The FWBO and 'Protestant Buddhism'
Wisdom Beyond Words
Forty-Three Years Ago
The Meaning of Conversion in Buddhism
Complete Poems 1941–1994
Was the Buddha a Bhikkhu?
In the Realm of the Lotus
Transforming Self and World
Buddhism for Today – and Tomorrow
Ritual and Devotion in Buddhism
The Inconceivable Emancipation
In the Sign of the Golden Wheel *(memoirs)*

Contents

Part 1

Part 2

Preface

One remarkable feature of the Buddha's spiritual genius was that he reached the goal of his spiritual quest, Enlightenment, without a guide. He made it on his own. He could see, however, that while others too might attain Enlightenment, they would need a lot of help, and so devoted the rest of his life to being a guide. One of the Buddha's titles is 'Shower of the Way'. Fortunately for us, he proved to be just as much a genius at showing others the Way as he had been in rediscovering it for himself. Many of his followers reached Enlightenment as a result of his help. They had to make the necessary effort, to learn, as he put it, to become lamps unto themselves. But their achievement was inspired by the Master's teaching; they would not have done it without his guidance.

Buddhists today need a guide on the Path to Enlightenment just as much as the Buddha's own followers did 2,500 years ago. In some respects they need one even more. There is now a vast Buddhist literature: thousands of pages of canonical scriptures of the different schools as well as countless commentaries by the great Buddhist teachers through the ages. All these millions of words were spoken or written in different languages in different periods of history for particular people or groups of people in specific circumstances, people with varying spiritual needs and from different cultural and social backgrounds. In addition to all this, hundreds of books have been written about Buddhism in the last fifty years, some of them accurate and inspiring, others less so.

If we are to derive spiritual nourishment from the Buddhist tradition, we need someone who can guide us through this daunting mass of literature: someone who is able not only to guarantee the accuracy of the translated word, but also to select and interpret it according to our individual needs. It is so easy, especially at the start of the journey, to be misled. For a very long distance along the spiritual path it is vital that we have someone to steer us away from the possible hazards ahead, someone we can trust to direct our progress towards the Goal.

Such a guide is Sangharakshita, one of the foremost teachers of the Buddha Dharma in the West, and founder of the Friends of the Western Buddhist Order (FWBO). Like all good guides, Sangharakshita knows the terrain extremely well. In the course of the twenty years he spent in India he acquired a firm and deep grounding in Buddhist teaching through systematic meditation and personal study, and benefited from the instruction of eminent teachers from all of the three great traditions of Buddhism, the Hīnayāna, the Mahāyāna, and the Vajrayāna.

Sangharakshita was born in London in 1925. In his teens he came across two Buddhist scriptures: the *Diamond Sūtra*, the famous discourse from the Perfection of Wisdom literature, and the *Platform Sūtra of Hui Neng*, one of the most important scriptures of the Zen School. He was convinced on reading them that he was a Buddhist. After serving in the army in India at the end of the Second World War, he stayed on and took the traditional step of renouncing the household life and 'going forth' in search of spiritual fulfilment. He was later ordained as a monk and studied for a while with the Ven. Jagdish Kashyap, a well-known scholar of the Theravāda School. Sangharakshita gives a vivid account of this period of his life in a volume of memoirs, *The Thousand-Petalled Lotus*.

He then went to Kalimpong, in the foothills of the Himalayas, where he founded his own vihara. There he studied under some eminent Tibetan lamas and the famous Zen hermit, Mr Chen, an expert on the Mahāyāna. He wrote the now well-known *A Survey of Buddhism* and was editor of the *Maha Bodhi Journal* for several years. (Two further volumes of memoirs, *Facing Mount Kanchenjunga* and *In the Sign of the Golden Wheel*, deal with this period.)

In the mid nineteen-fifties, Sangharakshita became intimately involved in helping the many thousands of ex-Untouchable Buddhists in Maharashtra who had converted to Buddhism just before the death of their leader, Dr B.R. Ambedkar. This work was resumed over twenty years later by some of his own Western disciples and culminated in the creation of Trailokya Bauddha Mahasangha Sahayak Gana (TBMSG), as the FWBO is known in India.

In the course of a two-year visit to England in 1964, Sangharakshita became convinced of the vital need for a new Buddhist movement. He therefore decided to move to the West and, in 1967, founded the Friends of the Western Buddhist Order. A year later he ordained the first members of the Western Buddhist Order.

From its beginning until recently he was very much personally involved in the activities of the FWBO, keeping a close watch on its early development and providing the vision for its further expansion. There gathered around him an ever-growing number of personal disciples; more and more men and women became members of the Order – the spiritual nucleus of the movement. Although very much concerned with the overall organization of the FWBO, Sangharakshita functioned chiefly, during the formative years of the movement, as a teacher of the Dharma; he communicated his vision and understanding of the Buddha's message in various writings, public lectures, and study seminars on Buddhist texts.

Between 1965 and 1987, he delivered almost two hundred public lectures on various aspects of Buddhism. Among others, there was a series on the Buddha's Noble Eightfold Path, another on aspects of the Bodhisattva Ideal, and two series in which Sangharakshita developed his account of the Buddhist spiritual path as a path of 'higher evolution'.

All these lectures were tape recorded, and it is from them that *A Guide to the Buddhist Path* has been compiled. It consists of carefully selected and edited extracts from the transcripts of the tapes. The original version was compiled as a study manual to be used on study retreats by people wishing to become members of the Western Buddhist Order. As the process of preparation for ordination developed over the years, some of the material was removed and more added. Eventually more changes were made with a wider readership in mind, and in this way the present version evolved.

It is as well for the reader to bear in mind that the *Guide* originated in this way and that it is essentially an anthology of edited excerpts from lectures which were given at different times and in different circumstances over a period of twenty years. Though they are arranged logically under clear headings, it is inevitable that they do not flow as naturally one into the other as they might had this book been conceived and written as a single work.

As well as being familiar with the terrain, the good guide is also alert to the kind of people he is guiding. A distinctive feature of Sangharakshita's work is his keen awareness of the need to translate the Buddha's teaching into a form to which the Western mind can readily respond. He is well equipped to do this, having immersed himself in Western literature and philosophy. His understanding of Western systems of thought is as impressive as is his grasp of Buddhism and other forms of Eastern philosophy.

Being so much at home in both worlds, the Eastern and the Western, he is a good translator: translator, that is, in the widest sense of the term. In one of his published papers, *St Jerome Revisited*, Sangharakshita reflects on his affinity with the figure of St Jerome, an embodiment in Western art of the translator archetype. The translator, in this sense, is the guide *par excellence*.

A Guide to the Buddhist Path gives a substantial taste of the main features of Sangharakshita's teaching and its underlying principles. At the outset he steers us away from the snare of sectarianism, the danger of mistaking the part for the whole. If we are really to approach Buddhism we are to approach it as a whole and not be misled into thinking that one particular school, be it Zen or the Vajrayāna, is the whole of Buddhism. We need to survey the whole in order to discover what is of most value to us. Sangharakshita has more than once suggested an analogy between the FWBO and the T'ien-T'ai School in China which flourished in the sixth century CE.* Both are wide-ranging and selective in their approach to the teachings; both choose, from the vast mass of material available, those particular insights, practices, and precepts that seem most conducive to the spiritual

* Buddhists and other non-Christians do not use the abbreviations AD – 'Year of our Lord' – and BC. They refer to years under this accepted dating convention as either CE (Common Era) or BCE (Before Common Era).

development of their own followers at a particular place and time in history.

Another important feature of Buddhist teaching which is not always appreciated, but which Sangharakshita often highlights in his work, appears early on in the *Guide*. This is the need to distinguish between the language of fact and the language of myth. He explores this distinction in a very illuminating way in the section 'Archetypal Symbolism in the Biography of the Buddha', showing the extent to which modern man, to his great detriment, has lost touch with the language of myth. We need to be able to speak and understand both languages and be wary of dismissing the highly-developed mythical side of Buddhism as 'mere legend'.

He also warns us against one of the worst traps of all, that of thinking that being a real Buddhist means being a monk. Much as he is in favour of the monastic life-style in principle, he is insistent that being a Buddhist essentially means Going for Refuge to the Three Jewels – the Buddha, the Dharma, and the Sangha – and placing those Three Jewels at the very centre of one's life. This emphasis on the primacy of Going for Refuge is, more than anything else, the distinguishing feature of Sangharakshita's message. The first part of the book is therefore devoted to those Three Jewels.

In the section on the Dharma, the second of the Three Jewels, another dominant theme in Sangharakshita's work emerges. In his earliest days back in England he soon became aware of how seriously people could be hampered in their spiritual progress by negative emotional states. He therefore stresses the need to develop positive emotion, in particular by practising the meditation known as the Metta Bhavana (the development of universal loving kindness). This keen awareness of our emotional plight has influenced the way he conveys the Buddha's profound teaching of conditionality, the teaching that all things or beings whatsoever, whether material 'things' or mental states, arise in dependence on conditions.

A fact that is often glossed over in books on Buddhism is that there are two basic modes of conditionality, not just one: two ways in which we can act, one unskilful, the other skilful. The first is known as the circular or, in Sangharakshita's term, 'reactive' mode. This is the mode in which we operate for much of the time, and it is the cause of all our suffering. But there is also a spiral or 'creative' mode, in which we can make spiritual progress, experience ever-expanding states of happiness and bliss. The more 'negative' reactive mode usually gets far more consideration and exposition than the more positive creative mode. In fairness to commentators both ancient and modern, it has to be admitted that the canonical texts themselves give curiously little space to the creative mode and to the affirmative stages of the spiritual path.

Determined to redress the balance in this respect, Sangharakshita gives much-needed emphasis to the spiral or creative mode of conditioning. He sees that in view of the conditioning which we have shaken off – or are in the process of shaking off – it is to positive stimulation rather than negative caution that we are more likely to respond.

The first part of the book concludes with a few sections on the meaning of Spiritual Community, the third of the Three Jewels. In view of his insistence on the primacy of Going for Refuge, it is not surprising that Sangharakshita should stress as he does the importance of Spiritual Community, which he defines as essentially 'those who go for Refuge'. This aspect of his teaching too counters the impression often given that the true Sangha is the monastic community.

The second part of the *Guide* deals with a traditional formulation of the Buddhist Path, the Threefold Path of Morality, Meditation, and Wisdom. In the section on morality Sangharakshita shows how Buddhist ethics are not based on any sense of obligation or law but on the fact that we are free to choose either of the two basic modes of conditionality open to us and that, having chosen, we are responsible for the consequences of our choice.

Meditation practice has always received a great deal of emphasis within the FWBO. In meditation we work directly on our mental states, and the systematic practice of meditation creates the necessary basis for the arising of Insight. People who become involved in the FWBO are encouraged to take up a regular meditation practice. In many of his lectures Sangharakshita deals with the subject of meditation and its various aspects. In one extract recorded here he discusses the five meditation practices which are the traditional antidotes to certain poisons or obstacles to spiritual growth; in another he explains the meditation techniques practised by members of the Western Buddhist Order in terms of an integrated system which reflects successive stages of spiritual progress.

From all I have said it should be clear that this book is not intended to be any kind of historical or geographical survey of Buddhism as a whole (as some of Sangharakshita's other works are). Rather, it is a personal interpretation of the teachings of the Buddhist tradition, a drawing together of its essential features to give the reader an idea of how to put those teachings into practice.

Giving as it does a substantial taste of Sangharakshita's teaching of the Dharma, *A Guide to the Buddhist Path* provides an excellent introduction to his work. But it is essentially, as the title indicates, a guide to actual practice. Many people have become Buddhists as a result of listening to Sangharakshita's lectures, either live or on tape. Perhaps for some who come across this book reading his words will be a bridge to listening to the voice of the guide. Whether that is the case or not, it is to be hoped that the following pages will be a source of inspiration to many people for many years to come and will provide them with the spiritual lead they have been looking for.

Dharmachari Abhaya

Part **1**

Introduction

The Approach to Buddhism

It is possible to approach Buddhism in many different ways, some of which are more adequate than others – a few being simply wrong. Ideally, one has to approach Buddhism *as Buddhism*. This surely seems obvious enough, but the fact is we do not always do this.

To understand what it means to approach Buddhism as Buddhism, we have to understand what Buddhism essentially is. I have defined religion as 'the achievement of the state of psychological and spiritual wholeness and in that state relating to other people and to Ultimate Reality'.[1] Religion is also the sum total of all the teachings and methods which conduce to that particular achievement. Buddhism reflects this definition – perhaps more purely than any other teaching; Buddhism is essentially a means to psychological and spiritual wholeness. In its own language, Buddhism is the 'way to Enlightenment'; Buddhism, or the Dharma, is compared to a raft,[2] a raft which carries us over to the farther shore which is nirvāṇa (Enlightenment, Perfect Peace of Mind, Freedom, Insight, Wisdom, Compassion). In more modern terms, Buddhism is the instrument of the Higher Evolution of mankind; that is to say, the instrument of the evolution of each individual human being from an unenlightened condition to the condition of supreme Enlightenment.

If therefore one is to approach Buddhism as Buddhism, one has to understand that essentially Buddhism is a means to psychological and spiritual wholeness; the way to Enlightenment; and the instrument of the Higher Evolution.[3] Unless one understands this, one cannot really approach Buddhism. One may approach *something*, but that will not be Buddhism. At best, it will be a rather unfortunate distortion of Buddhism.

I will give you a few examples of the way in which Buddhism is distorted because it is not approached as Buddhism. Some time ago I received a charming visitor from Japan – a Shin Buddhist[4] priest, who was on a world tour. In the course of conversation, he said to me, 'I must tell you about something which pleases me very much. On my way from Japan to London I called in at various places, among them Rome, where I had the honour of an audience with the Pope. Not only that, but the Pope gave me a letter in which he expressed a very high appreciation of Buddhism.' When I heard this, to be quite frank I became a little suspicious. I felt it was somewhat uncharacteristic of the Pope that he should express a high appreciation of Buddhism. So I said, 'Have you any objection to my seeing this letter?' My visitor was delighted to show it to me and produced it out of his briefcase. It was on a large thick sheet of parchment-like paper, with an enormous coat of arms embossed at the head. It was indeed from the Pope, though rather interestingly it did not actually carry his signature. The good Japanese priest, beaming, read the letter out to me. What the Pope had written was that Buddhism was to be commended because it was 'an excellent human teaching'.

To anyone who knows a little about Catholicism or orthodox Christianity it is very clear what this means. As far as Catholicism or orthodox Christianity is concerned, there are two kinds of religion: revealed religion and natural religion. Revealed religion is transcendental, one might say, while natural religion is merely humanistic. Because in Buddhism there is no supreme God who has revealed the religion to mankind, Buddhism is classified as a natural religion and described as a 'human teaching'. In other words, it is the teaching of *just* a human, not the teaching of a Son of God. It is nothing more than a system of ethics, certainly not something which is capable of leading one to salvation. The Japanese priest, because he was not familiar with Catholicism, did not realize this. He thought that Buddhism, in being described as 'an excellent human teaching', was being praised and appreciated, whereas in fact it was being subtly undermined and depreciated.

If one reads books written by orthodox Roman Catholics one finds that this is the general line that they take. They say that Buddhism on its own level is very fine and noble, but it is nevertheless a 'human' creation and you cannot therefore get salvation through it. In one book that I read, the Roman Catholic author, after a quite scholarly survey of certain Buddhist teachings, concluded his book by writing – in the very last paragraph of the last page – that it was a pity that so many millions of people should have embarked on the raft of the Dharma, considering that in the end the raft simply founders.[5] Such Roman Catholics do not regard Buddhism as a way to Enlightenment. In other words, they do not approach Buddhism as Buddhism, do not approach Buddhism on its own terms as a way to Enlightenment. If one does not approach Buddhism in that way there is just a very learned, scholarly missing of the mark.

In this respect, the Roman Catholics are not by any means the only offenders. One might cite also the example of the Hindus. Orthodox Hindus, especially the brahmins, have great difficulty in approaching Buddhism as Buddhism. In the course of many years spent in India, I came up against this very often. As soon as one mentions Buddhism to them – this has been my experience literally thousands of times – they say at once, without even waiting for another word on the subject, 'Yes, it is only a branch of Hinduism.' It is significant that they always use the word 'only'. Sometimes I asked, 'Why do you not say "It is a branch of Hinduism"? Why do you say, "It is *only* a branch of Hinduism"?' This little word 'only' gives one a clue to their attitude: the word implies depreciation and limitation.

Even some quite good Hindu scholars, when they take a look at Buddhism and find that certain doctrines of Buddhism are not found in Hinduism, say that these cannot really be a part of Buddhism at all. Buddhism, according to them, is just a branch of Hinduism, so if there are any doctrines in Buddhism which are not found in Hinduism, they must be 'corruptions' which have been introduced by the 'designing Buddhist monks'. This is what they explicitly state in some of their works. For instance, some Hindu scholars, including Radhakrishnan, try to argue quite seriously that the doctrine of no-self, *anātmavāda*, was not taught by the Buddha but was the invention of the monks later on. Similarly with the non-theistic attitude of Buddhism. Some Hindu scholars go so far as to argue that the Buddha did in fact believe in God, but did not like to tell his followers so because it might upset them – some scholars have actually put this down in 'scholarly' works. These then are some examples of the way in which Buddhism is distorted because people are not willing, or not ready, to approach Buddhism simply as Buddhism.

If we want really to approach Buddhism, we have to approach it *as Buddhism*: we have to approach it as a means to psychological and spiritual wholeness, as a way to Enlightenment, as the instrument of the Higher Evolution. Unless we understand this, we will not really be able to approach it at all. We may, as I have said, approach *something*, but it will just be our own distorted version of Buddhism, our own subjective interpretation of it, not the objective truth about Buddhism.

The culmination of approaching Buddhism as Buddhism is the 'Going for Refuge'.[6] We go for Refuge to the 'Three Jewels': the Buddha (the Enlightened teacher), the Dharma (the way to Enlightenment), and the Sangha (the community of those who, side by side, are walking that way which leads to Enlightenment). Even if we do not take the step of Going for Refuge to the Three Jewels, we should at least seriously ask ourselves whether we do regard Buddhism as the means to Enlightenment, or whether we have any other idea – or a lack of ideas – about it. We should ask ourselves whether in fact we are trying to approach Buddhism as a way to Enlightenment, whether in fact we are trying to lay hold of the instrument of our own individual Higher Evolution.

We now come to another important point. It is good to approach Buddhism as Buddhism, but that alone is not enough; we have to approach Buddhism also *as a whole*. Buddhism is a very ancient religion: it has behind it 2,500 years of history. During this time, especially during the earlier part, it spread over practically the whole of the East.[7] As it spread it underwent a process of continual transformation and development, and it adapted the expression of its fundamental doctrines to the different needs of the people in the midst of which it found itself. In this way many different schools and traditions came to be established. Historically speaking, we may say that Buddhism is all of these. 'Buddhism' represents the whole vast development that took place in the course of the 2,500 years during which the Dharma spread.

Broadly speaking, there are three major forms of Buddhism extant in the world. Firstly, there is South-east Asian Buddhism. This is the form of Buddhism current in Sri Lanka, Myanmar (Burma), Thailand, Cambodia, Laos, and a few other places. This form of Buddhism is based on the Theravāda Pali Canon (the version of the Buddhist scriptures in Pali handed down by the Theravāda, the 'school of the elders', which is one of the most ancient of all the schools of Buddhism).

Secondly, there is Chinese Buddhism. This includes Japanese, Korean, and Vietnamese Buddhism, all of which, at least in their early stages, were offshoots of Chinese Buddhism. Chinese Buddhism is based on the Chinese Tripiṭaka, or 'three treasuries' (the collection in Chinese of the translations of all the available Indian Buddhist scriptures of all schools: Mahāyāna, Sarvāstivāda, Sautrāntika, and so on).

Thirdly, there is Tibetan Buddhism, including the Buddhism of Mongolia, Bhutan, and Sikkim. This form of Buddhism is based on two great collections of canonical and semi-canonical works: the Kangyur, or translated word of the Buddha, and the Tangyur, the translated commentaries by the great *ācāryas*, the great Buddhist philosophers and spiritual teachers.[8]

These three major forms of Buddhism are all branches of the original trunk of Indian Buddhism. They represent forms of Buddhism which originally developed in India over a period of roughly 1,500 years. South-east Asian Buddhism represents the first phase of development of Buddhism in India. This first phase lasted roughly 500 years, from about the time of the *parinirvāṇa*, or death of the Buddha, up to about the beginning of the Christian era. This is known as the Hīnayāna phase of development. During this phase Buddhism was stated predominantly in ethical and psychological terms.

Chinese Buddhism represents Indian Buddhism in the second phase of its development. It represents a synthesis of Hīnayāna and Mahāyāna. The Mahāyāna comprises more devotional and metaphysical expressions of the Buddha's teachings. This phase lasted from about the time of the origins of Christianity up to about 500CE.

Tibetan Buddhism represents the third phase in the development of Buddhism in India. This final phase lasted from about 500CE to about 1,000CE – or a little longer. It represents a synthesis of Hīnayāna, Mahāyāna, and Vajrayāna. The Vajrayāna is a yogic and symbolically ritualistic Buddhism.

These further three major forms of Buddhism all include numerous schools and sub-schools. In South-east Asian Buddhism the differences are largely national – Sinhalese Buddhism differs from Burmese Buddhism, Burmese Buddhism differs from Thai Buddhism, and so on – although there are also individual schools within each particular country. In Chinese Buddhism there are very many schools indeed: the T'ien-t'ai School, the Hua-yen School, the Ch'an School (usually known as the Zen School), and so forth. Altogether in Chinese Buddhism there are about a dozen important schools. Japan too has schools of its own, which it developed independently of Chinese influence, notably the Shin School and the Nichiren School. In Tibet there are four major schools: the Gelugs, Nyingmas, Shakyas, and Kagyus.

I am not going into any details here and am mentioning all these names just to give you an idea of the richness of content of Buddhism. When we approach Buddhism, we approach all of these different schools and traditions, all of these adaptations and applications of the central fundamental principles of Buddhism. We approach Buddhism as a whole; we do not approach any one school only, but the total Buddhist tradition as it developed over 2,500 years throughout practically the whole of Asia.

We certainly do not treat one particular school of Buddhism as though it was identical with the whole Buddhist tradition, or *was*, in fact, the whole Buddhist tradition. Unfortunately this is sometimes done. I have selected just a few statements from some books on Buddhism to illustrate this.

In the introduction to one particular book on Buddhism, I found this statement: 'The Buddhist scriptures are to be found in the Pali Tipiṭaka.' This statement is incorrect. One *can* say that the Theravāda Buddhist scriptures are to be found in the Pali Tipiṭaka – that is quite correct. But if one says merely 'Buddhist scriptures', one is leaving out of consideration the Chinese Canon, the Tibetan Canon, and several other minor Canons also. So here the Pali Canon is being regarded as identical with the Buddhist scriptures as a whole, which is a mistake.

In another little pamphlet I found this statement: 'Buddhism teaches salvation by faith in Amitābha.'[9] It is quite correct to say that the Shin School of Japanese Buddhism teaches this, but it is not at all correct to say that Buddhism teaches this. Here, what is the teaching of one particular school is being attributed to Buddhism as a whole. That again is a mistake.

In another booklet I found this statement: 'The Dalai Lama is the head of the Buddhist religion.' The Dalai Lama is certainly the head of the Tibetan branch of the Buddhist religion, but he is not the head of the whole Buddhist religion. Here again, the part, Tibetan Buddhism, is being confused with the whole, the total tradition of Buddhism.

Each of these statements, allegedly about Buddhism, is really true only of one particular branch, or school, or line of tradition, of Buddhism. In every case, the part has been mistaken for the whole.

One's approach to Buddhism should therefore be not a sectarian approach, but a synoptic approach. One should approach the whole Buddhist tradition – whole in time and whole in space – and try to include, comprehend, and fathom the essence of it all.

I have said that one should approach Buddhism as Buddhism and as a whole. One should also approach Buddhism in a balanced manner. There are many sides to human nature: emotional, intellectual, introvert, extravert, etc. These sides are represented in Buddhism by the 'Five Spiritual Faculties' (faith, energy, mindfulness, meditation, and wisdom). These Five Spiritual Faculties have to be kept in balance. Faith and wisdom, which represent our emotional and intellectual sides, have to be balanced. Meditation and energy, which represent our introvert and extravert sides, have to be balanced. Mindfulness, or awareness, which is the equilibrating faculty, balances them all.

One should not have just an emotional approach to Buddhism, nor just an intellectual approach, nor just a meditative approach, nor just a practical, active approach; one should approach Buddhism in *all* these ways. One's nature comprises all these aspects – one feels, thinks, acts, also sometimes sits still – so one should approach Buddhism with all these aspects. In other words, one should approach Buddhism with one's total being. One should not just try to feel and not understand, nor just try to understand and not feel. One should not always look within and never look without, nor, on the other hand, always look without, never pausing to look within. There is a time and place for all these things. If possible, we should try to do all of these things all the time. As we ascend higher and higher in our spiritual development, we shall tend more and more to think and feel, act and not act, simultaneously. It sounds impossible, but that is only because of the limitations of our present way of thinking. Eventually, as one's spiritual life develops, all these four apparently contradictory senses are fused and harmonized into one spiritual faculty – into one 'being', as it were – which is forging ahead. Unless one has a balanced approach of head and heart, unless the whole of oneself is involved, there is no real commitment to Buddhism as a way to Enlightenment.

To summarize, we should firstly approach Buddhism as Buddhism, as the way to Enlightenment, as the instrument of the Higher Evolution, not on any other terms, since otherwise we cannot possibly hope to understand it or even begin to approach it. Secondly, we should approach Buddhism as a whole, not approach just the Theravāda, or just Zen, or just Shin. We should take in and try to assimilate the best elements in all these traditions. Thirdly, we should approach Buddhism in a balanced manner. We should approach Buddhism not with head or heart but with both – in fact with our total being.

The Buddha

Who is the Buddha?

The teaching or tradition which in the West we now call Buddhism sprang out of the Buddha's experience of Enlightenment beneath the Bodhi tree 2,500 years ago. It is with the Buddha, therefore, that Buddhism begins. But the question which at once arises is, 'Who was the Buddha?' It is useful, even for those who regard themselves as Buddhists of long standing, to think about this question.

The first thing we have to make clear is that the word 'Buddha' is not a proper name but a title. It means 'one who Knows, one who Understands'. It also means 'one who is Awake' – one who has woken up, as it were, from the dream of life, because he sees the Truth, sees Reality. This title was first applied to a man whose personal name was Siddhartha and whose clan or family name was Gautama, and who lived in the sixth century BCE in the area which is partly in southern Nepal, partly in northern India. Fortunately we know quite a lot about his early career. We know that he came from a well-to-do, even patrician family. Tradition sometimes represents his father as being the king of the *Śākya* clan or tribe. But it seems more likely that he wasn't so much the king as the elected president of the clan assembly, holding office for twelve years with the title of *rāja*, and that it was during this period that his son Siddhartha Gautama, who afterwards became the Buddha, was born.[10]

Siddhartha received what was, by the standards of those days, a very good education. He didn't go to school, of course, and it is not really clear whether he could read or write, but we know that he received an excellent training in all sorts of martial arts and exercises. In their more Buddhistic form some of these arts are still popular in the Far East today, and we can imagine the future Buddha spending his time more in that sort of way than in poring over books. From the wise old men of the clan he also learned, by word of mouth, various ancient traditions, genealogical lists, beliefs, and superstitions. He led on the whole quite a comfortable life, with no particular responsibilities. His father, a very affectionate, even doting, parent, married him off when he was quite young – some accounts say when he was only sixteen. (In India, in those days, as is usually the case today, marriage was arranged by one's parents, as it was not just one's personal affair but the concern of the whole family.) He married a cousin, and in due course a son was born.

The Four Sights

One might have thought that he led a happy enough existence, but the accounts make it clear that, despite his well-to-do way of life, Siddhartha Gautama was very deeply dissatisfied. H.G. Wells, describing this period in the Buddha's existence, rather appropriately says: 'It was the unhappiness of a fine mind that seeks employment.'[11] The legends that we find in the Buddhist scriptures speak of a sort of spiritual crisis, of a turning point, when the young patrician saw what are called the 'Four Sights'.[12] Scholars are not agreed whether he literally went out one day and saw these Four Sights in the streets of Kapilavastu or whether they represent a projection, externally, of essentially psychological and spiritual experiences. It would seem, however, that they do in fact represent psychological and spiritual experiences which later tradition transcribed, as it were, into arresting narrative form as the well-known legend of the Four Sights. These Four Sights crystallize in a powerful form certain fundamental teachings of Buddhism and throw a great deal of light on the Buddha's own early spiritual development.

The legend goes that one beautiful, bright morning Siddhartha felt like going out for a drive in his chariot, so he called his charioteer, whipped up the horses, and set out. They drove into the town and suddenly Siddhartha saw his first Sight: he saw an old man. According to the legend he had never seen an old man before. Taking the account literally, this means that he had been shut up in his palace and hadn't taken much notice of other people, hadn't realized that there was such a thing as old age. But one can take it another way. Sometimes we see something as though for the first time. In a sense we have seen it a hundred, even a thousand times already, but one day we see it as though we had never seen it before. It was probably something like this

The Four Sights

that happened in the case of Siddhartha, and it gave him a shock. He said to his charioteer, 'Who on earth is that?' And the charioteer, we are told, replied, 'That is an old man.' 'Why is he so frail, so bent?' 'Well, it's just that he's old.' And Siddhartha asked, 'But how did he get like that?' 'Well, everybody gets old sooner or later. It's natural. It just happens.' 'Will it happen to me too?' And the charioteer of course had to reply, 'Yes, young as you are, this will inevitably happen to you. One day you too will be old.' These words of the charioteer struck the future Buddha like a thunderbolt, and he exclaimed, 'What is the use of this youth, what is the use of this vitality and strength, if it all ends in this!' And very sick at heart he returned to his beautiful palace.

The second Sight was the sight of disease. It was as though he had never seen anyone sick before, and he realized that all human beings are subject to maladies of various kinds. He had to face the fact that, strong and healthy though he was, he might at any time be struck down by disease.

The third Sight was that of a corpse being carried to the burning ground on a stretcher. One can see this sight in India any day. In the West, when one dies one is smuggled away in a box. Nobody sees anything of you. You are disposed of like so much garbage that no one even wants to look at, which is just put into the incinerator or into a hole in the ground. But in India it isn't like that. When one dies one is laid out publicly in the best room in the house, and all one's friends and relations come and have a good look. Then the corpse is hoisted on the shoulders of four strong men and borne through the streets with the face uncovered. Crowds of people follow, accompanying the body to the burning ground. It was a procession of this sort that Siddhartha saw, and he asked the charioteer, 'What on earth is this?' The charioteer said, 'It is just a dead body', and Siddhartha said, 'Dead? What has happened to him?' 'Well, as you can see he's stiff, he's motionless. He doesn't breathe, doesn't see, doesn't hear. He's dead.' Siddhartha gave a gasp, and said, 'Does it happen to everybody, this death?' So the charioteer drew a long sigh and said, 'Yes, I'm afraid it does.' Thereupon Siddhartha realized that this would happen to him too one day. The revelation struck him very forcibly, like a thunderbolt. He saw how it was. You don't want to grow old, but you can't help it. You don't want to fall sick, but you can't help that either. So you start asking yourself, 'How do I come to be here? Here I am with this urge to live, and to go on living, but I have got to die. Why? What is the meaning of it all? Why this riddle, this mystery? Why have I been made like this? Is it God who is responsible? Is it fate, or destiny? Or has it just happened? Is there any explanation at all?'

In this way Siddhartha was brought up against these existential situations, and he started thinking about them very deeply. Then he saw a fourth Sight. This Sight was of what in India is called a sadhu, or holy man, walking along the street with his begging-bowl. He seemed so calm, so quiet, so peaceful, that the future Buddha thought, 'Maybe he knows. Maybe this is the way. Maybe I should do likewise – should cut off all ties, all worldly connections, and go forth as a yellow-robed homeless wanderer as this man has done. Maybe in this way I shall find an answer to the problems that are tormenting me.'

Going Forth

The beautiful, almost romantic, story goes on to relate how one night, when everything was quiet and there was a full moon in the sky, Siddhartha bade a last farewell to his sleeping wife and child. He wasn't happy to leave them, but he had to go. He rode many miles that night, till he reached the river that marked the boundary of *Śākya* territory. There he left his horse, left his princely garments, cut off his long hair and his beard, and became a homeless wanderer in search of the truth.

This 'going forth' is psychologically very significant. It is not just becoming a monk. It is much more than that. It means cutting oneself off from the incestuous ties to blood and soil and kindred and leaving oneself free as an individual to work out one's own salvation, one's own spiritual destiny.

This is what Siddhartha did. He got away from it all. He opted out. He'd had enough of worldly life and was now going to try to find out the truth, to try to see the truth for himself. The search was to last for six years.

In those days there were in India many people who taught, or professed to teach, ways leading to the realization of truth. One of the most popular of these ways was that of self-torture. Now in this country we can't really take this sort of thing seriously. With the possible exception of the hermits of the Egyptian desert in the second and third centuries CE, self-mortification has never really been a considered method of self-development in the West, and it is certainly not part of our daily life. We don't go to work and on the way see a man lying on a bed of nails. But in India such practices are very much part of the atmosphere, and even now many Indians do have the strong belief that self-torture is the way to heaven, or the way even to self-knowledge and Enlightenment.

So it was in the Buddha's day. There was a powerful movement of this sort, a movement teaching that if one wanted to gain the truth one had to subjugate, even mortify, the flesh. And that is exactly what Siddhartha did. For six years he practised the severest austerities. He limited his food and his sleep, he didn't wash, and he went around naked. All this the Buddha himself described when he was an old man, and his account is found in the Buddhist scriptures. As one of these accounts says, the fame of his austerities spread like the sound of a great bell hung in the canopy of the sky.[13] No one in India, he afterwards declared, had outdone him in self-torture and self-mortification. But he also said that it had led him nowhere. He had become famous as a great ascetic and had a number of disciples with him. But when he realized that this was not the way to Truth, not the way to Enlightenment, he had the courage to give it up.

He started eating again, and his disciples left him in disgust. And this is also significant. He had already left his family, left his friends, left his tribe, and in the end even his disciples deserted him. He was left utterly alone, and on his own he remained. He went about from place to place and eventually, we are told, he came to a beautiful spot on the banks of a fresh running river. There he sat down in the shade of a great tree, and made the resolution, 'I will not rise from this spot until I am Enlightened.'

There is a beautiful and dramatic verse which is put into his mouth by some of the early compilers of his teachings: 'Flesh may wither away, blood may dry up, but until I gain Enlightenment I shall not move from this seat.' So day after day, night after night, he sat there. As he sat he controlled and concentrated his mind, purified his mind, suppressed the mental hindrances, the defilements, and on Wesak night, the night of the full moon of May, just as the morning star was rising – just as he fixed his mind on that star glittering near the horizon – full Illumination, full Enlightenment, arose.

It is obviously very difficult to describe this sort of state. We can say it is the plenitude of Wisdom. We can say it is the fullness of Compassion. We can say that it is seeing the Truth face to face. But these are only words, and they do not convey very much. So let us simply say that at that moment the 'light' dawned, and Siddhartha Gautama became the Buddha.

In a sense this was the end of his quest. He had become the Buddha, the 'one who Knows'. He had found the solution to the riddle of existence. He was Enlightened, he was Awake. But in a sense it was only the beginning of his mission. Deciding to make known to humanity the Truth he had discovered, he left what we now call Bodh Gaya and walked to Sarnath, about one hundred miles away, gathered together the disciples who had left him when he gave up his austerities, and made known to them his great discovery. According to some accounts he preached to them the *sutta* which Westerners sometimes call 'The First Sermon'.[14] (I don't like this word 'sermon'. A *sutta* is really a connected discourse, a series of ideas and themes strung together as though on a thread, which is what *sutta* literally means.)

Gradually a spiritual community grew up around the Buddha. He didn't stay permanently in any one place, but roamed all over north-eastern India. He had a long life, gaining Enlightenment at the age of thirty-five and living to be eighty. So he had forty-five years of work, of

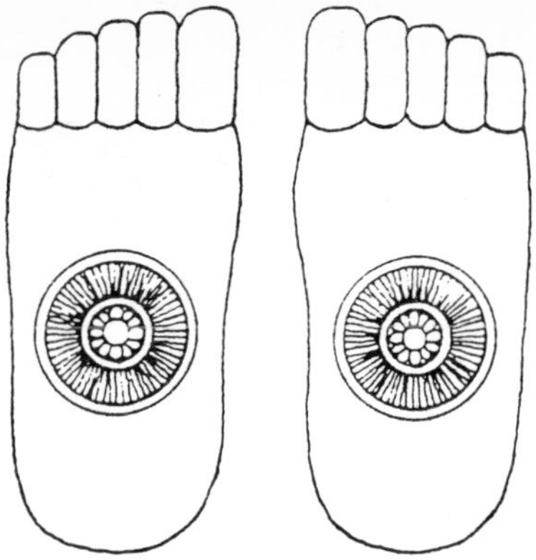

The Buddha's footprints

active life, spreading his teaching. The pattern seems to have been that for nine months of the year he wandered from place to place preaching, and then for three months took shelter from the torrential monsoon rains. Whenever he came to a village he would, if it was time for his one meal of the day, get out his begging-bowl and stand silently at the door of the huts, one after another. Having collected as much food as he needed, he would retire to the mango grove which, even now, is to be found on the outskirts of every Indian village, and sit down under a tree. When he had finished his meal the villagers would gather round and he would teach them. Sometimes brahmins would come, sometimes wealthy landowners, sometimes peasants, sometimes merchants, sometimes sweepers, sometimes prostitutes. The Buddha would teach them all. And sometimes in the big cities he would preach to kings and princes. In this way he gained a great following and became in his own day the greatest and best known of all the spiritual teachers in India. And when he died, when he gained what we call *parinirvāṇa*, there were thousands, even tens of thousands, of his disciples to mourn his departure, both monks and lay people, men and women.

In outline, at least, such is the traditional biography of Siddhartha Gautama, the Indian prince who became the Buddha, the Enlightened One, the Awakened One, the founder of the great spiritual tradition which we call Buddhism. But does it really answer the question, 'Who was the Buddha?'? It certainly gives us all the facts, but does such a biography, however well documented, really tell us who the Buddha was? Do we know the Buddha – and the emphasis is on the 'know' – from a description of the life of Siddhartha Gautama? What, in fact, do we mean by knowing the Buddha? Even from a worldly point of view, we may know a person's likes and dislikes, his opinions and beliefs, but do we really know that person? Sometimes even our closest friends do things which we find quite out of character, quite out of keeping with the ideas we had about them. This shows how little one really knows other people. We are not really able to plumb the deepest spring of their action, their fundamental motivation. Usually, the nearer people are to us, the less we really know them. There is an old saying: 'It's a wise child that knows its own father.' It is as though familiarity, or superficial closeness, gets in the way, so that what we know and relate to is not the other person but our own preconceptions, our own projected mental states, our own quite subjective reactions to that person. In other words, our 'ego' gets in the way. In order really to know another person we have to go much deeper than the ordinary level of communication, which isn't real communication at all.

It is the same with regard to this question of knowing the Buddha. This question in its deeper sense has been asked since the very dawn of Buddhism. In fact it is a question which was put to the Buddha himself, apparently, soon after his Enlightenment: 'Who are you?'

'I am a Buddha'

Journeying along the high road, the Buddha met a man called Doṇa.[15] Doṇa was a brahmin, and skilled in the science of bodily signs. Seeing on the Buddha's footprints the mark of a thousand-spoked wheel he followed in his track along the road until he eventually caught up with the Buddha, who was sitting beneath a tree. As the Buddha was fresh from his Enlightenment, there was a radiance about his whole being. We are told it was as though a light shone from his face – he was happy, serene, joyful. Doṇa was very impressed by his appearance, and he seems to have felt that this wasn't an ordinary human being, perhaps not a human being at all. Drawing near, he came straight to the point, as the custom is in India where religious matters are concerned. He said, 'Who are you?'

Now the ancient Indians believed that the universe is stratified into various levels of existence, that there are not just human beings and animals, as we believe, but gods, and ghosts, and *yakṣas*, and *gandharvas*, and all sorts of other mythological beings, inhabiting a multi-storey universe, the human plane being just one storey out of many. So Doṇa asked, 'Are you a *yakṣa*?' (a *yakṣa* being a rather terrifying sublime spirit living in the forest). But the Buddha said 'No'. Just 'No'. So Doṇa tried again. 'Are you a *gandharva*?' (a sort of celestial musician, a beautiful singing angel-like figure). Once again the Buddha said 'No', and again Doṇa asked, 'Well then, are you a *deva*?' (a god, a divine being, a sort of archangel). 'No.' Upon this Doṇa thought, 'That's strange, he must be a human being after all!' And he asked him that too, but yet again the Buddha said 'No'. By this time Doṇa was thoroughly perplexed, so he demanded, 'If you are not any of these things, then who are you?' The Buddha replied, 'Those mental conditionings on account of which I might have been described as a *yakṣa* or a *gandharva*, as a *deva* or a human being, all those conditionings have been destroyed by me. Therefore I am a Buddha.'

The word for mental conditionings is '*saṁskāra*', which means all kinds of conditioned mental attitudes. It is these conditioned mental attitudes, these volitions or karma-formations as they are sometimes called, which, according to Buddhism, and Indian belief in general, determine the nature of our rebirth. The Buddha was free from all these, and so there was nothing to cause him to be reborn as a *yakṣa*, a *gandharva*, a god, or even as a human being, and even here and now he was not in reality any of these things. He had reached the state of unconditioned consciousness, though his body might appear to be that of a man. Therefore he was called the Buddha, Buddha being as it were an incarnation, a personification, of the unconditioned mind.

The human mind proceeds by degrees, from the known to the unknown, and this is what Doṇa tried to do. Seeing the glorious figure of the Buddha, he tried to apply to it the only labels he had at his disposal – the labels of *yakṣa*, *gandharva*, etc. – but none of them would fit. This is very relevant to us because there are two of Doṇa's categories which represent mistakes which we still commit, here and now, when we try to understand who the Buddha was, or is. These are the categories of 'God' and 'man', the only two categories still available to us in the West. One school of thought says, 'The Buddha was a very good man, even a holy man, but just a man and no more than that.' This is the view taken by, for instance, some Christian writers about Buddhism. It is a rather insidious sort of approach. Though they may praise the Buddha for his wonderful love, wonderful compassion, wonderful wisdom, etc., they are careful to add that after all he was only a man, whereas Jesus Christ was the Son of God. The other school says, 'No, the Buddha is a sort of God for the Buddhists. Originally he was a man, of course, but after his death his followers deified him because they wanted something to worship.'

Both of these views are wrong. The Buddha was a man, yes, a human being, in the sense that he started off as every other human being starts off, but he wasn't an ordinary man, he was an Enlightened man. And such a being, or Buddha, is, according to Buddhist tradition, the highest being in the universe, higher even than the so-called gods. In Buddhist art the gods are represented in humble positions on either side of the Buddha, saluting him and listening to the teaching.

A certain amount of confusion has arisen in the West about the Buddha being a god, or God, because they see that he is worshipped – that Buddhists offer flowers to the altar, light candles, and bow down – and if you worship someone, we think, it means that for you that person is God. But that is quite wrong. Not only Buddhists, but people generally in the East, have got quite a different conception of worship. In India the same word '*pūjā*' is used for paying respect to the Buddha, to one's parents, to one's elder brothers and sisters, to one's teachers, spiritual or secular, and to any senior or respectable person. So what the Buddhists are doing when they offer flowers to the Buddha-image is respecting or honouring the Buddha as an Enlightened being, not worshipping him as God.

But let us get back to our main theme: knowing the Buddha. We have seen that 'Buddha' means 'unconditioned mind', or 'Enlightened mind'. Knowing the Buddha therefore means knowing the mind in its unconditioned state. So if at this stage we are asked, 'Who is the Buddha?' we can only reply, 'You yourself are the Buddha – potentially.' We can really and truly come to know the Buddha only in the process of actualizing – in our spiritual life, our meditation and so on – our own potential Buddhahood. It is only then that we can say from knowledge, from experience, who the Buddha is.

Now we cannot do this all at once. We have to establish, first of all, a living contact with Buddhism. We have to arrive at something which goes further than mere factual knowledge about Gautama the Buddha, about the details of his earthly career, even though it falls far short of knowing the unconditioned mind, of really knowing the Buddha. This something that comes in between the two is what we call Going for Refuge to the Buddha. This does not just mean reciting *'Buddhaṁ saraṇaṁ gacchāmi'*, though it does not exclude such recitation. It means taking Buddhahood, taking the idea or ideal of Enlightenment, as a living spiritual Ideal, as our ultimate objective, and trying our utmost to realize it. In other words, it is only by taking Refuge in the Buddha in the traditional sense that we can really know who the Buddha is. This is one of the reasons why I have always attached such great importance to the Refuges, not only to Going for Refuge to the Buddha, but also to the Dharma and to the Sangha.

In conclusion, it is only by taking Refuge in the Buddha, with all that that implies, that we can really and truly answer, from the heart, from the mind, and from the whole of our spiritual life, the question, 'Who is the Buddha?'

Archetypal Symbolism in the Biography of the Buddha

If we look below the rational, conceptual surface of man's mind, we find vast unplumbed depths which make up what we call the unconscious. The psyche in its wholeness consists of both the conscious and the unconscious. The unconscious, non-rational part of man is by far the larger part of his total nature, and its importance is far greater than we generally care to recognize. Consciousness is just like a light froth playing and sparkling on the surface, whilst the unconscious is like the vast ocean depths, dark and unfathomed, lying far beneath. In order to appeal to the whole person, it isn't enough to appeal just to the conscious, rational intelligence that floats upon the surface. We have to appeal to something more, and this means that we have to speak an entirely different language from the language of concepts, of abstract thought; we have to speak the language of images, of concrete form. If we want to reach this non-rational part of the human psyche, we have to use the language of poetry, of myth, of legend.

This other, no less important, language is one which many modern people have forgotten, or which they know only in a few distorted and broken forms. But Buddhism does very definitely speak this language and speaks it no less powerfully than it speaks the language of concepts, and it is through the latter that we are going to approach our subject, changing over from the conceptual approach to the non-conceptual, from the conscious mind to the unconscious. Here, we shall be beginning to descend into this language, encountering there some of what I have called the 'Archetypal Symbolism in the Biography of the Buddha'. To allow for this encounter, we have to be receptive, to open ourselves to these archetypal symbols, to listen to them and allow them to speak in their own way to us, especially to our unconscious depths, so that we do not just realize them mentally, but experience them and assimilate them, even allowing them eventually to transform our whole life.

The Language of Buddhism

Some people are under the impression that Buddhism speaks only the language of concepts, of reason; that it is a strictly rational system, even a sort of rationalism. When they hear the word Buddhism, they expect something very dry and abstract – it is as though they almost heard the skeleton rattle! Such a misunderstanding is in a way quite natural in the West. After all, ninety percent, if not ninety-nine percent, of our knowledge is derived from books, magazines, lectures, etc., so that, although we may not always be aware of this, our approach is in terms of mental understanding. It addresses our rational intelligence, our capacity to formulate concepts. In this way we get a very one-sided impression of Buddhism. But if we go to the East we see a very different picture. In fact, we may even say that in the Eastern Buddhist countries they tend to the other extreme. They tend to be moved and influenced by the divinities and images all about them without easily being able to give a mental formulation of what they actually believe. When I first went to live in Kalimpong, up in the Himalayas, I was surprised to find that many of my Tibetan, Sikkimese, and Bhutanese friends who were ardent, practising Buddhists had never heard of the Buddha! Or if his name was mentioned, they thought he was a very unreal, distant historical figure. Archetypal forms such as Padmasambhava, or the 'Five *Jinas*', or Maitreya, were real to them, but not the historical facts and figures.

So far as Buddhism in the West is concerned, much more attention has been given to the conceptual, analytical, intellectual approach. We now have to give much more time and much more serious attention to the other type of approach, to begin to try to combine both these approaches, unite both the conceptual and the non-conceptual. In other words, we need a balanced spiritual life in which both the conscious and unconscious mind play their part.

Now, let us define our key terms. What do we mean by archetypal symbolism? What is an archetype? Broadly speaking, an archetype is the original pattern or model of a work, or the model from which a thing is made or formed. In Jung's psychology – and it was Jung who familiarized this term in the modern psychological context – the term is used in a much more specialized sense.[16]

I must say, I found it rather difficult to elucidate the precise sense in which Jung uses this word. His use of it is very fluid and shifting. The meaning is not always conceptually clear and he tends to rely on examples, which he cites profusely. In doing this, he no doubt proceeds deliberately. Perhaps it is better to follow him in this and make the meaning of this term clear by citing examples.

And what do we mean by symbolism? A symbol is generally defined as a visible sign of something invisible. But philosophically and religiously speaking it is more than that: it is something existing on a lower plane which is in correspondence with something existing on a higher plane. Just to cite a common example, in the various theistic traditions, the sun is a symbol for God, because the sun performs in the physical universe the same function that God, according to these systems, performs in the spiritual universe: the sun sheds light, sheds heat, just as God sheds the light of knowledge, the warmth of love, into the spiritual universe. One can say that the sun is the god of the material world, and in the same way God is the sun of the spiritual world. It is the same principle manifesting on different levels in different ways. This is, of course, the old Hermetic idea: 'As above, so below.'[17]

Two Kinds of Truth

Now about the biography of the Buddha – various Western scholars in modern times have tried to write full, detailed biographies of the Buddha.[18] There is quite a lot of traditional material available. Quite a number of biographies were written in ancient India, for instance the *Mahāvastu* (which means the Great Relation). This is essentially a biography of the Buddha, though it does contain a great deal of other matter, especially *Jātakas* and *Avadānas*.[19] It is a bulky work – three volumes in the English translation, altogether about 1,500 pages – which contains some very ancient and interesting material. Then there are the *Lalita-vistara* and the *Abhiniṣkramana Sūtra*, both Mahāyāna sūtras. The *Lalita-vistara* is a highly poetic work and has great devotional appeal and literary value. In fact, Sir Edwin Arnold's famous poem, *The Light of Asia*, is primarily based on it.

These works are in Sanskrit, but we have also in Pali the *Nidāna*, Buddhaghośa's introduction to his own commentary on the *Jātaka* stories. Then again, we have Aśvaghoṣa's *Buddhacarita* (which means the Acts of the Buddha), a beautiful epic poem in classical Sanskrit.

Western scholars have explored this abundant material thoroughly, but having gone through the various episodes and incidents, they divide them into two great 'heaps': on one side, they put whatever they consider to be a historic fact – that the Buddha was born into a certain family, that he spoke a certain language, that he left home at a certain age, etc. On the other side, they put what they consider to be myth and legend. Now, this is all right so far as it goes, but most of them go a step further, and start indulging in value judgements, saying that only the historical facts – or what they consider the historical facts – are valuable and relevant. As for the myths and legends, all the poetry of the account, they usually see this as mere fiction and therefore to be discarded as completely worthless.

This is a very great mistake indeed, for we may say that there are two kinds of truth: there is what we call scientific truth, the truth of concepts, of reasoning; and in addition to this – some would even say above this – there is what we may call poetic truth, or truth of the imagination, of the intuition. Both are at least equally important. The latter kind of truth is manifested, or revealed, in what we call myths and legends, as well as in works of art, in symbolic ritual, and also quite importantly in dreams. And what we call the archetypal symbolism of the biography of the Buddha belongs to this second category – it is not meant to be historic truth, factual information, but poetic, even spiritual, truth. We may say that this biography – or partial biography – of the Buddha in terms of archetypal symbolism is not concerned with the external events of his career, but is meant to suggest to us something about his inner spiritual experience and, therefore, to shed light on the spiritual life for all of us.

This archetypal symbolism is often found in Buddhist

biographies, for example, in the life of Nāgārjuna,[20] of Padmasambhava,[21] of Milarepa.[22] In all these so-called biographies there are many incidents which are not based, and not supposed to be based, on historical facts, but which have an archetypal symbolic significance pointing to inner experience and inner realization. Sometimes it is difficult to distinguish between the two categories, to make up one's mind whether something belongs to the historical or to the symbolic order. Very often we find that the Buddhist tradition itself does not clearly distinguish between the two. It usually seems to take the myths and legends just as literally as the historical facts, as though in early times man almost didn't possess the capacity, or perhaps even the willingness, to distinguish in this way. Everything was true, everything was fact, of its own kind, in its own order. There is no harm in our trying to make up our minds what constitutes the factual, historical content of the Buddha's biography, and what represents its archetypal and symbolic content, but we should be careful not to undervalue the mythical and the legendary elements.

Buddhist Symbolism

I will now give a few examples of archetypal symbolism from the biography of the Buddha, drawing on some of the texts which I have mentioned. This will not be in chronological order as, with the exception of one particular sequence, it doesn't seem to be of any particular importance. I am going to start off with a comparatively simple example, known in Buddhist tradition as the Twin Miracle, or *yamaka-prātihārya* (Pali *yamaka-pāṭihāriya*), which, according to the scriptures, was performed by the Buddha at a place called Śrāvasti, and subsequently performed on a number of other occasions. It is described in the *Mahāvastu* as being performed by the Buddha at Kapilavastu.

The text says:

Then the Exalted One standing in the air at the height of a palm tree performed various and divers miracles of double appearance. The lower part of his body would be in flames, while from the upper part there streamed five hundred jets of cold water. While the upper part of his body was in flames, five hundred jets of cold water streamed from the lower part. Next, by his magic power the Exalted One transformed himself into a bull with a quivering hump. The bull vanished in the east and appeared in the west. It vanished in the north and appeared in the south. It vanished in the south and appeared in the north. And in this way the great miracle is to be described in detail. Several thousand koṭis[23] *of beings, seeing this great miracle of magic, became glad, joyful and pleased, and uttered thousands of bravos at witnessing the marvel.*[24]

I am not going to say anything here about the Buddha's transformation into a bull – the bull is a universal symbol in mythology and folklore, and it deserves a study of its own. I am going to concentrate here on the Twin Miracle proper. First of all, the Buddha stands in the air – in some versions, he is represented as walking up and down in the air as though making a promenade. This signifies a change of plane, and is highly significant. It represents the fact that what is described does not happen on the earth plane, or on the historical plane. The Twin Miracle is not a miracle in the usual sense, not something magical or supernormal happening here on this earth, but something spiritual, something symbolic, happening on a higher metaphysical plane of existence. The presence in Buddhist art, in any particular scene, of a lotus flower, for instance, has the same significance. If a Buddha-figure, or any other figure, is depicted sitting on a lotus flower, it means that the scene is on a transhuman, transcendental plane, where the lotus symbolizes severance of contact with the world. In fact, in sculptures of the Twin Miracle, since it is not possible to represent the Buddha up in the air – that would take him right up out of the picture – he is represented sitting on a lotus flower.

Having stood in the air, in this metaphysical dimension, as it were, the Buddha emits fire and water simultaneously: fire from the upper half of the body, water from the lower, and vice versa. If we were to take this literally, historically, at best it is just a conjuring trick, nothing more. But the Buddha certainly didn't indulge

in conjuring tricks. On the higher plane of existence where he now stands, fire and water are universal symbols. They are found all over the world, among all races, in all cultures, all religions. Fire always represents 'spirit', or 'the spiritual'; and water always represents matter, the material. Fire, again, represents the heavenly, the positive, the masculine principle; water the earthly, the negative, the feminine principle. Fire represents the intellect, water the emotions. Fire again represents consciousness, water the unconscious. In other words, fire and water between them represent all the cosmic opposites. They stand for what in the Chinese tradition are known as the yin and the yang.

The fact that the Buddha emitted fire and water simultaneously represents the conjugation of these great pairs of opposites. This conjunction on all levels, and on the highest level of all especially, is synonymous with what we call Enlightenment, what the Tantras[25] call *yuganaddha*, two-in-oneness.[26] This two-in-oneness, this union or harmony or integration of opposites represented here, has an interesting parallel in the Western alchemical tradition as explored by Jung for example, where the union of fire and water is said to be the whole secret of alchemy – of course not in the sense of producing gold, but in the sense of spiritual transmutation. In alchemy, sometimes this union of fire and water is spoken of as the marriage of the Red King and the White Queen. Here, this episode of the Twin Miracle tells us that Enlightenment is not a one-sided affair, not a partial experience, but the union, the conjunction, of opposites, of fire and water, at the highest possible level.

Let us now turn to another episode. According to the Theravāda tradition, the Buddha preached what became known as the Abhidharma to his deceased mother in the Heaven of the Thirty-three Gods (a higher heavenly world where she was reborn when she died, seven days after his birth). When he returned to the earth, he descended by means of a magnificent staircase, attended by different gods, divinities, and angels. In the Buddhist texts, this staircase is described, in very glorious terms, as being threefold, made up of gold, silver, and crystal.[27] Just imagine this magnificent staircase stretching all the way from the Heaven of the Thirty-three Gods right down to earth.

This also is a universal symbol – the staircase or the ladder between heaven and earth. Sometimes it is a silver or golden cord linking the two. For example, in the Bible there is Jacob's ladder, which has the same significance.[28] Again on a more popular level, there is the Indian rope trick where the magician or yogi throws a rope up into the air; it sticks up in the sky, and he climbs it with his disciple, and cuts his disciple into pieces; the pieces come falling down and the disciple is reconstituted. One finds this conception particularly strong in Shamanism,[29] all over the Arctic region. The staircase is that which unites the opposites, which links, draws together, heaven and earth. In the Buddhist texts, the archetypal significance of this episode of the Buddha's descent is enhanced by colourful, glowing descriptions in terms of gold and silver and crystal, and different coloured lights, and panoplies of coloured sun-shades and umbrellas, and flowers falling, and music sounding. These all make a strong appeal not to the conscious mind, but to the unconscious, to the depths.

Another important variant to the theme of the union of the opposites is what is generally known as the World Tree, or Cosmic Tree. The Buddha, according to the traditional account, gained Enlightenment at the foot of a peepul tree. It is significant that, from a historical, factual point of view, we don't really know whether he sat under a tree or not: the oldest accounts don't mention this. We may assume quite naturally that he did because, after all, he gained his Enlightenment in the month of May, which is the hottest time of year in India; so it is more than likely that he was sitting under a tree, just for the sake of shade and shelter from the heat. But we don't *know*. Gradually, it seems, as the legendary and mythical element grew in the biographies, the Buddha came to be more and more associated at the time of his Enlightenment with sitting at the foot of a tree. A tree's roots go deep down into the earth, but at the same time its branches tower high into the sky. So the tree also links

Calling the Earth Goddess to witness

The peepul tree, later known as the Bodhi tree

heaven and earth, is also a symbol of the union, or harmony, of opposites.

The World Tree is found in most mythologies. For instance, we have the Norse Yggdrasil, which is the World Ash – roots deep down, branches right up in the heavens, all the worlds as it were suspended on the branches. And one often gets this identification of the Christian cross with a World or Cosmic Tree. I have seen a representation of the crucifixion where branches were growing out of the sides of the cross, and the roots went deep down into the soil. The cross also, like the World Tree, links heaven and earth cosmically in the same way that Christ unites the human and the divine natures 'psychologically'.

Closely associated with the idea of a ladder, or a staircase, or a tree, is the image of the central point. In all the traditional legendary accounts of the Buddha's gaining Enlightenment, he is represented as sitting on what is called the *vajrāsana*, which literally means the Diamond Seat, or Diamond Throne as it is sometimes translated.[30] The diamond, the *vajra*, the *dorje*, in Buddhist tradition always represents the transcendental element, the metaphysical base.[31] According to tradition, the *vajrāsana* is the centre of the universe. One can compare this with the corresponding Christian tradition that the cross stood on the same spot as the Tree of Knowledge of Good and Evil, from which Adam and Eve had eaten the apple, and that this spot represents the exact centre of the world. This centrality in the cosmos of the *vajrāsana* suggests that Enlightenment consists in adopting a position of centrality. This metaphysical, or transcendental, centrality, which constitutes Enlightenment, amounts to the same as the union of opposites about which we have spoken.

We can go on in this way almost indefinitely – the scriptures, the traditional biographies, are full of material of this sort which, unfortunately, has not so far been explored in this way.[32]

The Buddha's Enlightenment

Now we are going to take up not just isolated archetypal symbols, but a whole sequence of symbols. This series is connected with the most important event in the Buddha's whole career, his attainment of Enlightenment. These symbols are represented by certain incidents usually regarded as historical, or partly historical, though their actual significance is much deeper.

The first of these incidents is traditionally known as the Victory over Māra,[33] the Evil One, the Satan of Buddhism. The Buddha – or the Bodhisattva (Pali *Bodhisatta*),[34] the Buddha-to-be – was seated in meditation at the foot of the tree – we are concerned with some of the later legendary accounts – when he was attacked by terrible demon hosts, by all sorts of foul, unsightly, misshapen figures, led by Māra. These hosts and their attack are vividly depicted in Buddhist art as well as in poetry. They were partly human, partly animal, hideously deformed, with snarling, leering, angry, and wrathful expressions, some of them lifting great clubs, others brandishing swords, all very menacing and frightful indeed. But all the stones, arrows, and flames, on reaching the edge of the Buddha's aura of light turned into flowers and fell at his feet.

The significance of this is obvious and doesn't need to be explained, only to be felt. The Buddha wasn't touched, wasn't moved, by this terrible attack. His eyes remained closed, he remained in meditation with the same smile on his lips. So Māra sent against the Buddha his three beautiful daughters, whose names are Lust, Passion, and Delight. They danced in front of the Buddha, exhibiting all their wiles, but the Buddha didn't even open his eyes. They retired discomfited.

All this represents the forces of the unconscious in their crude, unsublimated form. The demons, the terrible misshapen figures, represent anger, aversion, dislike, and so on. As for the daughters of Māra, they represent, of course, the various aspects of craving and desire. Māra himself represents primordial ignorance, or unawareness, on account of which we take birth again and again and again. Incidentally, the literal meaning of the name Māra is simply 'death'.

The second incident is known as the Calling of the Earth Goddess to Witness.[35] After he had been defeated,

after his hosts had returned discomfited, Māra tried another trick. He said to the Buddha-to-be, 'You are sitting on the central point of the universe, on the throne of the Buddhas of old. What right have you, just an ordinary person, to sit on that Diamond Throne where the previous Buddhas sat?' So the Buddha said, 'In my past lives I have practised all the *pāramitās*, all the Perfections, that is to say, Perfection of Giving, Perfection of Morality, Perfection of Patience, Perfection of Energy, Perfection of Meditation, Perfection of Wisdom.[36] I have practised all these, I have reached a point in my spiritual evolution where I am ready now, where I am about to gain Enlightenment. Therefore I am worthy to sit on this Diamond Throne like the previous Buddhas when they gained Enlightenment.'

Māra wasn't satisfied. He said, 'All right, you say that you practised all these Perfections in your previous lives, but who saw you? Who is your witness?' Māra takes on the guise of a lawyer, he wants a witness, he wants evidence. So the future Buddha, who was seated on the Diamond Throne in the position of meditation, with his hands resting in his lap, just tapped on the earth – this is the famous *bhūmisparśa mudrā*,[37] the earth-touching, or earth-witnessing *mudrā*, or position – and up rose the Earth Goddess, bearing a vase in her hand. She bore witness, saying, 'I have been here all the time. Men may come, men may go, but the earth always remains. I have seen all his previous lives. I have seen hundreds of thousands of lives in which he practised the Perfections. So I bear witness that on account of his practice of these Perfections he is worthy to sit in the seat of the Buddhas of old.'

This scene is also often depicted in Buddhist art – sometimes the Earth Goddess is shown as dark green in colour, sometimes a beautiful golden-brown, always half-emerged from the earth, very much like the figure of Mother Erda in Wagner's *The Ring*. (Erda, of course, means the earth, and Erda and the Earth Goddess are the same as Hertha, as in Swinburne's famous poem of that name.) The significance of the Earth Goddess is a whole subject in itself and there is a whole literature on it. Basically, she represents the same forces as those represented by Māra's daughters. But whereas Māra's daughters represent them in their crude, negative, unsublimated aspects, the Earth Goddess, as she bears witness, represents them in their tamed, subdued, even in their sublimated aspect, ready to help, not hinder.

The third incident is known as Brahmā's Request.[38] The Buddha, after his Enlightenment, was inclined to remain silent. He reflected, 'This Truth, this Reality which I have discovered, is so abstract, so difficult to see, so sublime, that ordinary people, their eyes covered with the dust of ignorance and passion, are not going to see it, to appreciate it. So it is better to remain silent, to remain under the Bodhi tree, better to remain with eyes closed, not to go out into the world and preach.' But then another great apparition arose. A great light shone forth, and in the midst of the light an ancient figure, the figure of Brahmā Sahampati, Brahmā the Great God, Lord of a Thousand Worlds, appeared before the Buddha with folded hands. He said, 'Please preach, preach the Truth – there are just a few with little dust on their eyes. They will appreciate, they will follow.' The Buddha opened his divine eye and looked forth over the universe. He saw all beings, just like lotuses in a pond, in various stages of development. And he said, 'For the sake of those with just a little dust over their eyes, those who are like lotuses half-way out, I will preach the Dharma.'

We shouldn't of course take this incident literally, in the historical sense – the Buddha was Enlightened, he didn't need to be asked to preach. Brahmā's Request represents the manifestation within the Buddha's own mind of the forces of Compassion which eventually compelled him to make known the Truth he had discovered, to preach to mankind.

The fourth and last episode is the Mucalinda episode.[39] For seven weeks the Buddha sat at the foot of the Bodhi tree and other trees in its vicinity, and in the middle of the seventh week there arose a great storm. The Buddha was Enlightened in the month of May, so seven weeks takes us to the middle of July, the beginning of the rainy season. In India, when the rainy season begins, in

Mucalinda salutes the Buddha

a matter of instants the whole sky becomes black and rain descends, not in bucketfuls, but in absolute reservoirfuls. The Buddha was out in the open, under a tree, with just a thin robe – he couldn't do much about it. But another figure arose out of the undergrowth, out of the shadows: a great snake, King Mucalinda, the Serpent-King. He came and wrapped his coils around the Buddha and stood with his hood over his head like an umbrella, and in this way protected him against the downpour. This episode is often depicted in Buddhist art, sometimes almost comically: you see a coil, like a coil of rope, with the Buddha's head just poking out, and the hood like an umbrella over him. Then the rain disappeared, the storm-clouds cleared up, and the Serpent-King assumed a different form, that of a beautiful youth about sixteen years of age, who saluted the Buddha.

Some scholars, I am afraid, try to take this episode literally, try to force some factual meaning from it, saying, 'Oh yes, it is well known that in the East snakes are sometimes quite friendly with holy men, and come and sit near them, and this is what must have happened.' But we cannot accept this pseudo-historical type of explanation. We are on a different plane, a different level of meaning altogether. All over the world, as we have seen, water, or the sea, or the ocean, represents the unconscious. And in Indian mythology – Hindu, Buddhist, and Jain – the *nāgas*, that is to say, the serpents, or the dragons, live in the depths of the ocean. So the *nāgas* represent the forces in the depths of the unconscious in their most positive and beneficent aspect – and Mucalinda is the king of the *nāgas*.

(The falling of the rain, the torrential downpour after seven weeks, represents a baptism, an aspersion. All over the world, pouring water on someone or on something represents the investiture of that person or that object with all the powers of the unconscious mind. As in Christianity, there is a baptism with water and with fire, an investiture with the forces of the unconscious mind and with the forces of the spirit.)

The rain, we saw, falls at the end of the seventh week, and Mucalinda wraps his coils seven times around the seated figure of the Buddha. This repetition of the figure seven is no coincidence. Mucalinda also stands for what the Tantras call the *Chandali*, the Fiery Power, or the Fiery One, what the Hindus call the *Kuṇḍalinī*, or the Coiled-up One, or the Serpent Power, which represents all the powerful psychic energies surging up inside a person, especially at the time of meditation, through the median nerve. The seven coils, or the winding seven times round the Buddha, represent the seven psychic centres[40] through which the *Kuṇḍalinī* passes in the course of its ascent. Mucalinda's assuming the form of a beautiful sixteen-year-old youth represents the new personality which is born as a result of this upward progression of the *Chandali*, or *Kuṇḍalinī*. Mucalinda in the new form salutes the Buddha: this represents the perfect submission of all the powers of the unconscious to the Enlightened mind.

It is obvious from all this that these four incidents all have a deep psychological and spiritual significance.

They are not just pseudo-history, and they are not just a fairy tale – though even fairy tales have a significance – but they are invested with a powerful symbolic and archetypal meaning.

The Four Principal Archetypes

Going a little further, we may say that the four main figures with which we have been concerned form a very definite set: Māra the Evil One, Vasundharā the Earth Goddess, Brahmā, and Mucalinda, in that order – and the order in which they appear is rather interesting. Now I am going to draw what some people may feel is a bold analogy, but I think it has great significance and suggestiveness. It seems to me that these four figures are to some extent analogous to the four principal archetypes according to Jung and that their appearance in this order represents an integration of these contents into the conscious mind – in other words represents, on a higher level, what Jung calls the individuation process.[41] Māra corresponds to what Jung calls the Shadow, that darker side of ourselves of which we are ashamed, which we usually try to keep under. The Earth Goddess represents the Anima. (The Buddha, being a man, had an Anima – in the case of a woman it would be an Animus.) Brahmā represents the archetype of the Wise Old Man. He is seen in Buddhist art with white hair and a beard, a sort of God-the-Father figure. And Mucalinda is the archetype of the Young Hero.

There is also a correspondence with the principal figures of Christian mythology: Māra corresponds to Satan, the Earth Goddess to the Virgin Mary, Brahmā to God, and Mucalinda to Christ. I don't think this is too far-fetched. If we study these matters carefully, go into them deeply, we should see the analogy. In Tantric Buddhism, there is a similar set: The Guardian (or the Protector, as he is sometimes called), the *ḍākinī*, the guru, and the *yidam*.[42]

Though I have drawn these analogies, there is a great difference of principle between the Buddhist and the Christian approaches to, or attitudes towards, the archetypes of their respective traditions. In Buddhism, it is always clearly, even categorically, stated that all these appearances, all these archetypal forms, are ultimately phenomena of one's own True Mind, or projections from one's own unconscious, and that they are all to be integrated. But in Christianity the corresponding archetypes are regarded as objectively existing beings. One cannot really resolve an archetype in the sense of incorporating it as representing unconscious contents into one's conscious mind, one's conscious attitudes, or one's new self, unless one realizes that, in the last analysis, it isn't something objectively existing, but something which one has projected from some depths, from some hidden source within oneself.

On account of this limitation, in the Christian tradition – with the exception perhaps of a few heretical mystics – there is no full resolution of the archetypal figure, whereas in Buddhism, on account of a more deeply metaphysical and spiritual background, such a resolution is possible. In Buddhism all the archetypes can be dissolved, can be drawn back into one's own conscious attitude, and integrated there so as to enrich, perfect, and beautify it. In other words, the individuation process can be carried to its absolute conclusion, Enlightenment.

We have only touched on a few of the archetypal symbols occurring in the biography of the Buddha. I would have liked to mention many more, for instance the Buddha's begging-bowl. There are many legends about it, some of them very interesting indeed. In fact, we may say without any exaggeration that it occupies in Buddhist legend and history a position analogous to that of the Holy Grail in Christianity, and carries much the same significance.

The archetypes, some of which I have mentioned, are not just of historic or literary interest, not something foreign to us. Each and every one of them is present within us all; or we can say that we are all present in them. We share them, we have them all in common, or they share us, have all of us in common. And in the course of our spiritual life, especially as we practise meditation, these archetypes tend to emerge in various ways into consciousness. Sometimes they show themselves, at least by way of a glimpse, in dreams, in meditation, or in waking fantasies. We all have to encounter the Shadow, for instance. This is the dark, unpleasant side of ourselves which appears in dreams, for example, as a black snarling hound, snapping at our heels, which we want to get rid of, but cannot; or as a dark man, etc. We have to face the Shadow, come to terms with it, even assimilate this darker side of ourselves, just as the Buddha faced and overcame Māra and his hosts. And here, just as in the case of Māra, repression is no solution. The Shadow, or the content represented by the Shadow, must be saturated with awareness and resolved. The Buddha himself didn't start emitting flames to counteract the flames of Māra's hosts; but when the flames touched his aura, they were just transformed into flowers, transmuted. This is also the sort of thing we have to do with our own Shadow – just see it, recognize it, accept it, and then transform and transmute it into what Tantric tradition calls a Guardian, or Protector.

We too have to call up the Earth Goddess, which means in psychoanalytical language that we have to face, and free ourselves from, the Anima – in the case of a man – that is to say, we have to bring up and integrate into our own conscious attitude our own unconscious femininity, just as a woman has to bring up and integrate her own unconscious masculinity. If this is done, there will no longer be any question of projecting these unconscious, unrealized contents on to members of the opposite sex, and the 'problem', as it is sometimes called, of sex will have been resolved. This is a very important aspect of the spiritual life.

Next, we all have to learn from the Wise Old Man. Sometimes, we may quite literally have to sit at the feet of a teacher, or at least have some ideal image to which we owe allegiance. Then, perhaps after many years, we have to incorporate into ourselves the qualities which that figure represents – wisdom, knowledge, and so on.

And then, finally, each one has to give birth within himself (or herself) to the Young Hero, in other words, create the nucleus of a new self, a new being, or in traditional Buddhist language, give birth within ourselves to the Buddha.

If we face our own Shadow, call up our own Anima or Animus, learn from our Wise Old Man and give birth within ourselves to our own Young Hero, we shall live out, we shall recapitulate within ourselves in our own lives, at all levels, in all aspects, the archetypal symbols which appear in the Buddha's biography.

The Symbolism of the Five Buddhas, 'Male' and 'Female'

Let us begin by going back to fundamentals, to the idea of Buddhahood. The first thing we have to understand – and this is very important – is that the Buddha is a human being. But a Buddha is a special kind of human being, in fact the highest kind, so far as we know. A Buddha is one who, in his spiritual development, so far transcends the ordinary run of humanity as to be, in a sense, no longer a human being at all. A Buddha is a human being who has attained *bodhi*, or, more technically, *samyaksambodhi*. *Bodhi* means 'Knowledge', or 'Understanding', even 'Awakening'. *Samyaksambodhi* means 'Supreme Knowledge', or 'Perfect Understanding', etc. *Bodhi*, however, is much more than knowledge, much more even than transcendental Knowledge. Broadly speaking *bodhi* – that which makes a Buddha a Buddha – has three main aspects. For the sake of convenience, we can call these the cognitive, the volitional, and the emotional.

The Cognitive Aspect of Bodhi

From this point of view, *bodhi* is a state of Insight, of Wisdom, of Awareness. But Insight into what? In the first place there is Insight into oneself. This means, in other words, taking a deep, clear, profound look into oneself and seeing how, on all the different levels of one's being, one is conditioned, governed by the reactive mind[43] (one reacts mechanically, automatically, on account of past psychological conditionings, of which only too often one is largely unconscious). It means seeing, moreover, the extent to which one is dominated, even against one's will (often without one's knowledge), by the negative emotions. Then there is Insight into others. This means extending one's vision and seeing the way others too are conditioned, even as one is conditioned oneself. Then, ranging even further afield, Insight consists in including in one's vision the whole of phenomena, the whole of nature, the universe itself on all its levels, and seeing how this too is conditioned, seeing this as transitory, ever changeful, frustrating, and unreal.

Insight is not only insight into universal conditionedness. It is seeing right through the conditioned and finding the Unconditioned. It is seeing the Eternal in the depths of the transitory, the Real in the depths of the unreal, and even, ultimately, seeing the two as one – as different facets of one and the same ultimate, absolute Reality.

The Volitional Aspect of Bodhi

Bodhi is not just a state of Knowledge. It is also a state of untrammelled Freedom, of Emancipation, both subjective and objective. Subjectively it is a state of freedom from all moral and spiritual defilements. In other words, it consists in freedom from, for instance, the 'Five Mental Poisons',[44] in freedom from all negative emotions, in freedom from the whole process of the reactive mind. Objectively it consists in freedom from the consequences of defilement. In other words, it consists in freedom from karma[45] and from rebirth – freedom from the turnings of the Wheel of Life.[46] More positively, one may say that this Freedom, the volitional aspect of *bodhi*, consists in a state of uninterrupted creativity, especially spiritual creativity, and spontaneity.

The Emotional Aspect of Bodhi

Bodhi is also a state of positive emotion, or perhaps we should say, of *spiritual* emotion. This too can be described as both subjective and objective. Subjectively it consists in a state or experience of supreme Joy, Bliss, Ecstasy. Objectively, in manifestation, it is a state of unbounded Love and Compassion for all living beings.

The Three Bodies of the Buddha

Thus a Buddha is a human being who, having attained the state of *samyaksambodhi*, is a living embodiment of Insight, Freedom, Happiness, and Love. I have been using the expression 'a Buddha', but at the beginning of the Buddhist tradition there was only one Buddha, *the* Buddha, the human, historical Śākyamuni. We find that even during the Buddha's lifetime a spiritually important distinction was drawn – it seems that even the Buddha himself drew it – between the Enlightened historical individual, on the one hand, and the abstract principle of Enlightenment, on the other; between

Buddha and Buddhahood. This distinction found expression in certain technical terms. The Enlightened historical personality was known as the *rūpakāya*, or 'Form-Body' (*rūpa* is 'form', *kāya* is 'body' or 'personality'). The principle of Enlightenment independent of the person realizing it was known as the *dharmakāya*, the 'Body of Truth', or 'Body of Reality'. In spite of this distinction, we must not consider that there is a difference: both the Form-Body and the Dharma-Body are bodies of the Buddha.

The distinction was not insisted on very strongly during the Buddha's own lifetime because in his case Buddha and Buddhahood, *rūpakāya* and *dharmakāya*, were united. But after the *parinirvāṇa* the distinction became more pronounced. After all, the Form-Body was dead and gone, the historical Buddha only existed in the form of relics in stupas,[47] whereas the Dharma-Body was eternally present. We can imagine the early Mahāyāna (which first elaborated the distinction between the two bodies) thinking vertically and seeing the Form-Body 'down there' in past time and the Dharma-Body 'up there' out of time, transcending time, so that there is a vertical relationship between the Enlightened individual and the principle of Enlightenment.

The late Mahāyāna continued to think vertically, but within that vertical thinking, or that vertical *experience*, a development took place. A third *kāya*, or 'body', appeared in between the other two. This was known eventually as the *sambhogakāya*, which means literally 'Body of Mutual Delight', or 'Body of Mutual Enjoyment'. This term, though it has a profound meaning of its own, is not very helpful in this context and can be better, more 'interpretatively', rendered as 'Ideal Buddha', or even 'Archetypal Buddha'. This Ideal Buddha is not an impersonal, abstract principle like the *dharmakāya*; it is definitely a person, but at the same time not a human, historical person. One could say that it is the Ideal person, even the archetypal person, below the level of the Absolute but above and beyond history.

Thus at this stage of development there were three *kāyas*, three 'bodies', vertically aligned. From top to bottom we have the Dharma-Body, then the Body of Mutual Delight, and finally the Created Body, or *nirmāṇakāya*, as it was now called, the term *rūpakāya* being at this stage applied to the Ideal Buddha and the historical Buddha collectively. What had developed was the famous *trikāya* doctrine, the doctrine of the Three Bodies of the Buddha, which is very important for the Mahāyāna and Vajrayāna. At present, however, we are just concerned with the fact that it became the basis for further developments in both the Mahāyāna and the Vajrayāna.

The Mandala of the Five Buddhas

Something rather dramatic happened next. The human historical Buddha, the *nirmāṇakāya*, disappeared into the past, almost out of sight (in Mahāyāna and Vajrayāna countries one finds that the historical Buddha Śākyamuni occupies a comparatively unimportant place), and Buddhahood, the *dharmakāya*, receded into the background – after all, the *dharmakāya* is rather abstract, not

to say vague, and rather difficult to grasp. What was left, occupying the centre of the stage as it were, was the Ideal, Archetypal Buddha. (This is *the* Buddha of the Mahāyāna, as, for example, in the *White Lotus Sūtra*,[48] where this Ideal Buddha is called Śākyamuni yet is obviously no longer the human personality of the Buddha; he is rather the Archetypal Buddha of Infinite Light and Eternal Life.)

The Mahāyāna did not rest there. A further development took place. So far the Mahāyāna had been thinking vertically. It now started thinking horizontally. Two more Buddhas appeared on either side of the Ideal Buddha. On his right appeared Amitābha, the Buddha of Infinite Light, and on his left Akṣobhya, the Imperturbable. These two Buddhas embodied – in the form of further Ideal Buddha-figures – the two principal aspects of Buddhahood itself. A clue to what these aspects are is provided by the emblems of the two new Buddhas. The emblem of Amitābha is the lotus flower. The emblem of Akṣobhya is the *vajra*. The lotus flower is soft, tender, and delicate; the *vajra* hard, strong, and powerful. The lotus flower is passive and receptive; the *vajra* active and dynamic. So we may say – in perhaps over-conceptual terms – that Amitābha is the embodiment of the Love aspect of the Ideal Buddha, the Love aspect of Enlightenment, whereas Akṣobhya is the embodiment of the aspect of transcendental Wisdom. (There are variations on this fundamental pattern. One can have, for instance, a Buddha flanked by two Bodhisattvas. The Buddha represents the Ideal Buddha, the Bodhisattvas his two principal aspects of Love and Wisdom.)

We have now to proceed to developments in the Vajrayāna, or Tantra. The Tantra thought both horizontally and vertically. As a result, two more Buddhas appeared. One appeared above the Ideal Buddha, the other below. For the time being we can call the one above 'the Buddha of Action' and the one below 'the Buddha of Beauty'. So now we have five Buddhas: one in the centre, one on the right, one on the left, one above, and one below. These five Buddhas make up what is called the Mandala of the Five Buddhas.

I have said that the Tantra thought both horizontally and vertically, but this is not quite correct. Those are only two dimensions, whereas the Tantra thought three-dimensionally. We must imagine the five Buddhas as occupying different directions on the same horizontal plane: one in the centre, one north, one south, one east, and one west. Then we must imagine, running through the centre of this plane, a central vertical axis, with the Dharma-Body in the zenith and the Created Body in the nadir. Thus the Ideal Buddha is in vertical alignment with the Dharma-Body and the Created Body, as well as in horizontal alignment with the two other pairs of Ideal Buddhas. In the vision of the Tantra, the Ideal Buddha is thus at the centre of the whole three-dimensional network.

I will now describe the symbolism of each of the Five Buddhas individually, starting with Vairocana, the Buddha of the centre, then moving round the mandala in a clockwise direction. As I describe them, we can try to 'see' them. For the most part, we shall leave the creative symbols to make their own impression. After all, symbols are essentially creative, i.e. capable of producing a direct impression without having to be rendered into their conceptual equivalents, equivalents which are, in any case, only approximate.

Vairocana

He is seated cross-legged. He wears monastic-type robes, but richly embroidered ones because he is on the archetypal plane. His hair is black, curly, and closely cropped. He has long ear-lobes. Sometimes he has a slight protuberance on the top of the head and a brilliant white curl of hair between the eyebrows.

Vairocana is brilliant white, like pure white light. White in the Tantra is the colour of the Absolute and the colour of centrality. (If we study some of the symbols of the Tantra, we find that the colour white is assumed by other Buddhas and Bodhisattvas, their own proper colour being left aside, as they move towards the centre of the mandala, either literally or metaphorically. Two Bodhisattvas who represent good examples of this

phenomenon are Avalokiteśvara and Tārā. Avalokiteśvara, technically speaking, is a Bodhisattva and his real colour is red, but in the course of time, in Tibet especially, Avalokiteśvara took on more and more importance, so much so that he became a sort of Buddha. Many people worshipped him and meditated upon him to the exclusion of all other Buddha or Bodhisattva figures. He occupied the centre of the mandala as far as their spiritual lives were concerned. To indicate this his colour was changed from red to white. The same sort of development occurred in the case of Tārā, whose real colour is green. Her position as a Bodhisattva of a particular Buddha family was forgotten. For her particular devotees she became all in all. As she assumed more and more importance, as she became *the* Buddha form, she took on the colour white, the colour of centrality and absoluteness.)

Vairocana's name literally means 'The Illuminator', the one who sheds light and radiance. The name 'Vairocana' was originally – from Vedic times – an epithet of the sun. In Japan, where the cult of Vairocana spread, he is generally known as the 'Sun Buddha' – he is a sort of sun of the spiritual universe. Vairocana has his own special emblem, the wheel, especially the eight-spoked golden wheel, the wheel of the Dharma. Sometimes in Tantric art he is depicted holding this wheel in his hands against his chest.

Vairocana's *mudrā* is that of the *dharmacakra*, representing the historical Buddha's initial proclamation of the Truth in the Deer Park at Sarnath. In early Buddhist art when the Buddha is depicted teaching for that first time in the Deer Park he is shown in this *mudrā*.

Vairocana also has a special animal, the lion, which is also associated with the proclamation of the Truth. In the Buddhist scriptures the Buddha's utterance is sometimes referred to as his *singha-nāda*, his 'lion's roar' (*singha* is 'lion', *nāda* is 'sound' or 'roar'). The lion roars in the jungle at night, without fear of other beasts. Other animals are afraid to make a sound, lest they be pounced on by their enemies. The lion roars, according to myth and legend, to proclaim his kingship of the whole jungle. So the Buddha's fearless proclamation of the Truth, his proclamation of his sovereignty over the whole spiritual universe, is compared to the roaring of the lion.

Vairocana is the head of the *Tathāgata* or Buddha family. This is very significant, as it suggests that Vairocana is *the* Buddha, of which the other Buddhas are only aspects. One of the most important members of that family is Mañjuśrī, the Bodhisattva of Transcendental Wisdom.

Akṣobhya

He occupies the eastern quarter of the mandala and is dark blue in colour – the colour of the midnight sky in the tropics. His name means 'Unshakeable', 'Immovable', 'Imperturbable', and his emblem is the *vajra*. Akṣobhya's *mudrā* is the *bhūmisparśa*, or 'earth-touching', *mudrā*.

His animal is the elephant, the biggest and strongest of all land animals – it is not very easy to push an elephant around! According to tradition, the elephant is also the wisest of animals. Akṣobhya is the head of the *Vajra* family, which includes the Bodhisattva or Buddha Vajrasattva and also many wrathful divinities (Buddhas, Bodhisattvas, guardians in wrathful form), such as Śaṁvara, Heruka, Hevajra, and Bhairava. In fact, there appear to be more wrathful deities in the *Vajra* family than in the family of any other Buddha. This may be due to the powerful associations of the *vajra*.

Ratnasambhava

He occupies the southern quarter of the mandala. His name means 'The Jewel-born One', or 'Jewel-producing One', and his emblem, naturally, is the jewel. His *mudrā* is the *vārada mudrā*, or *mudrā* of the supreme gift, the gift of the Three Jewels. Ratnasambhava's animal is the horse, which is associated with the historical Buddha's departure from home at night, on horseback. In Buddhism the horse is the embodiment of speed and energy, especially energy in the form of *prāṇa*, or vital breath. In Tibetan Buddhist art one often finds the figure of a horse galloping through the air, carrying the Three Jewels on

its back. This figure suggests that only through the concentration and proper direction of all one's energies can one gain Enlightenment. Ratnasambhava is the head of the Jewel family, which includes the Bodhisattva Ratnapāṇi, as well as Jambhala, the so-called god of riches, and Vasundharā, the Earth Goddess.

Amitābha

He occupies the western quarter of the mandala. He is red in colour. His name means 'Infinite Light'. His emblem is the lotus flower, which signifies spiritual rebirth and spiritual growth.

Amitābha occupies a particularly important place in Japanese Buddhism, right down to the present day, especially in the Jōdō Shin School, where they don't worship any other Buddha or Bodhisattva. The Jōdō Shin School recommends the invocation of the name of Amitābha not in order to gain Enlightenment but as an expression of gratitude for the gift of Enlightenment as already received. The devotee of the Jōdō Shin School aspires to be reborn after death in Sukhāvatī, the 'land, or realm, of bliss', the Pure Land[49] of Amitābha, situated in the western quarter of the universe. He aspires to rebirth there because there the conditions for gaining Enlightenment are said to be much more favourable than they are on Earth: one doesn't have to bother about food or drink, which appear automatically; one doesn't have to bother about clothes; the climate is beautiful; all the time one hears the Buddha Amitābha teaching – spiritual progress is assured.

The *mudrā* of Amitābha is that of meditation, in which one hand is placed on top of the other, the palms uppermost. Amitābha, being associated with the West, is associated with the setting sun, with the disappearance of light, as when in meditation the mind, withdrawing from material objects, enters a sort of darkness – a higher state of consciousness, a state which is, as it were, unconsciousness to the lower mind.

Amitābha's animal, or rather bird, is the peacock, the most splendid of all birds. Why it should be a peacock is not quite clear, and various explanations have been offered. On account of the eyes on the peacock's tail, the peacock is sometimes associated with consciousness, but that doesn't seem particularly relevant here. It might be because the peacock lives on snakes, including poisonous snakes, which suggests immunity to poison, immunity to defilement. Peacock feathers are quite often used in Tantric ritual. They are placed like flowers in the vase which contains the consecrated water.

Amitābha is the head of the Lotus family, which includes quite a number of well-known spiritual figures. The most important of these is Avalokiteśvara, the Bodhisattva of Compassion. There are also Kurukullā, Padmanarteśvara, and Padmasambhava.

Amoghasiddhi

He occupies the northern quarter of the mandala. He is green in colour. His name means 'Infallible Success' or 'Unobstructed Accomplishment'. His emblem is the double *vajra* (two *vajras* crossed). This is a very powerful and mysterious symbol indeed (it is connected with, among other things, a special aspect of the union of opposites). The *mudrā* of Amoghasiddhi is that of Fearlessness, one of the heroic virtues, which is greatly emphasized in all forms of Buddhism, most of all perhaps in the Tantra.[50] Amoghasiddhi's animal, or creature, is the garuḍa or 'bird-man', a fabulous hybrid creature, which is human (male or female) from the waist upwards, while having the feet and wings of a bird. Amoghasiddhi is the head of the Karma or Action family. Action is symbolized by a sword. The best known member of that family is Green Tārā.

'Male' and 'Female' Buddhas

Within the esoteric Tantra there were further developments of the fivefold Buddha pattern. We have seen that the early Mahāyāna, thinking vertically, envisaged the Ideal Body, the Body of Mutual Delight, in between the Dharma Body above and the Created Body below. We have seen that the late Mahāyāna, thinking horizontally, saw on either side of the Ideal Body two more Ideal Buddha-figures, one embodying the Love aspect of

(left) Amoghasiddhi
(below) A yab-yum

Enlightenment, the other the Wisdom aspect. We have seen that the Tantra, continuing to think horizontally but within the context of its own three-dimensional approach, envisaged another pair of Ideal Buddha-figures in the north and south, the 'Buddha of Action' and the 'Buddha of Beauty'. All the Buddhas, at each stage of development, were envisaged in male form. The original, historical Buddha was, of course, an Enlightened human being of the male sex. Nevertheless the esoteric Tantra, taking a dramatic new step, now envisaged the Ideal Buddha divided into two figures, one male and one female, locked in sexual union.

At this point we have to be careful not to misunderstand. At this level we are not concerned with sex, but with sexual *symbolism*, which is a very different thing. The 'male' and 'female' Buddha-figures represent the two principal aspects of Enlightenment: Love and Wisdom. What the Tantra is trying to express is the inseparable two-in-oneness of Love and Wisdom, *karuṇā* and *prajñā*. It is said that this two-in-oneness of Love and Wisdom is the very essence of Buddhahood. We must remember that the Tantra had no particular hang-ups about sex and so saw no objection to communicating its meaning in sexual terms. These were just as valid as any other terms. The content of the terms, however, was not itself sexual.

In Tibet and its cultural dependencies the 'male' and 'female' Buddha-figures in sexual union are known as *yab-yum*: *yab* meaning 'father' and *yum* 'mother' – the figures are as it were the archetypal father-mother. In the monasteries and temples of Tibet one finds many beautiful scroll paintings and images depicting these Buddha-figures in sexual union. For the Tibetans there is no sexual or erotic suggestion whatsoever. If one observes Tibetan Buddhists moving around their temples, one sees that when they come upon these figures, far from reacting in the way that Westerners often do, they seem to feel more reverence, more devotion, than ever. In some ways these figures are considered especially sacred inasmuch as the symbolism pertains to the highest level of spiritual experience, the level of Enlightenment, the level on which Love and Wisdom are finally integrated. For the Tibetans these figures are a symbolic expression of a profound spiritual truth, the truth of the inseparable two-in-oneness of Love and Wisdom. This is the way in which the Tibetans see them.

It is a real pity that these *yab-yum* figures are often regarded in the West as examples of Eastern erotic art, even pornographic art. This only goes to show that there is hardly anybody in the West, perhaps, who is free from sexual hang-ups, thanks largely to our Judaeo-Christian heritage.

Incidentally, one might have thought that the 'male' Buddha-figure represented the Wisdom aspect of Enlightenment and the 'female' Buddha-figure the Love aspect. This is not so. In the Buddhist Tantra it is the 'female' Buddha who embodies the Wisdom aspect and the 'male' Buddha who embodies the Love and Compassion aspect, which is also, incidentally, the Action aspect. This provides further evidence of the fact that this symbolism has got nothing whatsoever to do with ordinary sexual differences. Sometimes these two figures are symbolized by the *vajra* and the lotus or by the *vajra* and the bell.

We have not yet reached the end of the development. Not only does the Ideal Buddha, the Archetypal Buddha, divide into two figures – 'male' and 'female' sexually united – but the other four Buddhas similarly divide. So at this point there are not just five Buddhas but ten Buddhas: five 'male' Buddhas and five 'female' Buddhas. The 'female' Buddhas are regarded as the spiritual consorts of the 'male' Buddhas. I will say a little about each of the five 'female' Buddhas.

Ākāśadhātīśvarī

Ākāśadhātīśvarī is the consort of Vairocana, the white Buddha, the Buddha of the centre. Her name, Ākāśadhātīśvarī, means 'The Sovereign Lady of the Sphere of Infinite Space'. We recollect that Vairocana himself is the sun, the Sun Buddha, the sun of the whole spiritual cosmos. He is radiating light and heat in all directions, the light of Wisdom and the heat of Love. Ākāśadhātīśvarī, the Sovereign Lady of the Sphere of Infinite Space, represents the infinite space through which the rays of the light of Vairocana fall. She represents unlimited spiritual receptivity. She represents the whole of the phenomenal universe as completely pervaded by the influence, or the effluence, of the Absolute. In the language of *The Awakening of Faith* she represents the whole of phenomenal existence as thoroughly perfumed by the Absolute. Like Vairocana, Ākāśadhātīśvarī is white in colour. She is represented in *ḍākinī*[51] form, i.e. with loose flowing garments and long dishevelled hair.

Locanā

Locanā is the consort of Akṣobhya, the deep blue Buddha, the Buddha of the east. Her name means 'The Clear Visioned One', or literally 'The One with an Eye'. In Tibetan her name is translated as 'Lady Possessing the Buddha Eye'. She is the embodiment of pure Awareness; she represents pure, simple, direct awareness of things. Her consort Akṣobhya is especially connected with Transcendental Wisdom. (He is practically the only Buddha who appears in the Sūtras of Transcendental Wisdom, especially in the one in 8,000 lines.[52]) So the association between Locanā and Akṣobhya suggests that there is no Wisdom without Awareness and no Awareness without Wisdom: the two are inseparably connected, are in a sense different aspects of the same spiritual experience. Locanā is light blue in colour.

Māmakī

Māmakī is the consort of Ratnasambhava, the yellow Buddha, the Buddha of the south. Her name means 'Mine-maker'. She is the one who makes everything mine, though not in a selfish egoistic sense – one is now on the level of Enlightenment. Māmakī is that spiritual attitude that regards everything and everybody as mine, as my own, in a sense as my *very* own, as dear to me, precious to me, valuable to me. So Māmakī enjoys everybody, delights in everybody, rejoices in everybody, even, one might say, regards everybody as her own self. She sees no difference between herself and others. To her all other people are 'mine', are even 'me'. Her colour is yellow.

Pāṇḍaravāsinī

Pāṇḍaravāsinī is the consort of Amitābha, the red Buddha, the Buddha of the West. Her name means 'The White-Robed One', which suggests one who is vested in purity, or even insulated by purity. The imagery here recalls the Buddha's image for the fourth *dhyāna* (the fourth state of higher consciousness). The Buddha said that one's experience in the fourth *dhyāna* is like the experience of a man who, on a hot and dusty day, takes a bath in a beautiful pond and, having bathed, emerges from the water and wraps himself in a pure white sheet. This wrapping in a pure white sheet represents the gradual accumulation of all one's energies, especially one's emotional energies, and one's insulation of those energies from possibly harmful outside influences. So Pāṇḍaravāsinī is the White-Robed One, isolated, insulated, from outside influences. She is light red in colour.

Tārā:

Tārā is the consort of Amoghasiddhi, the deep green Buddha, the Buddha of the north. Her name means 'The One Who Ferries Across'. She ferries across the river of birth and death, the river of saṃsāra.[53] She recalls in her function the Buddha's parable of the raft. Just as a raft is something to help one cross a river and no more (one would not think of carrying a raft with one once one had reached the other shore), so the Dharma is solely a means to the end of crossing the river of birth and death and reaching the other shore, which is nirvāṇa. The name Tārā is often translated as 'Saviouress', but this can be rather misleading. We may say that Tārā represents the attitude of helping people to help themselves.

These are the five 'female' Buddhas: Ākāśadhātīśvarī, 'The Sovereign Lady of the Sphere of Infinite Space'; Locanā, 'The One with the Eye'; Māmakī, 'The Mine-maker'; Pāṇḍaravāsinī, 'The White-Robed One'; and Tārā, 'The One Who Ferries Across'. These five 'female' Buddhas together with their 'male' counterparts represent different aspects of the one integral Enlightenment experience, an experience which is in essence an experience of the inseparable two-in-oneness of Wisdom and Love.

The Wrathful Buddhas

There is one final development to be mentioned in the symbolic pattern with which we are concerned. In the esoteric Tantra, Buddhas and Bodhisattvas appear under two aspects: a peaceful aspect and a wrathful aspect. This applies to the Five Buddhas too. So far I have described the five 'male' Buddhas and the five 'female' Buddhas in their peaceful forms. Now I will say just a few words about them in their wrathful forms. The wrathful forms are much less highly individualized than the peaceful forms. In their wrathful forms the five 'male' Buddhas are known as the 'Five *Herukas*'. They are all named after their respective Buddha families. So there is the Buddha-Heruka, the Vajra-Heruka, the Ratna-Heruka, the Padma-Heruka, and the Karma-Heruka. Each one is represented as powerfully, even massively, built, as naked, except for a tiger skin and an elephant hide, and as wearing garlands of human skulls. Round their bodies and arms are twined snakes. They usually possess at least six arms, sometimes many more. Each has three bulging, inflamed eyes and a wrathful expression. They are usually represented as trampling on the enemies of the Dharma. They are pictured moving violently to the right. They are surrounded, each one, by a halo of flame. The Buddha-Heruka is either dark blue or black in colour, the others blue, yellow, red, and green respectively.

The consort of the Buddha-Heruka, the equivalent 'female' Heruka, is known simply as Krodheśvarī, which may be translated as 'Lady of Wrath'. The consorts of the other Herukas are, like the 'male' Herukas, named after

their respective Buddha families. So there is the Vajra Lady of Wrath, the Jewel Lady of Wrath, the Lotus Lady of Wrath, and the Action Lady of Wrath. They are all depicted in the same kind of way. They are naked, or practically naked. They are of the same colour as their consort, but the colour is lighter. They are somewhat smaller in size than their consort. In each case they cling on to the front of their consort, sometimes with their arms clasped round his neck.

Such then is the symbolism of the Five Buddhas, the 'male' and the 'female', the peaceful and the wrathful. This is one of the most important, most beautiful, and most meaningful patterns in the whole range of the Tantra.[54] It is a pattern that organizes part at least of the riches of the Tantra into a form that we can appreciate and perhaps assimilate. Yet in the midst of all these forms, we must never forget that *all* of them, whether 'male' or 'female', peaceful or wrathful, represent different aspects of the *one* Enlightenment experience, different aspects of Buddhahood. We must never forget that they all embody, indeed are the product of, spiritual experiences. If we remember this, perhaps we shall be able to respond to them. If we respond to them, we shall be helped by them – helped, in fact, by all the creative symbols of the Tantric Path to Enlightenment.

The Five Wisdoms

Each of the 'Five Buddhas' symbolizes a different aspect of Wisdom. These aspects of Wisdom are collectively known as the 'Five *Jñānas*', the 'Five Wisdoms', or the 'Five Knowledges'.

The first of the Five Wisdoms is the Wisdom of the *Dharmadhātu* and is symbolized by Vairocana. This is the basic Wisdom, of which the other four are special aspects. The term *Dharmadhātu* is a difficult one. *Dhātu* means a 'sphere', or 'realm', or 'field', and here represents the whole cosmos. *Dharma* here means 'Reality', 'Truth', the 'Ultimate'. So the *Dharmadhātu* means the universe considered as the sphere of the manifestation of Reality, or the universe conceived of as fully pervaded by Reality. Just as the whole of space is filled by the sun's rays, so the whole of existence, with its galactic systems, its suns, its worlds, its gods, and its men, is pervaded by Reality itself. It is a field for the manifestation of, the play of, the expression of, the exuberance of Reality.

The Wisdom of the *Dharmadhātu* therefore means direct knowledge of the whole cosmos as non-different from Reality. Not that the cosmos is wiped out or obliterated. The cosmos is still there and you see it still. The houses, the trees, the fields, the men and the women, the sun, the moon, and the stars are all there, just as they were before, but now they are pervaded by Reality. You see both the cosmos and Reality at the same time – the one does not obstruct the other. You see the cosmos; you see Reality. You see Reality; you see the cosmos. Cosmos is Reality; Reality is cosmos. *Rūpa* is *śūnyatā*; *śūnyatā* is *rūpa*.[55]

Then, secondly, there is the Mirror-like Wisdom, symbolized by Akṣobhya. This Wisdom is like a mirror, because just as a mirror reflects all objects, so the Enlightened mind reflects everything: it sees everything, it understands the true nature of everything. If you look into the depths of the Enlightened mind you see everything.

All the objects of the world are reflected in the depths of the Enlightened mind, but the Enlightened mind is not affected by them – they do not stick. If you take a mirror and place an object in front of it, the object is reflected. If you take that object away and put another object in front of the mirror, the mirror now reflects that. When you move the object – or when you move the mirror – you do not find the reflection sticking. The Enlightened mind is just like that: it reflects but nothing sticks. *Our* mind, however, is quite different. If you pursue the illustration, you may say that our mind is a sort of mirror, but all the reflections stick. In fact they not only stick, but they congeal. They get all jammed up together. Sometimes the mirror even sticks to the object so that you cannot separate them. In other words, in the Enlightened mind there is no subjective reaction, no subjective attachment, there is pure, perfect objectivity – just like a mirror reflecting everything that exists.

The third of the Five Wisdoms is the Wisdom of Equality or Sameness. This is symbolized by Ratnasambhava. The Enlightened mind sees everything with complete objectivity. The Enlightened mind sees the same Reality in all, the same *śūnyatā* in all, and so has the same attitude towards all. It sees that a man is a man, a woman is a woman, a flower is a flower, a tree is a tree, a house is a house, the sun is the sun, and the moon is the moon. It sees all that, but at the same time it sees the common Reality in all and so has a common attitude towards all. The Enlightened mind is equal-minded towards all. There is the same Love, the same Compassion, for all, without any distinction or discrimination. Sometimes it is said that the Love and the Compassion of the Enlightened mind fall without discrimination on all beings, on all objects, on all things, just as the sun's rays fall now on the golden roofs of a palace and now on a dung-hill – it is the same sun. The Enlightened mind shines with its Love and its Compassion on high and low, on 'good' and 'bad'.

The fourth of the Five Wisdoms is the All-distinguishing Wisdom. This Wisdom is symbolized by Amitābha. The mirror, as we have seen, reflects all things equally, but at the same time does not confuse or blur their distinctive features: the mirror will reflect the tiniest detail. This is very important. It means that the Enlightened mind does not see things only in their unity, or only in their diversity, but sees both together.

The Enlightened mind, especially under its aspect of the All-distinguishing Wisdom, does not see only the unity of things, it also sees the differences of things, the uniqueness of things, and it sees both of these together. It does not reduce the plurality to a unity; it does not reduce the unity to a plurality: it sees the unity *and* the plurality.

Buddhism, on the philosophical level, is neither a monism, in which all differences are cancelled out, nor a pluralism, in which all unity disappears. It is neither monistic nor pluralistic. In the Buddhist vision of existence unity does not obliterate difference, difference does not obliterate unity. *We* cannot help perceiving now one, now the other, but the Enlightened mind sees unity and difference at one and the same time. It sees that you are uniquely yourselves; at the same time it sees that you are all one. And you are one at the same time that you are yourselves individually; and at the same time that you are yourselves individually, blossoming with all your idiosyncrasies, you are all one. These two, the unity and the difference, the monism and the pluralism, are not two different things – we do not say that they are one, but they are not two.

Fifthly and lastly there is the All-performing Wisdom, symbolized by Amoghasiddhi. The Enlightened mind devotes itself to the welfare of all living beings. In doing so, it devises many 'skilful means'[56] of helping people. The Enlightened mind helps living beings naturally and spontaneously. We must not imagine the Bodhisattva, or the Enlightened mind, sitting down one morning and thinking, 'How can I go and help someone today? Is this person more in need of help, or that? Perhaps I will go and help so-and-so today.' The Enlightened mind does not function like that: it functions freely, spontaneously, naturally.

The Dharma

The Word of the Buddha

The Dharma, as taught personally by the Buddha to his disciples, as transmitted orally by the disciples after the Buddha's *parinirvāṇa*, and as written down much later in the form of scriptures, is known by the special term *Buddhavacana*. This means 'the word of the Buddha'. The term *Buddhavacana* is often used to refer simply to the Buddhist scriptures; but it has deeper implications, some of which we shall examine here.

Firstly we must emphasize that *Buddhavacana* is the word of *the Buddha*. Buddha is not just a personal name, like Rahula or Ānanda. Buddha is a title, literally meaning 'one who Knows'. A Buddha is one who has realized Truth, or Reality. So the word of a Buddha is not like that of an ordinary person. The *Buddhavacana* is the expression in terms of human speech of an Enlightened state of consciousness. Even though we know the meaning of Buddha and *Buddhavacana* we do not always realize this. We tend, perhaps unconsciously, to think of the Buddha as speaking in much the same way as an ordinary person speaks, because, after all, he uses much the same words. But, even though the words may be the same, behind the Buddha's words there is something that is not behind our words. Behind the Buddha's words there stands the Enlightened consciousness. Thus 'for those who have ears to hear' the word of the Buddha expresses that Enlightened consciousness.

Furthermore we must understand that although the Buddha's words express his Enlightened consciousness, they do not express it directly. We should not think that here is the Enlightened consciousness, and straight out of that come words expressive of that Enlightened consciousness. It is not as simple as that, because intervening between the Enlightened consciousness and its expression in terms of ordinary human speech there are several intermediate levels of being and experience. These levels are also included, in principle, in what we call the *Buddhavacana*. We will look at these levels in turn.

The Buddha Mind

Firstly, there is the level – beyond all levels – of the Enlightened mind itself, the Buddha mind. We use the expression 'the Enlightened mind', but it is very difficult for us to have any idea of what this is like, because in that Enlightened mind there is no subject and no object; the ordinary consciousness which is dominated by the subject–object distinction can barely conceive the Enlightened mind. We can only say – though even this is misleading – that the Enlightened mind is pure, undifferentiated Awareness; that it is absolutely Void;[57] that it is absolutely Luminous – one continuous mass of spiritual luminosity; that it is completely satisfying, and is therefore Peace and Bliss beyond all human understanding; that it is above and beyond space and time; and that in that everything is known because in that there is nothing to be known. We might describe it, more metaphorically, as being a vast and shoreless ocean, in which millions of universes are just one tiny wave, even just a single drop of foam.

Within this Enlightened mind – we can only speak of it in terms of space and time, even though it transcends them – there arises the desire to communicate with the non-enlightened mind on the level of the non-enlightened mind. Enlightenment desires to communicate Enlightenment (after all, there is nothing else that it has to communicate; Enlightenment can only communicate Enlightenment). We can identify this desire as Compassion. This communication, at this highest level, is very subtle; there is nothing gross or obvious about it. It is like a tremor, or a subtle vibration, that passes between the Enlightened mind and the mind that is just a little short of Enlightenment.

We can think in imaginative terms of this vibration as an extremely subtle sound: not gross, physical, external sound which we can hear with our ears, nor even sound that we can hear with our inner ear in the ordinary psychological sense, but a kind of primeval, primordial, mantric sound. This is something which is equivalent on the spiritual plane to what we know as sound. This sound, this soundless sound even, is the *Buddhavacana* in the highest sense of the term.

This sound is given off by the Buddha mind, by Reality itself. The Enlightened consciousness is not

The seed syllable OṀ

limited by time or place. Therefore it gives off this sound all the time and in all places. Some Indian traditions identify this primordial cosmic sound with the mantra[58] *oṁ*: not *oṁ* as pronounced by any human tongue, but a subtle, inner, spiritual *oṁ*, which can sometimes be heard in meditation or in other higher states of consciousness. One can even hear it coming from all phenomenal objects in the universe, because the Buddha mind is, as it were, behind them all, sounding through them all. One can even say, pursuing our earlier analogy that the Enlightened consciousness is like the ocean and phenomenal objects like the waves or the foam, that it is as though every wave, every drop of foam, every phenomenon in the universe, is repeating, all the time, this mantra *oṁ* – and nothing but *oṁ*.

Hearing this mantra one listens to the word of the Buddha. In hearing it one hears and understands everything; everything is in this undifferentiated sound. No words are necessary. No thoughts are necessary. There is no need for images. From this one primordial sound, sounding forth from the Buddha mind, one hears all, knows all, and understands all.

The Level of Archetypal Images

The second level is the level of archetypal images. The Enlightened mind comes down a step, as it were, to the level of archetypal images. On this level are images of the sun and moon, light and darkness, the heavens and the earth; images of birds, beasts, and flowers; images of rain, wind, thunder, lightning; images of Buddhas and Bodhisattvas; images of gods and goddesses; images benign and wrathful; images, perhaps above all, that are brilliantly coloured and luminous, arising out of the depths of infinite space.

They are not created by the individual human mind, nor by the collective consciousness, nor even by the collective unconscious. Perhaps these images are not created at all, but are, as it were, co-eternal with the Enlightened consciousness itself – at least in so far as this level of communication is concerned. These images too reveal everything. They reveal it in terms of form and colour. On this level no thoughts, or ideas, or words are necessary. Communication is perhaps not so subtle as on the level of mantric sound, but it is still far subtler and far more comprehensive than anything we ordinarily experience.

The Level of Conceptual Thought

The third level is the level of conceptual thought. Here we have come down yet another step, but we must remember that it is still the *Enlightened* mind which is 'coming down': it is not a question of the unenlightened consciousness expressing itself in terms of thought. Conceptual thought is a medium common to both the Enlightened and the unenlightened mind. Conceptual thought is created by the unenlightened mind, but it can be used, and even be transformed, by the Enlightened mind in accordance with its own higher purposes. This gives us a clue to the real nature of 'Buddhist philosophy' or 'Buddhist thought'. Buddhist thought does not consist of the speculations of the unenlightened minds of ordinary, relatively nominal Buddhists. Buddhist thought is a series of attempts on the part of the Enlightened mind, whether that of Gautama the Buddha or of others, to communicate with unenlightened minds through the medium of concepts. Doctrines such as that of Conditioned Co-production (*pratītya-samutpāda*) have to be understood in this light.

The Level of Words

Lastly we come down to the level of words. Some people say that one cannot really separate words and thoughts. Certainly the connection between the two is very close (it is closer than the connection between images and thoughts). Nevertheless they are not quite the same. We do sometimes have thoughts which we do not, or even cannot, put into words, even sub-vocally.

Having explored to some extent these four levels, we can now see the enormous gulf that separates the Enlightened consciousness, the mind of a Buddha, from its expressions in terms of ordinary human speech. We can see through how many levels the Buddha had to 'descend' after his Enlightenment before he could begin to teach. We must be careful, however, when we think of the Buddha coming down through the various levels, that we do not think of him as leaving behind the preceding levels: this is a coming down without a leaving behind. The word of the Buddha consists of all these four things: the primordial mantric sound, the archetypal images, the concepts, and the words. The Dharma is transmitted on all these levels, not just through ordinary words.

Wrong View, Right View, Perfect view

In Buddhism there is no such thing as philosophy. In fact, in the Indian languages, including Sanskrit and Pali (the languages of the Indian Buddhist scriptures), there is no word corresponding to 'philosophy', either literally or metaphorically. There is a word which used often to be translated as 'philosophy', but it does not mean that at all. That word is *darśana* (Pali *dassana*). *Darśana* comes from a word meaning 'to see' and means 'that which is seen', or 'a sight', 'a view', 'a perspective', even 'a vision'.

This is clearly not the same thing as philosophy. The word philosophy literally means 'love of wisdom', but is more generally understood to mean 'a system of abstract ideas'. It suggests something thought rather than seen. *Darśana*, on the other hand, is very much a matter of direct perception and direct experience – *darśana* does not represent something mediated by concepts.

In Buddhism the term is not *darśana*, but *dṛṣṭi*. *Dṛṣṭi* also comes from a root meaning simply 'to see', and *dṛṣṭi* also means 'a sight', 'a view', 'a perspective', 'a vision'. Buddhism traditionally distinguishes two kinds of view: wrong view and right view. This is an important distinction. In order to understand the difference between the two let us look at the question of sight in the literal sense, because a view, whether wrong or right, is, metaphorically speaking, a kind of seeing.

We may say that there are two kinds of sight: bad and good. Bad sight is sight which is, in the first place, weak. Our sight is said to be weak if we do not see very far or very distinctly. In the second place, bad sight is blinkered. It is restricted to a very narrow field. We see only what is straight in front of our nose. We do not see what is to this side or that side – much less still do we see all the way round. Thirdly, bad sight is distorted, as when we look through a distorting medium – a piece of bottle glass, or a stained-glass window which makes everything look multi-coloured, through a thick fog. Sight which is weak, blinkered, and distorted is bad sight.

Good sight is the opposite of all this. Good sight is sight which is strong, as when we see for a great distance and see clearly. It is sight which is unblinkered, as when we have a wide field of vision. It is sight which is undistorted. We do not see things through a distorting or refracting medium, but see them directly.

The Factors of Wrong View

With the help of this distinction between bad sight and good sight, in the quite ordinary sense, we can perhaps see something of the difference between wrong view and right view. Wrong view is, in the first place, weak. We mean by this that it does not have any energy behind it. If there is no energy behind our vision, then our 'insight' into things is weak; we do not see clearly into the true nature of things; we do not see things as they are. The energy that we need comes from meditation – meditation in the sense of *dhyāna* experience. This concentrated energy, which we derive from meditation experience, transforms a purely conceptual understanding of the truth into a matter of direct experience.

Secondly, wrong view is blinkered. It is limited to a narrow range of experience. This range is what we experience through the five physical senses and the rational mind. Someone whose experience is confined within this narrow range nevertheless often generalizes and draws conclusions from it, unaware of other possibilities of perception and experience. There is, for instance, the example of the man who is interested only in his job, his family, the football pools, and so on. That exhausts his interests. He has no interest in world affairs, or in the arts, or in personal development. So his experience is limited, yet he sees existence itself, life itself, simply in terms of his limited existence.

Thirdly, wrong view is distorted. Our view of things can be distorted in all sorts of ways. It can be distorted by emotion. When we are in a happy mood we see things in quite a different way to the way we see them when we are in a gloomy mood. If we dislike someone, we see all sorts of faults; whereas if we like someone, then we see in them all sorts of perfections, which perhaps they do not in fact possess. Our vision is also distorted by prejudice of various kinds – on account of race or class or religion or nationality.

Wrong view is therefore view which is weak (it does

not have the force of meditation behind it), blinkered (it is limited to a narrow range of experience), and distorted (by one-sided emotions and by prejudices).[59]

The Factors of Right View

Right view is the opposite of wrong view. Right view is view which is strong and powerful. It has behind it the concentrated energy of meditation, so it gives rise not just to a conceptual understanding of things, but to a direct experience of the truth. It does not remain on the surface, but penetrates deep into the heart of things. It sees everything clearly and distinctly. Right view is unblinkered and unlimited. It ranges over the whole field of human experience. It is not confined to what can be experienced through the physical senses or the rational mind. If it generalizes at all, it generalizes from the entire range of human experience in all fields, on all levels. Lastly, right view is undistorted. It is not distorted by emotion or prejudice, but sees things as they are.

So far I have spoken in terms of views, but views do not exist in the abstract: views are always somebody's view. Inasmuch as there are two kinds of view – wrong view and right view – there are two kinds of people. There are people who have wrong view and there are people who have right view. There are people whose view of existence is limited, restricted, and distorted. There are people whose view of existence is unlimited in extent, unrestricted in scope, and without any distortion whatsoever.

People who have wrong view are known technically in Buddhism as *pṛthagjanas*, or 'ordinary folk'; those who have right view are known as the *āryas*, or 'spiritually noble'. We could say that the first are those who are without any degree of personal development, who have not worked at all on themselves, who are, as it were, just as nature made them. The second are those who have attained some degree of personal development, who have worked on themselves, and are not as nature made them: they have remade, recreated, remodelled themselves, at least to some extent.

The 'ordinary folk' are, of course, in the majority; the 'spiritually noble' are in the minority. However, it is possible to change from one category to the other. The *pṛthagjanas* can become the *āryas*. The ordinary person can become one of the 'spiritually noble'. One does this by developing awareness, by cultivating positive emotions, by raising one's level of consciousness, and, above all, by discarding wrong view and developing right view.

Perfect Vision

I have only spoken so far of two kinds of view – wrong and right. Really there are three kinds. The third is Perfect View, or rather, Perfect Vision. Perfect Vision is right view developed to the fullest possible extent. It is the total vision of the total man, at the highest conceivable level of his development. Perfect Vision is vision without limits; it is the unconditioned Vision of the unconditioned Reality; it is vision that transcends space and time; it is vision that transcends the ordinary framework of perception, the subject–object relation itself. Perfect Vision is the vision of the Enlightened One – the one who sees with Wisdom and Compassion. Perfect Vision, thus, is the vision of the Buddha.

Our view is wrong view. Only occasionally do we have a flash of right view. We see things, for the most part, wrongly. Not only that, we rationalize our wrong views. We present them in systematic conceptual form. These are all our so-called worldly philosophies, our various -isms and -ologies. If, however, we can have a glimpse of how the Buddha sees, we shall be momentarily raised to that level, at least in imagination, and we shall be able to see exactly where we ourselves stand. We shall have a true philosophy, which will give purpose to our lives and enable us to understand the general principles that underlie the whole process of personal individual development.

The Tibetan Wheel of Life

The Wheel of Life and the Spiral Path

The Buddha, when he gained Enlightenment beneath the Bodhi tree, saw a vision of human existence, a vision he was never to lose and which was in a sense identical with the experience of Enlightenment itself. He communicated his vision in four ways. He communicated it by means of concepts, by means of symbols, by his actions, and by silence. I am only going to deal here with the Buddha's communication of his vision by means of concepts and symbols.

The Law of Conditionality

In terms of concepts, the Buddha, seated beneath the Bodhi tree, saw the truth of change. He saw that everything was process. He saw that this was true at all levels: not only was there process on the material plane, there was process also on the mental plane. He saw that there was, in fact, nothing anywhere in the world – in conditioned existence – that did not change, that was not process. (In terms of Indian thought, the Buddha saw that there was in Reality no such thing as 'being', nor any such thing as 'non-being'.) He saw that things arise and then pass away.

But the Buddha also saw that this change was not fortuitous – things do not arise and pass away by chance. Whatever arises, arises in dependence on conditions; whatever ceases, ceases because those conditions cease. (The conditions are purely natural conditions; there is no room here for any such explanation as the will of God.) The Buddha, therefore, saw not only the truth of change, but also the law of conditionality. This law is the fundamental principle of Buddhist thought.

The law of conditionality, though it is the fundamental principle of Buddhist thought, can be stated in a very simple form: A being present, B arises; in the absence of A, B does not arise. This is the famous principle that Aśvajit proclaimed to Śāriputra.[60] Aśvajit was one of the Buddha's first five disciples (those who had originally left him when he gave up self-mortification but whom he reclaimed after his Enlightenment). Śāriputra at that time was a wandering ascetic looking for a teacher. Śāriputra met Aśvajit and was very impressed by his appearance: he seemed calm, happy, and radiant. So he asked Aśvajit, 'Who is your teacher and what teaching does he profess?' (These were standard questions in ancient India. Even nowadays you often get asked such questions.) Aśvajit replied, 'I am only a beginner. I don't know very much. But what I do know, I shall tell you.' He thereupon recited a verse in Pali. The verse, which we still have in the scriptures, goes like this: 'Of those things which proceed from a cause, the *Tathāgata*[61] has explained the origin. Their cessation too he has explained. This is the doctrine of the great ascetic.' With one possible exception, this is the most famous verse in all the Buddhist scriptures. It is often regarded as a summary of the Dharma. On hearing this verse, Śāriputra at once attained a high degree of spiritual insight.

Now conditionality is not all of the same kind. There are two great orders of conditionality at work in the universe and in human life. The first we can call the cyclical or reactive order; the second we can call the spiral or progressive order. In the cyclical order of conditionality there is a process of action and reaction between pairs of factors which are opposites, e.g. pleasure and pain, happiness and misery, loss and gain, and, within the wider context of a whole series of lifetimes, birth and death. In the spiral order, on the other hand, there is a gradual progression as between factors which progressively augment each other. Here the succeeding factor augments the effect of the preceding factor, rather than counteracting it or cancelling it out. For instance, in dependence upon pleasure arises not pain but happiness; in dependence upon happiness arises not unhappiness but joy; in dependence upon joy arises delight, then bliss, then rapture, then ecstasy.

The Reactive Mind and the Creative Mind

In the life of the individual human being these two orders of conditionality are reflected in two different kinds of mind: the reactive mind and the creative mind. This does not mean that there are literally two minds, but rather that there are two different ways in which the one mind can function. We can function either reactively or creatively. To function reactively means to 'react' – which is not to act at all. To react means to be essentially passive. It means to respond automatically to whatever stimuli are presented to us. To function creatively, on the other hand, means to 'act', to originate – to bring into existence something that was not there before, whether that something be a work of art or a higher state of consciousness. To function reactively means to be mechanical; to function creatively means to be spontaneous. When we are reactive we go on repeating ourselves. We repeat the same old pattern of our lives: we do today what we did yesterday; we do this week what we did last week; we do this year what we did last year; we do this decade what we did last decade; if you even extend the context, we do in this life exactly what we did in all our previous lives. But when we are creative we change and develop ourselves: we become new men and new women.

Personal development, therefore, is based on the progressive order of conditionality. Personal development means ceasing to live reactively and learning to live creatively. This, of course, is by no means easy. It requires, among other things, awareness of the two kinds of conditionality not simply as abstract principles but as concrete alternatives actually confronting us. After all, they confront us as alternatives not just once or twice in a lifetime, but virtually every minute of the day, because virtually every minute of the day we have to choose whether to react or whether to create. Suppose, for instance, someone speaks to us a little unkindly. We can either react, by getting angry or feeling hurt, or we can respond creatively, by trying to understand what has happened (perhaps reflecting on why he or she spoke like that), by trying to sympathize, by trying at least to be patient. If we react we will remain as we are or even deteriorate, but if we create we will take a step forward in our personal development.

The Symbol of the Wheel

In terms of symbols, the Buddha, seated beneath the Bodhi tree, saw two things. First, he saw a great Wheel. This Wheel embraces the whole of conditioned existence; it is conterminous with the cosmos; it contains all living things. It is constantly turning: it turns by day and night; it turns life after life; it turns age after age. We cannot see when it first began turning and we cannot see, as yet, when it will cease turning – only a Buddha sees that.

This great Wheel is revolving on a hub. Its hub is made up of three creatures: a red cock, greedily scratching the earth; a green serpent, its red eyes glaring with anger; and a black pig, ignorantly wallowing in the mud. These three creatures themselves form a circle and each bites the tail of the one in front.

Surrounding the hub, which is the first circle of the Wheel, there is a second, larger circle. This is divided vertically into two halves: a white and a black half. In both halves there are figures of men and women. The figures in the white half are moving upwards, even floating upwards, as though to the sound of beautiful music. They all have rapt, blissful expressions. Some are holding hands. All are gazing upwards to the zenith. The figures in the black half, on the other hand, are moving downwards. In fact, they are not just moving, but are plunging down headlong. Some are holding their hands to their heads. Some are naked and deformed. Some are chained together. All have expressions of anguish and terror.

The next circle of the Wheel is by far the largest. It is divided by six spokes into six segments. In each segment a whole world (or number of worlds) is depicted. If you prefer, each segment may be seen as a state of mind, or a plane of consciousness. The order varies, but always, right at the top, we see the gods, or *devas*. They live in wonderful palaces. They are provided with all manner of delights. For them, existence is like a pleasant dream. Some of the gods have bodies made entirely of light and they communicate by pure thought.

Next, going round this circle in clockwise order, we see the *asuras*. The *asuras* live in a state of constant hostility and jealousy. They are always fighting. They all wear armour and grasp weapons. They are fighting for possession of the fruits of the wish-fulfilling tree.

In the next segment up we see the *pretas* or hungry ghosts. They have enormous swollen bellies but thin necks and tiny mouths like the eyes of needles. All are ravenously hungry, but whatever food they touch turns to either fire or filth.

In the bottom segment we see beings in states of torment. Some are freezing in blocks of ice; others are burning in flames. Some are being decapitated. Some are being sawn in two. Some are being devoured by monsters.

Next we see various species of animals: fish, insects, birds, reptiles, mammals. Some are large, some small. Some are peaceful, some predatory. We notice that they are all in pairs, male and female, and that they are all in search of food.

In the last segment we see human beings. We see houses and lands. We see gardens and fields. Some people are cultivating the earth. They are ploughing, sowing, and reaping. Some people are buying and selling. Some are giving alms. Some are meditating.

These are the six segments of this circle of the Wheel, which make up six worlds or six kinds of mental state. The inhabitants of these worlds do not remain in them indefinitely. They disappear from one world and reappear in another. Even the gods, though they stay a very long time in their world, disappear and reappear somewhere else.

The final circle in the Wheel – the rim of the Wheel – is divided into twelve segments. In these segments we see twelve scenes depicting stages of the process by which living beings pass from world to world of the previous circle (in some cases they reappear in the same world). In clockwise order these twelve scenes are: (1) a blind man with a stick; (2) a potter with a wheel and pots; (3) a monkey climbing a flowering tree; (4) a boat with four passengers, one of whom is steering; (5) an empty house; (6) a man and woman embracing; (7) a man with an arrow in his eye; (8) a woman offering a drink to a seated man; (9) a man gathering fruit from a tree; (10) a pregnant woman; (11) a woman giving birth to a child; (12) a man carrying a corpse to the cremation ground.

The Wheel is clutched from behind by a fearful monster – half demon, half beast. His head peers over the top. He has three eyes, long fangs, and a crown of skulls. At either side of the Wheel appear his clawed feet, and his tail hangs down below. This then is the ever-revolving Wheel of Life.

But there is something more. Above the Wheel, to the right, there is a figure in a yellow robe, who is pointing. He is pointing to a space between the seventh and the eighth segment of the outermost circle of the Wheel (the space between the picture of the man with the arrow in his eye and the picture of the woman offering a drink to a seated man). Here, rising out of this space, we see the second thing that the Buddha saw in his vision of human existence. It is not so much a symbol as a group of symbols. It seems to change its form as we look at it.

At first it seems like a path, which stretches far away into the distance. It winds, now through cultivated fields, now through dense forest. It traverses swamps and deserts, broad rivers and deep ravines. It winds around the base of mighty mountains, on the tops of which rest clouds. Eventually it disappears over the horizon. But the symbol changes. The path seems to straighten out; it stands upright. The path becomes a great ladder or a stair. It is a ladder that stretches from heaven to earth and from earth to heaven. It is a ladder of gold, of silver, of crystal. But again the symbol changes. The ladder becomes slender, solid, three-dimensional, and green in colour. It becomes the stem of a gigantic tree. On this tree are enormous blossoms. The blossoms lower down are relatively small; those higher up are much bigger. At the top of the tree, shining like a sun, is the biggest blossom of all. In the calyxes of all these blossoms sit all kinds of beautiful and radiant figures: figures of Buddhas and Bodhisattvas, Arhants, *ḍākas*, and *ḍākinīs*.

So this is what the Buddha saw as he sat beneath the Bodhi tree. This is his vision of human existence as communicated by concepts and symbols. The significance of his vision is quite clear. It is a vision of possibilities. It is a vision of alternatives. On the one hand, there is the cyclical type of conditionality; on the other, there is the spiral type of conditionality. On the one hand, there is the reactive mind; on the other, the creative mind. One can either stagnate or one can grow. One can either remain seated and accept the drink from the hand of the woman or one can refuse the drink and stand up on one's own two feet. One can either continue to revolve passively and helplessly on the Wheel or one can follow the Path, climb the ladder, become the plant, become the blossoms. Our fate is in our own hands.

The Six Realms

The Wheel of Life is depicted on the walls of temples and monasteries, as well as on painted scrolls, all over Tibet and the adjacent, especially Himalayan, area. But the Wheel of Life is not a painting. It is something quite different. I am going to ask you, therefore, to look at the Wheel of Life again, not only look *at* it but look *into* it, because the Wheel of Life is in fact a mirror. The Wheel of Life is a mirror in which we see ourselves.

We could even say that the Wheel of Life is made up not of four concentric circles, but of four mirrors, each mirror bigger than the last. Or we could say that we look into the mirror four times, and each time we look we see more of ourselves. The Wheel of Life is a magic mirror, even a crystal ball into which we can gaze. So let us look now into that mirror, into that crystal ball. Let us look into it not just four times but as many times as may be necessary, and let us have the courage to see ourselves.

Looking in the Mirror

The first time we look into the mirror we see three animals – the cock, the snake, and the pig. We are usually taught that these represent the 'Three Mental Poisons' of greed, aversion, and ignorance and that these are present in our own hearts. But this, if I may say so, is letting us off far too lightly. This sort of explanation represents a kind of defensive rationalization. It is, after all, much more of a shock when we look into the mirror and see – actually – not the allegedly human face that we expected but the face of a bird (a cock), the face of a reptile (a snake), and the face of an animal (a pig). In the mirror we see just that. That is us. In other words, we have a direct experience of our own animal nature – we are just an animal, even just a beast; we see that we are really not so human, not so civilized, as we had thought. This realization is the beginning of spiritual life. We see ourselves as we really are at rock bottom. We see ourselves as we are, recognize that we are such, and go on from there.

Going on from there means, to begin with, that – after we have recovered from our first look – we take a second look in the mirror. Looking in the mirror this time, we see two paths. One path goes up, the other down. One path is white, the other black. We see, in other words, that we are faced with two alternatives: to go up or to go down, to evolve or to regress. It is as simple as that, and the choice is before us. The choice is before us every minute of the day: in every situation in which we find ourselves we have to decide whether we shall ascend or descend, follow the white path or follow the black path. It is up to us to decide.

Suppose we decide, after thinking it all over, to go up, to follow the white path, to evolve, then the question arises: what must we do to evolve? What constitutes the next step? The nature of the next step depends on where we are now. To find out where we are now we look into the mirror for the third time.

Sometimes when we look into the mirror this third time we see a happy, smiling, cheerful face – we see the face of a god. Sometimes we see an angry, aggressive face – the face of a titan. Sometimes we see a famished, hollow-eyed face, with a pinched mouth and dissatisfied expression – the face of a hungry ghost. On other occasions we see an unhappy, miserable, even tormented face – the face of someone in hell. Again when sometimes we look we see a face with a long snout, or whiskers, or big sharp teeth – the face of an animal. Sometimes when we look in the mirror we see just an ordinary human face. But whatever, at any given moment, we see in the mirror, it is ourselves that we see.

The Six Worlds

The six segments into which the third circle of the Wheel of Life is divided can be seen as six worlds, six actual realms of existence (the realms of the gods, titans, hungry ghosts, hell beings, animals, and humans); and living beings are reborn in a particular realm as a result of their karma and live in that realm until that karma has been exhausted. This is quite true, but it is only half the truth. The six segments of the third circle also represent six states of mind which we can experience here and now, in the course of our present human existence. Sometimes we experience these states of mind so strongly that for the time being we seem actually to be living in another

world – in heaven, or in hell, or among the hungry ghosts, etc. In other words, we experience them almost as states of being, rather than just as states of mind. So let us look at each of the six worlds in this light: as states of mind or being, rather than as realms of existence.

Firstly, the world of the gods. The world of the gods represents a happy, pleased state of mind, a state of relaxation, content, repose. It is a state in which everything goes smoothly, a state in which there are no obstacles, difficulties, or problems. It is also a state of aesthetic experience. It is even the state of meditation, in the more limited sense of the term (meditation as an experience of higher states of consciousness not giving direct access to the transcendental).

Secondly, the world of the *asuras*, or titans. This is an aggressive, competitive state of mind. Here there is lots of energy – maybe too much energy – which all turns outward. There is restlessness, suspicion, jealousy. The *asuras* are depicted in the Wheel of Life as fighting with the gods for possession of the wish-fulfilling tree.[62] So this state of mind is one that strives after endless material wealth, strives, we might say, after a higher and ever higher standard of living, strives after increased and yet more increased wages, and so on. It is a state of assertive egotism: one always wants to be better than others, or in some way superior to others. It is a state in which one even wants to control others, exercise power over others, dominate others.

Thirdly, the world of the *pretas*, or hungry ghosts. This is the state of neurotic desire. Desire is neurotic when it seeks from its object either more than the object by its very nature is able to give or even something quite different from that which the object is able to give. Let me take for example the neurotic desire for food. Sometimes people gobble down huge quantities of food – usually it is sweet food of some sort. Very often they do not really want food at all. They want something else. Food in this case is a substitute for something else. Psychologists tell us that people who consume unnecessarily large quantities of food for psychological reasons are really wanting affection. Neurotic desire is very often present in personal relationships, especially personal relationships of the more intimate kind. In some cases it is present to such an extent that the relationship looks like one hungry ghost trying to devour another.

Fourthly, the world of the tormented beings, the hell-beings. This is the state of acute mental suffering, of nervous frustration, of mental breakdown. Ultimately it is even the state of insanity. This state of mind is brought about in various ways. It may, for instance, be brought about by long-continued frustration of natural human impulses, or by sudden unexpected bereavements, or by unconscious mental conflicts. Whatever the particular cause, it adds up to a state of intense mental suffering. This is the state represented by the beings in hell.

Fifthly, the world of the animals. This is the state of purely sensual indulgence. In this state one is interested in only food, sex, and simple material comforts. When one's desires for these things are satisfied, one is quite gentle, quite tame even, but when they are frustrated, one becomes dangerous, rather like the wild animal.

Sixthly, the world of men. This is the state of distinctively human consciousness. This state of consciousness is neither ecstatic nor agonized, neither fiercely competitive nor mindlessly sensual, nor yet neurotically desirous. In this state we are aware of ourselves and aware of other people. In this state we satisfy, in a reasonable manner, objective human needs, but at the same time we see that they have their limitations. In this state we devote ourselves to spiritual development. This is the truly human state, but it is a state which most 'human beings' only intermittently, or perhaps never, experience.

If we wanted to sum all this up in a rather epigrammatic manner, we could say that the world of the gods equals the world of higher aesthetic enjoyment – whether achieved by the fine arts or by meditation; the world of the titans equals the world of politics, business, and trade unionism; the world of hungry ghosts equals the world of romance or symbiotic personal relationships; the world of tormented beings equals the world of mental illness; and the world of men equals the world of truly human beings, leading truly human lives.

The Six Buddhas

In depictions of the Wheel of Life, six Buddhas appear in the midst of the six worlds, one Buddha to each world. These Buddhas, according to the Tibetan Buddhist teaching, are all manifestations of the Bodhisattva Avalokiteśvara. Avalokiteśvara is the Bodhisattva who embodies the Compassion aspect of the Enlightenment experience. Each of these six Buddhas, these six manifestations of Avalokiteśvara, holds a particular object. The particular object that each Buddha holds is something that is needed by the beings of the world in which he appears, or, we may say, indicates the next step to be taken by a person in a certain state of mind.

In the world of the gods there appears a white Buddha. The object he holds is a *vina*, or lute. He plays on the lute the melody of impermanence. This means that when we are in the state of aesthetic enjoyment, the next step for us is to remind ourselves that it does not last. We need to remind ourselves that such aesthetic enjoyments, however great, are not to be mistaken for the supreme bliss of nirvāṇa; though things seem to be going well now, though we seem to be happy, pleased, contented, joyful, delighted, we have not as yet reached nirvāṇa, in fact nirvāṇa is still a long way off.

This brings us to a point that is much insisted on in the Buddhist tradition. The point is that prolonged happiness can be spiritually dangerous – if not disastrous. If we are happy all the time, if we always get our own way, if we never have any problems, then we tend to become self-satisfied, complacent, even careless and unmindful: we tend to forget that we are mortal, that life is short, that time is precious. This applies to the enjoyment of the fine arts and even to the enjoyment of the higher aesthetic experience of meditation itself (meditation in the narrow sense of the term). We need to go on, as it were, even from the heights of our mundane, in this case aesthetic, experience to the experience of the transcendental.

It is interesting incidentally to note that the Buddha in the realm of the gods does not stand up and deliver a lecture on impermanence, but rather plays the melody of impermanence on a lute. The gods – or people in the state of mind of gods – are in this state of higher aesthetic experience, which, though admittedly a higher state, is nevertheless a somewhat complacent and self-satisfied state. The white Buddha wakes them up to higher transcendental truths and realities – the melody of impermanence does communicate the message of impermanence. But he does this not through a philosophical, religious, or intellectual medium, but through an artistic medium.

In the world of the *asuras* there appears a green Buddha, who brandishes a flaming sword. This sword is the sword of Transcendental Wisdom. This means that when we are in the state of competitiveness and aggressiveness, the next step for us is to develop intellectual insight into Truth and Reality.

This brings us to an interesting point, which is briefly discussed by Dr Conze in an essay entitled 'Hate, Love and Perfect Wisdom'.[63] The *asura*-like person, the titan, the enemy of the gods, is dominated by hate. Hate, according to the Buddhist tradition, has an affinity for Wisdom, or, even, Wisdom has an affinity for hate. If you have got lots of anger and hatred, you can, strange as it may seem, fairly easily develop Wisdom (this is not wisdom in the ordinary sense of intellectual knowledge, but Wisdom in the sense of the intellectual penetration into Truth and Reality, which is a spiritual experience). The characteristic of hatred is that it seeks to destroy the hated object. If you really hate something, you want to destroy it, smash it up; if you really hate someone, you want to annihilate them, finish them off, make just one big nothing where they were before! You may not always admit this to yourself, but this is what sometimes you would like to do to something or someone that you hate. The characteristic of hatred is to destroy and to kill – in the widest sense of the term. The characteristic, or the function, of Transcendental Wisdom too is to destroy and to kill. Transcendental Wisdom seeks to destroy everything that is unreal or illusory; it seeks to smash through everything which stands in its way, everything which is not Reality, is not Truth, is not Buddhahood. (Transcendental Wisdom is symbolized by the thunderbolt, because the thunderbolt, it is said, is the most powerful thing in the universe, able to destroy all obstacles. The *Vajracchedīka Prajñā Pāramitā Sūtra*, the famous *Diamond Sūtra*,[64] is literally the discourse on the Perfection of Wisdom that cuts like the thunderbolt, or the diamond.) It is through this common characteristic of destructiveness, in the one case unskilful and in the other case highly skilful,[65] that we find this affinity between hatred and Transcendental Wisdom.

We do in fact see that people with hot tempers often have well developed, not to say highly developed, intellects. I must say, quite frankly, that I have noticed this among oriental scholars (scholars who specialize in Pali, Sanskrit, Tibetan, Chinese, and Japanese studies). Such scholars, who may specialize in Buddhism and write, from a scholarly point of view, about love, meditation, and higher spiritual experiences, are often bad tempered and quarrelsome, especially among themselves.

The tremendous energy which is in hatred can be diverted into purely intellectual channels and used for the discovery and realization of truth. The *asura*-type person can fight not only with the gods, but can as it were fight with and conquer truth itself, at least through the intellectual approach, and can do this more effectively than other people who may be easier to get on with.

In the world of the *pretas*, the hungry ghosts, there appears a red Buddha. He showers the hungry ghosts with food and drink that they can actually consume. This means that when we are in a state of neurotic desire, the next step for us is to get back to objectivity, which also means getting back to the present. We must see what the desired object can actually give us and what it cannot give us. We must see what it is that we really desire – whether or not it is really the desired object. We must see where the desire is coming from. Eventually we have either to give the desire its proper satisfaction or just resolve it.

In the world of tormented beings there appears a smoke-coloured Buddha. He regales the beings in hell with *amṛta*, nectar, ambrosia. There are two meanings here, which are a bit contradictory. One meaning is rather profounder than the other. The less profound meaning is that when we are in a state of intense suffering, especially mental suffering, the next step for us is simply to gain some respite from that suffering: we need to gain some sort of ease, or relaxation. For many people that is the best that they can do in the circumstances; very often, when people are in a state of intense mental suffering, the only thing they can think of is respite from it.

The more profound meaning, which is a better, more challenging meaning, is connected with this word *amṛta*. *Amṛta* is usually translated as nectar or ambrosia, but it is also in many Buddhist texts a synonym for nirvāṇa itself. Nirvāṇa is often spoken of as the *amṛtapada* (Pali *amatapada*), the deathless or eternal state, the state of ambrosia. The smoke-coloured Buddha gives the beings in hell not just ambrosia, but nirvāṇa. This means that when we are in a state of intense suffering, the next step is to gain nirvāṇa. It is as though there is nothing left for us to do about our suffering except go, as it were, straight to nirvāṇa. There is no other hope for us: all worldly hope has foundered. It is as though there is an affinity even between intense mental suffering and susceptibility to higher spiritual attainment.

In the world of animals there appears a blue Buddha. He is showing the animals a book. This means that when we are in a state of barbarism and savagery, the state represented by the animals, the next step for us is simply to become civilized, to make ourselves acquainted with the arts and the sciences, the cultural life of mankind, because these things have a refining influence, and it is difficult, if not impossible, to go from a state of barbarism, a state of mental savagery, straight into the spiritual life.

We see historically that Buddhism in the East was always a bearer of culture. It took not only the spiritual teaching of Buddhism all over Asia, but also Indian higher culture. It did this for the quite definite spiritual reason that the secular, humanistic culture formed a foundation for the higher spiritual life. This is also why we are often told in Mahāyāna texts that the Bodhisattva, the ideal Buddhist, should be a master of arts and sciences.

Lastly, in the world of men there appears a saffron-coloured Buddha. He carries a begging-bowl and a three-ringed staff, which are the insignia of the religious mendicant and therefore of the spiritual life in general. This means that when we find ourselves in a truly human state, the next step for us is to devote ourselves wholeheartedly to the task of spiritual development: once we have reached the human state this should be our main interest in life.

The Twelve Links

The twelve links (*nidānas*) of Conditioned Co-production represent the application of the general Buddhist philosophical principle of universal conditionality to the process of rebirth. Rebirth is not one of those aspects of Buddhism that tend to attract people most nowadays. None the less it is of great importance, especially historical importance; it is an integral part of the whole Buddhist teaching. Different aspects of Buddhism are of great interest at different times, nevertheless we should try to achieve a balance as between these different aspects. This is only possible if we ourselves become psychologically and spiritually balanced. If we find that one aspect appeals to us very strongly it is usually because there is some imbalance in ourselves – a certain need in ourselves to which that aspect of the teaching corresponds. As we become more and more balanced we find that it is less and less this or that particular aspect which attracts us (more or less) exclusively, but rather that it is the whole body of the teaching which attracts us.

Conditioned Co-Production

Pratītya-samutpāda, or Conditioned Co-production, deals with production or origination, and consists of twelve *nidānas*, or twelve links, in a series, or chain. Each of these links arises in dependence on, or is conditioned by, the preceding. That is why we speak of the Conditioned Co-production or dependent origination of these successive links, one by one in the series.

We will see what each of these *nidānas* is. But first of all I should observe that some texts enumerate five *nidānas* and other texts enumerate ten *nidānas*, though twelve is the standard number. We should not forget the existence of the fivefold and tenfold enumerations, because they serve to remind us that lists of this sort should not be taken too literally. You must not think of any particular subject as literally divided into a specific number of parts. You should not really think of the 'Eightfold Path'[66] as quite literally consisting of eight distinct parts. These are divisions just for practical convenience. In studying – in this case – the twelve *nidānas*, we should try to understand, through them and with their help, the spirit of conditionality, rather than pin it down in a particular set framework.

Ignorance

The first *nidāna* is *avidyā* (Pali *avijjā*), or ignorance. This *nidāna* is in some ways the most important *nidāna* of all. *Avidyā* is not ignorance in the intellectual sense, so much as a lack or deprivation of spiritual awareness – even of spiritual consciousness and spiritual being. *Avidyā* in this sense is the direct antithesis of *bodhi*, Enlightenment. *Bodhi* is the goal of the whole evolutionary process, especially of the whole process of the Higher Evolution.[67] In the same way, *avidyā* represents all that lies behind us – or below us – in that evolutionary process. If Enlightenment represents the goal, then ignorance represents the depths from which we have come. If Enlightenment represents the mountain peak, then ignorance represents the valleys from which we are gradually emerging and which lie wrapped in darkness.

More specifically, *avidyā* is made up of various wrong views. A number of these are specified in the canonical texts. For instance, there is the wrong view which consists in seeing the conditioned as Unconditioned: thinking that anything phenomenal can last for ever. This is not an intellectual conviction, of course, but an unconscious assumption: we behave as though certain things were going to last for ever; we therefore cling to them; and we are unhappy when we finally have to surrender them.

Another wrong view is belief in a personal God, a supreme being. Buddhism, like psychoanalysis, tends to regard the God-figure as a sort of projected father-figure, a glorified representation of the father of our childhood, on which we depend for help when we get into difficulties. Buddhism tends to regard belief of this sort, dependence of this sort, as a manifestation of spiritual immaturity.

Various beliefs, whether rationalized or not, in the efficacy of purely external actions, are considered to be based on a wrong view. So far as most readers are concerned, this might seem to be a case of flogging a dead horse. But having spent twenty years in India, and having seen so much of popular Hinduism, it does not seem to me that in other parts of the world this is so much of a dead horse. Even now there are very many orthodox Hindus who genuinely believe that the waters of the Ganges, for instance, have definitely a purifying effect. If you take a dip in those waters your sins will really be washed away. Well-educated, intelligent Hindus, some of them Western-educated, will quite seriously and quite honestly defend this belief.

This reminds me of a little story about Ramakrishna, the great Hindu mystic at the end of the last century. He was once asked, 'Is it true, as the orthodox say, that when you take a dip in the Ganges all your sins are washed away?' He did not like to offend the feelings of the orthodox. At the same time he did not like to commit himself to the orthodox belief. So he said to the questioner, 'Yes, it is quite true that when you take a dip in the sacred Ganges all your sins are washed away. But when you go down into the water your sins take the form of crows and perch on the trees nearby and when you come out of the water they come back again.' So this is how he got round the difficulty. This example reflects the tendency of people to attach importance to external acts.

One might say that the Reformation inaugurated by Luther was really about this question – whether external observances have a value of their own. In this case the question was that of indulgences[68] and the whole sacramental side of religion. In those days it was one of the teachings of the Church – I think that it still is in the Roman Catholic Church – that the sinfulness of the priest in no way impairs the efficacy of the sacrament. The priest can be as sinful as you like, but when he performs the sacrament, because he utters certain words in a certain way, its efficacy is unimpaired. Luther protested against this sort of external view of religion.

This external view of religion is still quite strong in certain quarters. Only recently I was reading several accounts of the proceedings of the recent Vatican Council.[69] It is quite clear that in the Council there were two groups of Fathers participating. One group – a smaller group admittedly – wanted to hang on to all the old mechanical external ritualistic ways of regarding religion, and the other group, of more progressive Fathers, wanted to abolish them, or at least modify them. It seems that this is a permanent element in the religious character: trying to treat things external (actions, ceremonies, rituals, and sacraments) as possessing efficacy and value by themselves, quite apart from the state of mind with which they are performed. This sort of belief, though ostensibly religious, is really a part of spiritual unawareness, *avidyā*.

Above all, spiritual unawareness includes ignorance of the law of universal conditionality itself.

Karma-Formations

According to the formula in the texts, in dependence on ignorance arise karma-formations (Sanskrit *saṁskāras*, Pali *sankhārās*). *Saṁskāra* literally means 'preparation' or 'set-up'. The word stands for volitions or acts of will. In this context the word is used to mean the aggregate of those mental conditions which, under the law of karma, are responsible for the production – or preparation or setting up – of the first moment of consciousness in a 'new' life. In this context the word *saṁskāras* is often translated as 'karma-formations'; when it appears in the context of the 'Five *Skandhas*'[70] (the 'Five Aggregates') it is usually translated as 'volitions'.

Essentially the *saṁskāras* are acts of will connected with different states of mind. These states of mind can be either 'skilful' or 'unskilful' (Buddhism in its original texts tends to avoid words like good and bad, and uses instead skilful and unskilful). The unskilful mental states are those dominated by greed, hatred, and mental confusion. The skilful mental states are dominated by generosity, love, and clarity of mind. All these acts of will can be expressed through body, speech, and mind.

Those acts of will which are rooted in unskilful mental states result in what is popularly called a 'bad rebirth'; those which are rooted in skilful states result in a 'good rebirth'. However, it is important to note that Buddhism regards both of these as ultimately rooted in ignorance.

Buddhism would say that the desire for a good rebirth or even working towards a good rebirth is just as much a product of ignorance in the spiritual sense as working towards a bad one, because rebirth is not the goal of Buddhism – not even a good rebirth. The goal of Buddhism is the complete emancipation from the round of conditioned existence itself: from the round of birth and death and rebirth.

The Buddha gives a rather pointed comparison for the relationship between ignorance and the karma-formations. He says that the state of ignorance is like the state of drunkenness and the *saṁskāras* are like the actions which you perform in that state. In effect he is saying that most people in their ordinary everyday actions, even in their conventionally religious actions, are no better, from a spiritual point of view, than drunken men or women behaving foolishly in various ways. That is really the state of most of us. We are drunk because we are 'overcome' by this spiritual unawareness, and everything we do, say, and think is the product, in one way or another, of that spiritual unawareness. When a man is drunk whatever he does and whatever he thinks might seem wise and clear to himself but is in fact just the expression of his drunkenness; in just the same way, we may do, say, and think all sorts of things – we may indulge in all sorts of charitable activities, all sorts of conventional religious practices – but it is all the expression, basically, of spiritual unawareness.

Consciousness

In dependence on the karma-formations arises consciousness (Sanskrit *vijñāna*, Pali *viññāna*). This is not consciousness in general, but consciousness in the specific sense of the 're-linking consciousness'. This is so called because it re-links the person, or psyche, to the psycho-physical organism of the new life.

According to Buddhism, for conception (of a human being) to take place three factors are necessary. Firstly, there must be sexual intercourse. Secondly, it must be the prospective mother's season. Thirdly, there must be what the texts popularly describe as 'the being to be reborn'. 'The being' here represents the last moment of consciousness belonging to the previous existence, in other words, the re-linking consciousness. According to the Theravāda School there is no interval between death and the following rebirth. But other schools, the Sarvastivādins and following them the Tibetans, teach that in between there is an intermediate state. (This is described in the *Tibetan Book of the Dead*.[71])

Now a very important question arises: who or what is reborn? One is often asked this. People like to ask tricky questions and, especially when you have spoken about *anātman* (Pali *anattā*, the doctrine of no-self or no-soul), they think that they are being very clever when they ask, 'If there is no self, who or what is reborn?' There are two extremes to be avoided. One extreme is maintaining that the person in the previous life and the person in the present life are the *same* person. If someone is reborn it is the same Tom or Dick or Harry or Gertrude or Mary that you had before; it is the same old mind in a new body. This sort of belief is expressed for instance in the *Bhagavad-Gītā* where Sri Krishna says, 'What is rebirth? It is just like changing your clothes. In just the same way as you get up in the morning and decide to wear a new set of clothes, so you cast aside the old body and take a new body.' You yourself, as it were, remain unchanged.

The other extreme is maintaining that the person in the previous life and the person in the present life are *quite different* persons. This position holds that the conditioning coming from the body is so basic that you cannot speak of the same person: it is a different person entirely. The two extremes therefore are that the person reborn is the same as the one who died or different to the one who died.

These two extremes are connected historically with an ancient Indian dispute about the nature of causation. There were, even now in India there are, two schools. One, the Satkāryavāda School, maintains that cause and effect are identical. The followers of this school say that when a so-called effect is produced, all that has really happened is that the cause has changed its form. They say, for instance, that supposing you have a lump of gold (the cause), which is made into ornaments (the effect), it is the same gold whether you call it cause or effect: it is one, is the same, is uninterrupted. The Asatkāryavāda School, on the other hand, says that cause is one thing and effect another. Both these views, the Satkāryavāda and Asatkāryavāda, if they are pressed logically, make causation impossible. If cause and effect are really identical, you cannot really speak of cause and effect at all. If, on the other hand, cause and effect are quite different, how can you relate them? In that case also there is no causation. Buddhism avoids this whole argument, regarding it as proceeding from wrong premises. Buddhism teaches neither Satkāryavāda, identity of cause and effect, nor Asatkāryavāda, difference of cause and effect, but *pratītya-samutpāda*, conditionality. It says, symbolically or abstractly, that in dependence on A, B arises. It says that the relationship between the two terms, A and B, cannot be described in terms of identity and cannot be described in terms of difference: these two categories just do not fit.

The same idea is also applied to this question of rebirth. Buddhism says that it is beside the point to ask whether it is the same or a different person who is reborn. The one who is reborn is neither the same as, nor different from, the one who died. If one puts it paradoxically, the really strict orthodox Buddhist position is that there is rebirth but there is no one who is reborn.

It is for this reason that Buddhism avoids terms like reincarnation. Incarnation is getting into a body; reincarnation is getting into a body again. The term reincarnation implies, just as in the case of the *Bhagavad-Gītā* passage which I referred to, that you have got a little soul (or fixed self) which pops into one body after another, while remaining itself unchanged. The correct Buddhist term is *punarbhava* (Pali *punabhava*), which means 'again-becoming' or 're-becoming' – not even 'rebirth'.

Name-and-Form

In dependence on consciousness arises name-and-form (*nāma-rūpa*). Here *nāma-rūpa* means simply the physical body (at first the embryonic physical body) together with the other three mental aggregates of feeling (*vedanā*), perception (*saṁjñā*), and volitions (*saṁskāras*).

The Six Bases

In dependence on name-and-form arise the six bases (Sanskrit *śadāyatana*, Pali *salāyatana*). The six bases are simply the five physical sense organs together with the mind (which is treated as a sort of sixth sense, even sixth sense-organ). They are called the six bases because they constitute the bases for our experience of the external world.

Contact

In dependence on the six bases arises contact (Sanskrit *sparśa*, Pali *phassa*). This represents the mutual impact of organ and appropriate object. The eye, for instance, comes into contact with visual form, giving rise to eye contact. In the same way the other five senses come into contact with their respective sense-objects.

Feeling

In dependence on contact arises feeling (*vedanā*). With regard to its origin, feeling is sixfold, according to whether it is born of eye contact, or ear contact, etc. Each of these in turn is threefold, that is to say, pleasant, painful, or neutral (neither pleasant nor painful).

Craving

In dependence on feeling arises craving (Sanskrit *tṛṣṇā*, Pali *taṇhā*). *Tṛṣṇā*, craving or thirst, is of three kinds: *kāma-tṛṣṇā*, *bhava-tṛṣṇā*, and *vibhava-tṛṣṇā*. *Kāma-tṛṣṇā* is craving for sensuous experience. *Bhava-tṛṣṇā* is craving for continued existence, especially continued existence after death in heaven. *Vibhava-tṛṣṇā* is craving for annihilation or death. This particular stage, in which craving arises in dependence on feeling, is a very important stage, even the crucial stage, in the whole series, because it is here – if one is able not to react to feeling with craving – that the chain can be broken.[72]

Attachment

In dependence on craving arises attachment (*upādāna*). It is interesting to note that there are four kinds of attachment. Usually we think just in terms of attachment to material things – to pleasures and possessions. This is indeed the first kind of attachment: the attachment to sensuous pleasure, i.e. attachment to pleasant experiences coming through the eye, or the ear, or the nose, etc. We all know what they are, so there is no need to elaborate on that.

But then, secondly, there is attachment to *dṛṣṭi*. *Dṛṣṭi* means literally 'views', but also means opinions, speculations, beliefs, including all sorts of philosophical and religious opinions. This is very significant. Buddhism represents attachment to our own beliefs and convictions as unhealthy. It is not that you should not entertain beliefs, but you should not be attached to them. You might ask, 'How can you tell whether or not you are attached to your beliefs?' In fact it is quite easy to tell. Very often when you are engaged in argument with someone, and you challenge what they say – you refuse to accept it, you want to discuss it, for you it isn't axiomatic – they become upset or even angry. If someone behaves in this way it is not that their opinions are right or wrong intrinsically, objectively considered, but they are attached to them. It is the attachment which is wrong. Attachment is a fetter that binds us to the wheel of birth and death. This is something very salutary for us to remember. By all means accept the 'Three Refuges', accept karma and rebirth, accept the teaching of the Five Aggregates, accept the Buddha's teaching about meditation and about nirvāṇa. Yes, accept it all. Try to put it into practice. But do not be attached to it: do not cling to it in such a way that if anyone questions you or challenges you, you feel threatened and react in a hostile, unsympathetic manner.

Thirdly, there is attachment to *śīla* and *vrata*. *Śīla* is ethics and *vrata* is religious observances. Again it is not that these things are necessarily wrong in themselves – it is not that you should not be ethical, should not practise the 'Five Precepts'.[73] But don't cling to them: don't cling to your own practice of the Precepts; don't think that this is an end in itself; don't think that by practising you are differentiated from other people. The practices themselves are all right – just as the beliefs and convictions were – but the attachment to them, the one-sidedness psychologically with regard to them, is not all right – it is all wrong.

Then, fourthly, there is attachment to the belief in a permanent unchanging self, or soul (in the orthodox Christian sense), existing apart from the Five Aggregates.

Becoming

In dependence on attachment arises becoming (*bhava*). *Bhava* is life, or existence as conditioned by our attachment, on any plane.

Birth

In dependence on becoming arises birth (*jāti*).

Decay and Death

In dependence on birth arises decay-and-death (*jarā-marana*). Once you have been born, nothing on this earth can prevent you from decaying and eventually dying.

These are the Twelve *Nidānas*, the Twelve Links of Conditioned Co-production. They are a concrete, serial exemplification of this universal Buddhist principle of conditionality, especially as that principle is applied to the process of rebirth.[74]

The first two *nidānas* (ignorance and karma-formations) are together called the 'cause process of the past life'. In other words, our primordial spiritual ignorance and our actions based upon that ignorance in the past, in previous existences, have been the 'cause' of us coming again into this new existence, our present life.

The next five *nidānas* together make up what is called the 'effect process of the present life'. In other words, in this our present life the consciousness arising in the womb of the mother, the psychophysical organism, the six senses, contact, and feeling, are all the 'effect' of ignorance and activities based on ignorance in the previous life.

The next three *nidānas* (craving, grasping, and becoming) constitute the 'cause process of the present life'. Whereas the previous five *nidānas* were all 'effects' (the 'effects' of previous actions), these three *nidānas* are all 'causes': they set up actions which must bear fruit in the future (either in this life or in some future life).

The last two *nidānas* (birth and decay-and-death) constitute the 'effect process of the future life'. As the 'effect' of our actions in this life we will be born, grow old, and die in a future life.

As we go round the outermost circle of the Wheel of Life in this way, we see how these Twelve *Nidānas* are spread out over three lives. We see how, due to our original ignorance and activities based on ignorance, the seed of consciousness arises again in a new existence. That seed develops into a whole new psychophysical organism. That psychophysical organism is endowed with the six senses, which make contact with the six sense-objects. As a result of that contact, feelings arise. As the feelings arise, we start craving and then trying to cling on to those that are pleasant, while rejecting those that are unpleasant. So, by way of conditioned existence, we grow and precipitate ourselves into another life in the future, which is again subject to old age, disease, and death.

We see not only that the Twelve Links are spread out over three lives, but also that they comprise an alternation of 'cause process' and 'effect process' ('cause process of the previous life', 'effect process of the present life', 'cause process of the present life', and 'effect process of the future life'). This alternation represents a cyclical movement between pairs of opposites.

The Three Junctures

Since we have this alternation within the context of three lives we see that there are three points at which one type of process changes into the other ('cause process' into 'effect process' or 'effect process' into 'cause process'). These three points are known as the 'Three Junctures', *sandhis*. (This is the same word which is used in Pali and Sanskrit for dawn and dusk, where either night passes over into day or day passes over into night.)

The first of the Three Junctures is between the second and third links, where the *saṁskāras*, volitional activities based on ignorance, which constitute the last link in the 'cause process of the past life', are succeeded by *vijñāna*, the germinal consciousness arising in the womb of the mother, which represents the first link in the 'effect process of the present life'.

The second of the Three Junctures is between the seventh and eighth links, where, in dependence upon *vedanā*, feeling, which is the last link in the 'effect process of the present life', there arises *tṛṣṇā*, craving, which is the first link in the 'cause process of the present life'.

The third of the Three Junctures is between the tenth and eleventh link, where *bhava*, becoming, the last link in the 'cause process of the present life', gives rise to *jāti*, birth, the first link in the 'effect process of the future life'.

It is with the second of these Three Junctures that we are at present concerned. This second juncture, between feeling and craving, is important because it represents the point of intersection between the cyclical and the progressive type of conditionality. It is the point of intersection between the Round and the Spiral. It is the point where we either go wrong completely and revolve once more in the Round, or start going right and begin to ascend in the Spiral. Let us examine this juncture a little more closely and try to see what happens.

Suppose we are just sitting doing nothing – there is no

need to go further than this. All the time various feelings are arising in us. These feelings are either pleasant, or painful, or neutral. Most of the time we react to pleasant feelings with craving: we try to cling on to them; we want to perpetuate them; we do not want to lose them. If we have a pleasant experience, our natural tendency is to try to repeat it. That is the fatal mistake which we always make. We are never content to let it come and let it go. If the feelings are unpleasant, painful, or at least unsatisfactory, then instinctively – one might almost say compulsively – we try to thrust them away from us. We do not want anything to do with them. We try to escape them. This is aversion (*dveṣa*). If we are confronted by a feeling which is neither pleasant nor painful, then we just remain confused. We do not know whether to grasp it or reject it. This, in other words, is bewilderment (*moha*).

We react in one of these three ways all the time to all the sensations, feelings, and experiences, which are continually, from all sides – through all the senses and through the mind – impinging upon our consciousness. We react in this cyclical order: dependent upon the feeling arises craving – or aversion, or bewilderment, as the case may be. In this way, an 'effect process' is succeeded by a 'cause process', the Wheel of Life makes one more revolution, and all the conditions are created – or re-created – for a fresh rebirth. This very point, where dependent upon feelings there arises craving, is where it all happens.

Suppose, however, that we do not react in the way I have described. Suppose, when feelings befall us, we do not react with craving, or aversion, or confusion. Suppose we can stop this process. Then, we gain Enlightenment. Then mundane, conditioned existence just ceases and only the transcendental is left. This, of course, is easier to say than to do.

Getting off the Wheel

Broadly speaking, we may say that there are two ways of ensuring that feeling is not succeeded by craving, of ensuring that the Wheel does not make another revolution. There is a 'sudden way', when the Wheel is, as it were, shattered with a single blow, and a 'gradual way', in which it is gradually slowed down – a brake is gently applied, bringing the Wheel slowly to a standstill.

The first way, the 'sudden way', the abrupt way, is illustrated, you may be surprised to hear, not by a story from the Zen scriptures, but by one from the *Udāna* in the Sutta Piṭaka of the Pali Canon.[75] The story goes that a certain monk called Bahiya came to the place where the Buddha was staying. He wanted to meet the Buddha. He had been admitted to the Sangha in some distant part of the country, and so had never had the opportunity of meeting him. At the time of Bahiya's arrival, the Buddha was, apparently, out on his daily almsround.[76] Bahiya enquired the direction in which he had gone and followed him. Before long he caught up with him. Walking just behind the Buddha as the Buddha went from door to door, Bahiya called out to him, 'Please give me a teaching.' It was, we are told, the Buddha's custom that when he went on his almsround he never spoke, so he said nothing to Bahiya but just walked quietly on. A second time Bahiya asked, even more urgently this time, 'Please give me a teaching.' Again the Buddha ignored him and walked on. A third time Bahiya made his request. It was another custom of the Buddha's that, if anyone asked him something a third time, whatever the question and however terrible the consequences might be for the questioner, he answered it. So he halted in his tracks, turned around, gave Bahiya a direct look, and said, 'In the seen, only the seen. In the heard, only the heard. In the touched, only the touched. In the tasted, only the tasted. In the smelt, only the smelt. In the thought, only the thought.' Having said just this, he turned again and continued on his almsround. Bahiya became Enlightened on the spot.

This is the 'sudden way'. The Buddha in effect was saying, 'Do not react.' 'In the heard, only the heard.' If a sound impinges on your eardrums, that is just a sound. You do not have to react to that sound – that you like it or do not like it, want it to continue or want it to stop. Similarly with 'the seen', 'the tasted', 'the touched', 'the smelt', and 'the thought', do not react. Let the bare experience be there. Do not make that experience the basis for any reaction in the cyclical order. If you can do that, you are Enlightened on the spot, as Bahiya was: at a single stroke, you cut off the whole of saṁsāra, you stop the Wheel revolving.

Some of you may be thinking that this 'sudden way' is impossible. The case of Bahiya shows that it is not actually impossible, but it is certainly very difficult. Therefore for most of us – if not for all of us – it is better to try to follow the 'gradual way'. (Though it is called the 'gradual way', it is not the never-never way.)

The Twelve Positive Links

The 'gradual way' may be explained in terms of the 'Eightfold Path', or in terms of the 'Seven Stages of Purification', or in terms of the 'Ten *Bhūmis*', and so on. Perhaps, however, it is best explained in terms of the 'Twelve Positive Links'.[77] These constitute, psychologically and spiritually, the successive stages of the path, or the successive spirals of this progressive movement of conditionality as it winds out of the Round.

Here we are concerned only with the first two of the Twelve Positive Links. These are *duḥkha* (Pali *dukkha*), which means 'pain', 'suffering', or 'unsatisfactoriness', and *śraddhā* (Pali *saddhā*), which means 'faith', or 'confidence'.

Duḥkha corresponds, in the Twelve *Nidānas* of the *pratītya-samutpāda*, to *vedanā*, which is the last link in the 'effect process of the present life'; *śraddhā* corresponds to *tṛṣṇā*, which is the first link in the 'cause process of the future life'.

We have seen how sensations, feelings, are impinging upon us from all sides, and how we can react to them with craving, thus perpetuating the cyclical movement of existence. However, it is possible for us to react in a different, positive way. As all these sensations, feelings, experiences – pleasant, painful, and neutral – impinge upon us, we can begin to see that none of them, not even the pleasant ones, are really satisfactory. We can begin to see that even if we really could isolate and perpetuate the pleasant experiences, while eliminating the painful ones, that would still not be enough: there would still be some hidden lack, something not satisfied, something frustrated. We can begin to realize that this whole conditioned existence, our life, our experience in the ordinary sense, is not enough: it cannot give us permanent, true satisfaction or happiness. In other words, if we analyse it deeply, our life, in the long run, is unsatisfactory (*duḥkha*).

Because we see our everyday experience in this way, we begin to sit loose to it. We begin to detach ourselves from it. We do not care so much about it. We lose interest in it. We start to think that there must be something higher, something beyond, something which *can* give us deeper satisfaction. We start to think that there must be something spiritual, even something transcendental. So we begin to shift our attention and eventually we place our heart – the word '*śraddhā*' comes from a verb meaning 'to place the heart' – not so much on the conditioned, not so much on the things of everyday experience, but more and more on the Unconditioned, on the spiritual, on the transcendental. In this way faith develops.

At first, our faith is confused, vague, and inchoate, but gradually it strengthens and eventually becomes faith in the 'Three Jewels'.[78] We begin to see the Buddha, the Dharma, and the Sangha as the embodiments of those higher spiritual values which stand above and beyond the world but which at the same time give meaning and significance to the world. We 'place the heart' more and more on them, until we are galvanized into action and go for Refuge.[79]

Instead of craving arising in dependence upon feeling, faith arises in dependence upon unsatisfactoriness. In dependence upon the experience of the unsatisfactoriness of the whole of conditioned existence there arises faith in the Unconditioned, as represented by the Buddha, the Dharma, and the Sangha. At this juncture, therefore, we have left the Round and we have entered upon the Spiral: we have begun to move not in a cyclical order but progressively in a spiral order. At this juncture we have entered upon the path that leads to nirvāṇa.

The Spiral Path

Buddhism can be looked at, in a very general way, from two points of view: from a more theoretical, philosophical, or even speculative point of view, or from one which is more practical, even pragmatic. Here we are going to be concerned with the practical aspect of Buddhism. We are going to leave aside the theory and concern ourselves with what is pre-eminently practical. We are going to try to understand something of the stages of the spiritual path. Hardly anything, from a Buddhist point of view, could be more practical than that.

Buddhism is not just a religious teaching, but is primarily the path to the attainment of Enlightenment. What we describe as the stages of the spiritual path are simply the successive, cumulative stages in our progress to that state of Enlightenment. These stages are not laid down in accordance with any purely external criterion. They are psychological; they are dictated by the very nature, or structure, of our own spiritual experience. They represent a certain sequence of experiences, one experience arising in dependence upon another. Just as out of the bud grows the flower, and out of the flower the fruit, so out of one spiritual experience there blossoms another, and out of that yet another, and out of that another still. Each succeeding stage is higher, more refined, more beautiful, a little nearer to nirvāṇa, than the preceding one. The whole sequence of stages is progressive and cumulative.

Here we are going to deal, somewhat briefly, with the twelve stages of the spiritual path, each stage arising in dependence upon, or conditioned by, the preceding stage. There are other formulations of the path which enumerate different numbers of stages. There is the 'Noble Eightfold Path',[80] the 'Threefold Path' (of ethics, meditation, and Wisdom), the 'Path of the Perfections' (*pāramitās*) practised by the Bodhisattva, which are either six or ten in number.[81] But here we are concerned with the twelve successive stages because this formulation exhibits more clearly, perhaps, than any other the nature of the spiritual path itself.

We shall take up these stages one by one and try to understand what they represent. First, however, we must stress that each of the stages represents a spiritual experience in process of transition to another experience which is more advanced. The experiences are not fixed and static, like steps in a staircase or on a ladder. Each experience is all the time in process of developing into something greater than itself. We speak of the spiritual *path*, but we must not be misled by metaphors. It is not that the spiritual path is something fixed and rigid, which we simply go up. The path itself grows, just as a plant grows. One stage passes over into the next, so that there is a constant ascending movement. This is made clear by the formula by which the stages of the path are described: in dependence upon A arises B. If we traverse these stages, and try to understand these experiences, we shall find that we have arrived at a sort of progressive phenomenology of the spirit.

Suffering and Faith

In dependence upon suffering (Sanskrit *duḥkha*, Pali *dukkha*) arises faith (Sanskrit *śraddhā*, Pali *saddhā*). This is where the spiritual path begins. Here we have two experiences: an experience of suffering and another experience which is called the experience of faith. We are further told by this formula that the former experience, suffering, gives rise to the latter experience, faith. Suffering here means not just individual painful experience, like toothache, or a cut finger, or when someone disappoints you bitterly – though these are painful experiences – but suffering in the sense of unsatisfactoriness.

One of the traditional explanations of the word *dukkha* (Pali) is that the prefix *du-* means 'ill', 'bad', 'incorrect', or 'improper', and that the suffix *-kk(h)a* corresponds to the second syllable of the word *cakka*, which means 'wheel'. So *dukkha* is explained – this may not be etymologically correct in the scientific sense, but it throws a great deal of light on the Buddhistic meaning of the term – as being originated from a chariot wheel which fits badly – *du-(ca)kkha*, 'the ill-fitting chariot wheel'.

If you have an ill-fitting chariot wheel and you are driving along in the chariot, then you have a bumpy and uncomfortable journey. (In ancient India there were no springs on chariots and no proper roads.) Thus *duḥkha* means the sort of discomfort which arises in the course of our lives when things do not fit properly, when there is a lot of jarring and a lot of discomfort. This is what is really meant by *duḥkha*: a disharmony, a jarring quality that we experience in the course of our everyday life in the world.

We all know what this means. Things are never one hundred percent right. There is always something, even if it is a little something, that goes wrong. Even in the course of the most beautiful day, it seems, only too often a cloud has to float across the face of the sky. You may have prepared expectantly for a very beautiful day. You are going to meet somebody whom you like. Things are going to be so lovely. But then some absurd incident happens and it all goes wrong. Then you feel completely out of tune, completely jangled by whatever has happened. Very often this is our experience of life. We find that everything from which we expected so much fails and does not live up to our expectations. This sort of experience is *duḥkha*, unsatisfactoriness or suffering.

Then we start becoming dissatisfied. We start feeling that nothing is going to give us any lasting satisfaction. We might have tried all sorts of things – worldly success, pleasure, comfort and luxury, wealth, learning. But in the end we find them all unsatisfactory. There is a vague restlessness inside us. It is not that we are actually suffering pain all the time, but we are just not really happy. We feel a vague discomfort all the time; we can't really settle down; we feel that we don't belong; we perhaps feel, in the words of the Bible, that 'here we have no abiding city'.

So we start, at first almost unconsciously, looking for something else – searching for something higher. At first, very often, we do not know what we are looking for. This is the paradoxical situation in which we find ourselves. We are looking, but we do not know what we are looking for. We are driven by this vague restlessness to grope in all directions for we know not what.

But eventually, searching in this way – if it can be called searching – we come into contact with something which, for want of a better term, we label 'spiritual'. This word spiritual is not one that I really like, but we don't seem to have a better one in English. I use it to mean something higher, something which is not of this world, even something, as the idiom goes, out of this world. When we come into contact with it – howsoever we come into contact with it – it at once evokes a response in us. We get the feeling, or at least an inkling of a feeling, that this is what I have been searching for all the time, even though I did not know it when I was actually searching. This emotional response to this spiritual something, when we first come into contact with it, is what, in the context of Buddhist tradition, we call faith (*śraddhā*).

Śraddhā is not faith in the sense of belief, or in the sense of believing to be true something which cannot be rationally demonstrated. If we want a definition of faith we may say that it is 'the emotional response of what is ultimate in us to what is ultimate in the universe'. Faith is an intuitive, emotional, even mystical response to what is of ultimate value. For Buddhism, faith means specifically faith in the 'Three Jewels': the Buddha, the Enlightened teacher; the Dharma, the way leading to Enlightenment; and the Sangha, the Spiritual Community of those who are treading the way. The Buddha, the Dharma, and the Sangha represent for Buddhism the highest values of existence. They are called the Three Jewels because in the same way that jewels are the most precious things in the material world, so these three represent for Buddhism the highest values in the spiritual world.

Joy

In dependence upon faith arises joy (Sanskrit *prāmodya*, Pali *pāmojja*). We have found what we were looking for. We might not have been able to seize hold of it, but at least we have had a glimpse of it. So naturally, after what has perhaps been a long period of struggling and discontent, we are pleased and happy. More than that, our contact with these higher values has begun to transform our lives.

The contact is not something merely intellectual or theoretical; our hearts have actually been placed on something higher (*śraddhā* literally means 'a placing on of the heart') and as a result a change begins to take place in our lives. We begin to become just a little less self-centred; our egotism is just a little disturbed. We begin to become just a little more generous and outward-going. We tend not to hang on to things so very compulsively.

What may be described as the lower part of our human nature (that part which belongs to the Lower Evolution) starts to come under the conscious control of the higher part of our human nature (that part which belongs to the Higher Evolution[82]); things like food, sex, and sleep begin to come under the control of that higher nature. We begin to lead a life which is simpler and more harmless than before. This too makes us feel more contented. We feel more at ease within ourselves and do not rely so much on external things – we don't care if we haven't got a beautiful house in the suburbs or a beautiful car, etc. We are much freer, more detached, than we were before. We are at peace with ourselves. We have a good conscience – though there is no complacency.

Buddhism attaches great importance to this particular stage of the path, to our having a clear conscience and feeling happy and joyful on account of our spiritual life. This is one of the things that you can notice in the East, certainly in the Buddhist East. There spiritual life is much more associated with joy than it is in the West. In the West we tend to think that in order to be religious you must be at least a bit gloomy, be serious, keep a straight face, certainly not laugh in church – that would be very improper. But it is not like that in the East. There they tend to think that if you are a Buddhist, or leading a spiritual life, you should be happier, more open, more carefree, more joyful than other people. I was surprised when I came back to this country after twenty years in the East to find that the Buddhist movement here was, on the whole, such a gloomy and serious affair, with people hardly daring to smile when you made a joke in the course of a lecture.

If you have found this precious 'something' that you were looking for, and if this has really begun to transform your life, then why should you not be happy? If you are not happier than other people who have not got these Three Jewels, what is the use of being a Buddhist? What does being a Buddhist mean? People who come into contact with those who have discovered the Three Jewels ought to feel that those people are more happy than people they normally meet. If they are not, one can only put the question: 'Why not?'

Indeed, so much importance does Buddhism attach to this stage of joy that if, for any reason, you lapse from it – you may have done something that you should not have done so that you get all sad and serious and start beating your breast in the good old pre-Buddhistic fashion – Buddhism considers this state – of guilt and remorse – a very unhealthy state to be in and says that the sooner you get out of it the better. This does not mean that what you did was not wrong. You made a mistake. It is best to admit that, and try to make up for it and not do it again. But once you have understood that and have tried to put it right, it is best to put it out of your mind. Just move on and leave the mistake behind. It will not do you any good whatsoever to carry it with you.

In Buddhism we even have special ceremonies to bring about this psychological effect. If you feel weighed down by any fault that you have committed just go in front of the shrine, bow down in front of the Buddha, think it all over, and say to yourself, 'Well, what a fool I've been! I really should not have done that. I really am sorry. I won't do it again.' Then recite some texts and try to fix your mind on the teaching in order to recollect the Ideal. Perhaps light some candles and burn some incense. In this way you purge your mind of the feeling of guilt. You restore your state of clear conscience and joy in the Three Jewels. The state of joy should be the hallmark of the true Buddhist.

Rapture

In dependence upon joy arises rapture (Sanskrit *prīti*, Pali *piti*). Even joy is not enough. *Prīti* is a very strong word. It is an emotion of intense, thrilling, even ecstatic joy. *Prīti* could well be translated as 'ecstasy', because it is an emotion so powerful that it is experienced not just mentally, but also physically. We all know that when we are deeply moved by an experience, perhaps in connection with human relationships, or with art, as when we listen to a marvellous symphony beautifully played, or with nature, as when we look at a beautiful sunset, then it sometimes happens that there is not only an emotion, something mental, but there is a physical innervation at the same time. We may be so deeply moved that our hair stands on end. Some people shed tears. (You can sometimes see people at symphony concerts so moved that they have to wipe their eyes, maybe in a rather shamefaced way because in this country we are not supposed to do that sort of thing.) *Prīti* is an overwhelming psychophysical experience of rapture, bliss, ecstasy, and is the sort of experience which will be generated as we follow the path.

Calm

In dependence upon rapture arises calm (Sanskrit *praśrabdhi*, Pali *passaddhi*). *Praśrabdhi* represents the calming down, or the pacification, of all the physical side effects of rapture. We saw that rapture, or ecstasy, which arises in the previous stage, is something psychophysical. In this fourth stage the physical side of the experience subsides and you are left with the purely emotional experience of rapture. The physical innervations die away, not because the rapture is less, but because it has become greater: it has gone beyond all possibility of physical expression.

The texts give an interesting simile to illustrate this. Suppose an elephant steps down into a small pond – a pond, in fact, which is not much bigger than the elephant itself. When this great beast gets into that small pond the water splashes out at the sides. In the same way, in the previous stage the experience of rapture is very great, yet our capacity to receive it is very small, so some of it spills over in the form of these physical innervations. But then, the illustration goes on to say, suppose the elephant steps down into a great pool of water, a huge lake, or an enormous river. Big as the elephant is, when he steps into the water there is hardly a ripple. Though the elephant is big, the body of water is immeasurably bigger still. In the same way, when you come as far as this stage of calm, even though the experience of rapture may be very great indeed, you are more able to receive it (there is less external disturbance), and the physical innervations therefore die down, leaving only the inner, purely emotional experience of rapture.

Bliss

In dependence upon calm arises bliss (*sukha*). You see how far we are going. We started off with joy, then went on to rapture, and after a period of calm we come now to bliss. It is extraordinary that some of the early books written in the West on Buddhism describe it as a gloomy, pessimistic, and negative religion. Here we see exactly the opposite. Bliss is a state of intense happiness. It represents the complete unification of all our emotional energies. They are not divided; there is no split or flaw; they are all flowing together in a great stream, strongly and powerfully, in a single direction. Here, we are told, there is not only bliss, there is peace, love, compassion, joy, and equanimity. There are no negative emotions: no craving, no fear, no hatred, no anxiety, no guilt, no remorse. All the negative emotions have been purged. Whatever energy we had invested in those negative emotions now flows positively in the form of bliss.

Concentration

In dependence upon bliss arises concentration (*samādhi*). *Samādhi* has several different meanings.[83] Here it means concentration. This is not concentration in the sense of the forcible fixation of the mind on a single object, but concentration in the sense of the unification and integration that come about quite naturally when, in that state of intense happiness, all our emotional energies are flowing together in the same direction.

This stage is based upon the very important principle that when we are completely happy, we are concentrated – in the true sense. Hence we may say that a concentrated person is a happy person and a happy person is a concentrated person. The happier we are, the longer we are able to stay concentrated. We find it difficult to stay concentrated for long because we are not happy with our present state. If we were really and truly happy, we would just stay still, enjoying that happiness. But we are not happy, we are dissatisfied, and so we get restless and go searching for some distraction.

The connection between happiness and concentration is illustrated by a rather interesting story from the scriptures. We are told that one day a king came to the Buddha to ask him about his teaching. In the course of their discussion the question arose who was the more happy: was the Buddha happier than the king or the king happier than the Buddha? The king was quite sure that he was by far the happier. He said, 'Look, I've got palaces; I've got an army; I've got wealth; I've got beautiful women. But you have got nothing. Here you are sitting under a tree outside some wretched hut. All that you have got is a yellow robe and a begging-bowl. So, obviously, I am the happier of the two.' The Buddha replied, 'Let me ask you a question. Could you sit here perfectly still for an hour, enjoying complete and perfect happiness?' The king replied, 'Yes, I suppose I could.' The Buddha asked, 'Could you sit here, without moving, enjoying complete and perfect happiness, for six hours?' The king replied, 'That would be rather difficult.' The Buddha asked, 'Could you sit here for a whole day and a whole night, without moving, absolutely happy the whole time?' The king had to admit that that would be beyond him. Then the Buddha said, 'I can sit here for seven days and seven nights without stirring, and experience all the time complete and perfect happiness. Therefore I think I am happier than you.'

From this story we can see that the Buddha's happiness arose out of his concentration and his concentration arose out of his happiness. Because he was happy he was able to concentrate; because he was able to concentrate he was happy. The fact that the king was unable to concentrate showed that he was not really as happy as he had thought.

All this is related very closely to our practice of meditation. We know that meditation begins with concentration. Many of us, however, find concentration very difficult. We find it difficult simply because we are not happy. We are split; our emotional energies are not integrated. Because our emotional energies are not integrated we cannot concentrate, we cannot focus those energies on a single point. Therefore we try forcibly to fix our mind on that point. But then all sorts of disturbances arise and we get distracted. Concentration is thus something which pertains to the whole being, not just to the conscious mind.

It is very significant that concentration in this higher sense (the sense of *samādhi*) arises only at this stage of the path – when we are half-way along. This points to the importance of preparation for meditation. We cannot just come along and sit down and think that we can meditate. This is not possible. If we really want to meditate we have to go through all these previous stages. If we have done that then the concentration exercises that we do just put the finishing touch. Quite a lot of people, however, have no experience of the unsatisfactoriness of life; no faith has arisen; they do not have much experience of joy; they certainly do not have much experience of rapture or calm: they are just in their ordinary, restless, dissatisfied state. It is only when we have reached this stage of the path, the stage of *samādhi*, that we can really and truly begin to concentrate, because our emotional energies have been unified and we are now, perhaps for the first time in our lives, happy.

Knowledge and Vision

In dependence upon concentration arises Knowledge and Vision of things as they really are (Sanskrit *yathābhūta-jñānadarśana*, Pali *yathābhūta-ñāṇa-dassana*). Once we are truly happy and truly concentrated we can look into things with a concentrated mind and begin to see them as they really are. We begin to see Reality. This stage is of the utmost importance because here is the transition from meditation to Wisdom, from what is psychological to what is spiritual.[84] Once we have reached this stage there can be no falling back; according to the traditional teaching, the attainment of Enlightenment is now assured.[85]

So far as conditioned existence is concerned, this Knowledge and Vision is threefold.[86] Firstly, it consists in Insight into the truth that all conditioned things are impermanent: they are constantly changing; they do not remain the same for two consecutive instants. Secondly, it consists in Insight into the truth that all conditioned things are ultimately unsatisfactory: they may give us some happiness for a time, but they cannot give us permanent happiness – to expect that from them is pure and simple delusion. Thirdly, there is Insight into the fact that all conditioned things are insubstantial or ultimately unreal: not that we do not experience them; not that they are not there, empirically speaking; but as we experience them it is all only superficial (it does not penetrate into the depths but is all on the surface) and not truly real.

This Knowledge and Vision represents a direct perception. You actually see through the conditioned. Not only that, but you see through the conditioned to the Unconditioned. Piercing through the impermanence of the conditioned you see the permanence of the Unconditioned. Piercing through the unsatisfactoriness of the conditioned you see the ultimately satisfying nature of the Unconditioned. Piercing through the insubstantial, the unreal, you see that which is eternally Real, what the Mahāyāna calls the *dharmakāya*, the Body of Spiritual Truth.[87]

When your concentration becomes so keen that this Knowledge and Vision of things as they really are arises, and you can see the conditioned in its true nature and through the conditioned to the Unconditioned, your whole outlook and attitude radically changes: you cannot be the same as you were before. It is just as when a man sees a ghost. When a man sees a ghost he is never the same afterwards. Once Hamlet, in Shakespeare's play, had seen that ghost stalking along the battlements he was a changed man. He saw something from another dimension. In the same way here, though in a much more positive sense, once you have caught a glimpse (which is not a speculation, nor an idea, but a real contact or 'communication') of the Unconditioned, of that higher dimension, then you cannot be the same. A permanent change takes place in your life. There is a permanent reorientation. To use the Yogācāra expression, you have begun to 'turn about in the deepest seat of consciousness'.[88]

Withdrawal

In dependence upon Knowledge and Vision of things as they really are there arises Withdrawal (Sanskrit *nirvid*, *nirveda*, Pali *nibbidā*). This is sometimes translated as 'Revulsion' or 'Disgust', but that is too strong and too psychological. This particular stage represents the serene withdrawal from involvement with the things which we have seen through. If we have seen through something, we are no longer involved in it: we withdraw from it. It is like seeing a mirage in a desert. At first we may be very interested in those palm trees and that oasis, and we may be hastening in that direction. But as soon as we see that it is a *fata morgana* and is not really there then we are no longer really interested. We stop and do not hasten in that direction any longer.

This stage of Withdrawal is a 'sitting loose' to life. You play all the games that other people play, but *you* know that they are games. A child takes his game very seriously: to the child, his game is life. But the adult, although he can join in the child's game and play with the child, knows it is all a game. If the child beats him in the game, the adult doesn't mind and doesn't get upset – because it is only a game. In the same way, once we have seen through the 'games people play' we can go on playing the games, but knowing that they are just games, we withdraw from them. There is an inner withdrawal, even if there is not an external withdrawal; we may be doing what is necessary objectively, but subjectively we are not caught up. This is what is meant by Withdrawal.

Dispassion

In dependence upon Withdrawal arises Dispassion (Sanskrit *vairāgya*, Pali *virāga*). Withdrawal, the previous stage, is the movement of detachment from conditioned existence; Dispassion represents the fixed state of actually being detached. In this state we cannot be moved by any worldly happening. Anything may happen to us, but we cannot really be disturbed. It is a state of complete spiritual imperturbability. It is not a state of hardness, or stoniness, or insensitivity, or 'stoic' apathy, but a state of serene imperturbability, like that displayed by the Buddha when he sat underneath the Bodhi tree. On that occasion, we are told, along came Māra, the embodiment of evil, with his forces. This scene is often depicted in Buddhist art. Māra is shown leading his army, complete with hundreds of thousands of monstrous demons throwing great rocks, spitting fire, and releasing arrows against the Buddha. But the Buddha does not take any notice: he does not even see them. He is in a state of complete imperturbability. When all the arrows, stones, and flames hurled by these demon hosts touch the edge of the Buddha's aura they just turn into flowers and drop to the ground.

Freedom

In dependence upon Dispassion arises Freedom (Sanskrit *vimukti*, Pali *vimutti*). This is spiritual freedom. Nowadays there is quite a lot of talk about freedom. Most people, it seems, think that to be free means simply to do as one likes. The Buddhist conception of freedom is rather different. In the earliest Buddhist teaching freedom is twofold. Firstly, there is *ceto-vimukti*, Freedom of mind, which means complete freedom from all subjective, emotional, and psychological bias. Secondly, there is *prajñā-vimukti*, Freedom of wisdom, which means freedom from all wrong views, all ignorance, all false philosophy, all opinion. It is this total spiritual freedom – freedom of heart and mind at the summit of one's existence – which is the aim and object of Buddhism.

On one occasion the Buddha addressed his disciples and said, 'O monks, just as the water of the four great oceans has one taste, the taste of salt, just so my teaching, my doctrine, has one taste, the taste of Freedom (*vimukti-rasa*).'[89] From wherever in the oceans you take water – whether you take it from the Atlantic Ocean, or the Bay of Bengal, or the Straits of Dover, or the Suez Canal – it tastes of salt. In the same way, whatever aspect of the Buddha's teaching you may look at – whether it is the 'Four Noble Truths', the 'Noble Eightfold Path', the 'Four Foundations of Mindfulness', the 'Four *Brahma-vihāras*', the 'Three Trainings', the 'Three Refuges' – it will have the taste of Freedom.

This state of complete spiritual freedom, freedom from everything conditioned, even, as the Mahāyāna goes on to say, freedom from the very distinction between the conditioned and the Unconditioned, is the final objective of Buddhism.

Knowledge of the Destruction of the Āśravas

In dependence upon Freedom arises Knowledge of the Destruction of the *Āśravas* (Sanskrit *āśravakṣayajñāna*, Pali *āsavakkhayañāṇa*). One is not only free, one also knows that one is free. One knows that one is free because one is free from the *āśravas*. *Āśrava* is one of those untranslatable Pali and Sanskrit words. It means a sort of mental poison that floods the mind. It is a very expressive word. The *āśravas* are three in number. There is *kāmāśrava*, which means the poison of craving for experience through the five senses. Then there is *bhavāśrava*, which is the poison of craving for any form of conditioned existence, even, we are told, for existence as a god in a heaven. Lastly, there is *avidyāśrava*, the poison of spiritual ignorance. When these poisons are extinct, and one knows that they are extinct, then one is said to be Enlightened: one has reached the end of the spiritual path.

These twelve stages, from 'suffering' right up to 'knowledge of the destruction of the *āśravas*', constitute the spiritual path. (They also constitute the whole process of what we call the Higher Evolution.) We can see very easily from this formulation how the whole spiritual life is a natural process of growth. Each succeeding stage of the path is the product of the overflow – the product of the very excess, of the very prodigality – of the preceding stage. As soon as one stage reaches its fullness, it inevitably passes over into the next. We find this in meditation also. Sometimes people ask, 'When we get to a certain stage in meditation, how shall we get on to the next?' Well, there is no need to ask that question. If you get up to a certain stage and go on cultivating that stage, so that it becomes more perfect, full, and complete, then out of its very fullness, under its own momentum, it will move forward into the next stage. When you perfect any lower stage, then automatically the transition to a higher stage of perfection of development begins. This is what happens here. The succeeding stage of the path is given birth to by the preceding stage when that preceding stage reaches a point of fullness. We do not really have to bother about the next step, the next stage. All we need to do is bother about this one. Cultivate that. Maybe have a theoretical idea of the next stage, but do not bother about it too much. Once the present stage is fully developed, it will automatically pass over into the next. By fully developing, cultivating within ourselves, each successive stage of the spiritual path, we shall attain Buddhahood.

The Sangha

The Traditional Significance of the Sangha

The Sangha, or Spiritual Community, is the third of the Three Jewels. According to Buddhist tradition, there are three levels of the Sangha. These are known as the *ārya-sangha*, the *bhikṣu-saṅgha*, and the *mahā-saṅgha*. An examination of the meaning of each of these terms will lead to a fuller understanding of the traditionally accepted significance of the Sangha.[90]

The Ārya-saṅgha

In *ārya-saṅgha*, *ārya* literally means 'noble'; by extension of meaning, it means 'holy'. In Buddhist terminology *ārya* always means 'holy' in the sense of 'in touch with the transcendental'. So the *ārya-saṅgha* is so called because it consists of Holy Persons, *ārya-pudgalas*, who have certain transcendental attainments and experiences in common.

These people may or may not be in physical contact, but are united on a spiritual plane, because of the spiritual experiences they have in common. The Sangha on this level is a purely spiritual body: a number of people living at distant places, at different times, but sharing, above space and time, the same spiritual attainments and experiences.

According to the substratum of belief and doctrine shared by all the different Buddhist schools, four types of Holy Persons are distinguished: the Stream-Entrant (*srotāpanna*), the Once-Returner (*sakṛdāgāmin*), the Non-Returner (*anāgāmin*), and the Arhant. These Holy Persons constitute a spiritual hierarchy intermediate between Buddhahood and ordinary unenlightened humanity.

The path to Enlightenment, as taught by the Buddha, can be divided into successive stages in different ways. The basic division, however, is into three great stages. These are the stages of Ethics (Sanskrit *śīla*, Pali *sīla*), Meditation (*samādhi*), and Wisdom (Sanskrit *prajñā*, Pali *paññā*). Wisdom, the culminating stage, comes in the form of flashes of Insight revealing the nature of Reality. These flashes of Insight are not conceptual, but are immediate, direct, and intuitive. They usually arise in the midst of deep meditation.

In the spiritual life we find that nothing comes all at once; everything comes gradually, by degrees. At all stages we have to proceed slowly and systematically. We find therefore that there are insights of different degrees of intensity. You can have a feeble flash of insight (if your meditation is weak, that is all it can support); or you can have a very strong, brilliant flash of Insight, which illumines far into the depths of Reality. It is according to the degree of intensity of Insight that the different types of Holy Persons are distinguished one from another.

This raises the important question: How do you measure the intensity of Insight? In Buddhism Insight is traditionally measured in two ways: subjectively, according to the number of spiritual Fetters (Pali *saṁyojana*) which it is capable of breaking (there are 'Ten Fetters' chaining us to the Wheel of Life on which we revolve); and objectively, according to the number of rebirths remaining after the Insight is attained.

The Stream-Entrant. The first Holy Person is the Stream-Entrant (*srotāpanna*). *Srotāpanna* literally means 'one who has entered the stream', i.e. the stream which eventually leads to nirvāṇa.[91] The Stream-Entrant has developed a degree of Insight powerful enough to break the first three of the Ten Fetters.[92] We shall dwell on these Fetters longer than on the others because they concern us very directly.

The first Fetter is known as *satkāya-dṛṣṭi* (Pali *sakkāya-diṭṭhi*), which means 'personality-view'. This is of two kinds. The first is called *śāśvata-dṛṣṭi*. This view holds that after death personal identity persists unchanging. This is a form of traditional soul-belief. You have got a soul (an unchanging ego-identity) within you, which is quite distinct from your body and continues after your death (it either goes to heaven or reincarnates). The basic point is that, like a sort of spiritual billiard ball, it rolls on unchanged; it is an entity, not a process. The other kind of personality-view holds that after death comes oblivion: death is the end; everything finishes; everything is cut off dead (the traditional term for this, *uccheda* (Pali), literally means 'cut off'). This view holds, in other words, that the psychical side of life, like the material and the physical side, ends at the time of death.

According to Buddhism, these two views are both

misconceived extremes. Buddhism teaches a middle view. It teaches that death is not the end, in the sense that when the physical body dies there is no complete stop to the mental, psychological, spiritual processes: these continue. But it is not an unchanging ego-soul which continues. It is the process – mental, psychological, spiritual – which continues, in all its complexity, ever-changing, flowing on like a stream. The Buddhist view is that what goes on after death is, as it were, a flow of psychical events.[93]

The second Fetter is *vicikitsā* (Pali *vicikicchā*), which is usually translated as 'sceptical doubt', sometimes as 'indecision'. This is not that 'honest doubt' of which Tennyson says,

There lives more faith in honest doubt,
Believe me, than in half the creeds.[94]

Rather, *vicikitsā* represents an unwillingness to come to a definite conclusion. People waver; they like to sit on the fence; they do not want to commit themselves. They remain in this state of indecision, not making up their minds and not really trying to. If asked about the question of life after death, they would admit to one day thinking one way and another day thinking differently. They will not commit themselves to pursuing the matter to the end and thinking things out clearly. This complacent state of wavering is therefore a Fetter, which, according to the Buddha's teaching, has to be broken.

The third Fetter is called *śīlavrata-parāmarśa* (Pali *sīlabbata-parāmāsa*). It is usually translated as 'attachment to rites and ceremonies', but this is quite wrong. The literal meaning of *śīlavrata-parāmarśa* is 'grasping ethical rules and religious observances as ends in themselves'. *Śīla* here is not a rite at all; *śīla* is an ethical observance or rule. (If you say that according to Buddhism you must not take life, this is a *śīla*, an ethical rule.) *Vrata* is a Vedic term for a vow, but in the sense of 'religious observance'. The operative word – in the wording of the Fetter – is *parāmarśa*, which means 'grasping'. The whole Fetter is: *grasping* even ethical rules, even (good) religious observances, as ends in themselves.

This brings us back to the Buddha's parable of the raft.[95] Through that parable the Buddha teaches that the Dharma in all its aspects is a means to an end. If we start thinking that ethical rules or religious observances – even meditation, even the study of the scriptures – are ends in themselves, then they become Fetters, and Fetters have to be broken. So this Fetter means: treating as ends in themselves religious practices and observances, which are quite good as means to an end, but which are not in fact themselves the end.

These are the first three Fetters. Stream-Entry is attained, therefore, by realizing the limitations of the self, by realizing the need for definite commitment, and by realizing the relativity of all religious practices and observances. Once Stream-Entry is attained, there remain, according to Buddhist tradition, no more than seven rebirths within the Wheel of Life – there may be less, but there will not be more. Stream-Entry represents, therefore, an important stage in the spiritual life. We may even go so far as to say that it represents conversion, in the true sense.

Furthermore Stream-Entry is within the reach, and should be considered to be within the reach, of all serious Buddhists. It is no use jogging along with a little meditation and a perfunctory observance of the Precepts, with perhaps just an odd glance at nirvāṇa. One must think seriously that it is possible, in this life, to break the Three Fetters, enter the Stream, and get well on the way to Enlightenment.

The Once-Returner. The second Holy Person is the Once-Returner (*sakṛdāgāmin*), the one who returns only once more to this earth as a human being. He has broken the first three Fetters and he weakens two more. He weakens the fourth Fetter, 'desire for sensuous existence' (*kāma-rāga*), and the fifth Fetter, 'animosity' or 'anger' (*vyāpāda*). These are both very powerful Fetters. The first three Fetters are broken comparatively easily. They are 'intellectual Fetters' and can therefore be broken by clear Intellection, that is, Insight. The fourth and fifth Fetters, on the other hand, are emotional Fetters, so they go much deeper and are much more difficult to break. Therefore even only weakening these two Fetters is sufficient to make one a Once-Returner.

I will make just a few comments on these two Fetters. *Kāma-rāga* is the desire or urge for sensuous existence. It takes a little reflection to realize how strong this urge is. Imagine that you are suddenly deprived of all your senses. What sort of state would your mind be in? You would be in a terrible state of deprivation. Your one urge would be to make contact: you would want to see, hear, smell, taste, touch. By thinking in this way we can gain some realization of how strong our desire for sensuous existence really is. (We know that at the time of death we do lose our senses; we no longer see, hear, smell, taste, or touch. The mind is torn away from these things and suspended in a dreadful void – 'dreadful', that is, for those who want to contact the external world through the five senses.)

Just as the fourth Fetter is strong and difficult even to weaken, so also is the fifth Fetter of anger (*vyāpāda*). Sometimes we feel as though there is a well-spring of anger within us searching for an outlet. It is not as though something happens and we become angry, but rather as though the anger is already there and we are looking around for a target against which to direct it. This anger is deep-rooted within us.

The Non-Returner. The third Holy Person is the Non-Returner (*anāgāmin*). Whereas the Once-Returner only weakens the fourth and fifth Fetters, the Non-Returner breaks them; he breaks all the five lower Fetters – the three intellectual Fetters and the two emotional Fetters. Having broken these Fetters, the Non-Returner does not come back to the human plane at all. He is reborn, according to the Buddhist tradition, in a sphere called the 'pure abodes'[96] (*śuddhāvāsa*) at the peak of the 'world of pure form' (*rūpa-dhātu*).[97] After death he attains nirvāṇa from there.

The Arhant. The fourth Holy Person is the Arhant. Arhant means simply 'the worthy' or 'the worshipful'. He is one who has gained Enlightenment in this life. He breaks all Ten Fetters – the five lower and the five higher. I will briefly enumerate these five higher Fetters.

The sixth Fetter is 'desire for existence in the world of form' (*rūpa-rāga*). Instead of 'the world of form', we might translate this as 'the archetypal realm'. Seventhly, there is the Fetter of 'desire for existence in the formless worlds' (*arūpa-rāga*). Eighth is the Fetter of 'conceit' (*māna*). This is not conceit in the ordinary sense (as when someone says 'I am very beautiful' or 'I am very clever'), but the conceit that I am I, that I am not the not-I, or, as the Buddha said, that I am either better than, or worse than, or equal to, others. Conceit, in this sense, is altogether dispelled by the Arhant (he does not even think 'I gain nirvāṇa'). Ninthly, there is 'instability' or 'trembling' (Sanskrit *auddhatya*, Pali *uddhacca*). This is something very subtle. It is as though the Arhant-to-be is poised between the last reaches of the phenomenal world and nirvāṇa and just oscillates slightly: he has not quite settled down in nirvāṇa. Finally, there is the tenth Fetter – the most basic and the strongest of them all. This is 'ignorance' (Sanskrit *avidyā*, Pali *avijjā*). It is primordial ignorance, spiritual darkness. The Arhant dispels this darkness with the light of Wisdom and, having broken all ten Fetters, realizes nirvāṇa.

These are the four Holy Persons who make up the *ārya-saṅgha*. When we say, '*Saṅghaṁ saraṇaṁ gacchāmi*' as part of our recitation of the 'Three Refuges' it is primarily in the Sangha as an *ārya-saṅgha* that we take Refuge.

The Bhikṣu-saṅgha

Secondly, we come to the *bhikṣu-saṅgha*. This consists of those who have 'gone forth from the household life'[98] and joined the monastic order founded by the Buddha. The *bhikṣu-saṅgha* follows a common set of 150 rules (*prātimokṣa*).[99]

One enters the *bhikṣu-saṅgha* when one is ordained as a monk by a local Sangha, or chapter. This must consist of at least five fully-ordained monks, including at least one 'elder' (*sthāvira*). The tradition is that at the time of ordination you are handed over to a *sthāvira* – he may or may not be the one who presided at your ordination – and you remain with him, under his tutelage, for at least five, preferably for ten, years. (It is significant that only *sthāviras*, only those who have been in the order for ten years, may act as teachers in this way.)

The duties of the monk in Buddhism are manifold: firstly, to study and practise the Dharma, especially meditation; secondly, to set an example to the laity; thirdly, to preach and teach; fourthly, to protect from unwholesome psychic influences; fifthly, to give advice about worldly affairs.

Nowadays in Buddhist countries there are two branches of the monastic order: the Theravāda branch (which is found in Sri Lanka, Myanmar (Burma), Thailand, Cambodia, and Laos) and the Sarvastivāda branch (which is found in Tibet, China, Vietnam, and Korea). There is little difference between the way of life and the rules observed by the monks of these two great traditions – they have the same *prātimokṣa*. (Japan is a special case, because although the monastic ordination was introduced there some centuries ago it died out, its place being taken by the Bodhisattva ordination and other ordinations.)

The Mahā-saṅgha

Thirdly, there is the *mahā-saṅgha*, or 'Great Sangha'. It is so called because it is great in size. It is the collectivity of those who accept certain spiritual principles and truths, regardless of vocation (i.e. regardless of whether they are separated from the world as a monastic order or whether they are in the world, if not exactly of it). The *mahā-saṅgha* includes *āryas* and *anāryas*; it includes the monks and the laity. It is the whole Buddhist community, on all levels, united by a common allegiance to the Buddha, the Dharma, and the Sangha. The *mahā-saṅgha* comprises all those who take Refuge in the Three Jewels. The common Going for Refuge is the bond between them.

The Primacy of Going for Refuge

How does one know who is committed to Buddhism? How does one know who is spiritually motivated? What is the criterion? What is a Buddhist? Although not all Buddhists would agree with me, I personally would say without hesitation that a Buddhist is one who goes for Refuge: one who commits himself to the Buddha, the Dharma, and the Sangha with body, speech, and mind – in other words, totally.

There are many examples of this in the Buddhist scriptures, especially in the Pali scriptures. When we read those scriptures we encounter the Buddha wandering from place to place, begging his food as he goes. In the course of his wanderings he meets somebody – it may be a brahmin priest, or a farmer, or a young man about town, or a wandering ascetic, or a housewife, or a prince. They get into conversation and sooner or later this person asks the Buddha a question (perhaps about the meaning of life or about what happens after death) and the Buddha replies.

The Buddha might reply at considerable length or in just a few words; if he was very inspired he might reply in verse, breathing out what is called an *udāna*; occasionally he might reply with complete silence; or he might give one of his famous 'lion's roars' (Pali *sīhanāda*) – a full and frank, almost defiant, declaration of his own great spiritual experience and the path that he taught.

Whatever the Buddha said – or did not say – in reply, if that listener was receptive, the result was the same. He or she would feel deeply affected. Sometimes there were external manifestations of this: their hair might stand on end; they might shed tears; they might be seized by a violent fit of trembling. They would perhaps feel completely overwhelmed. They would have a tremendous experience of illumination (it would be like seeing a great light). They would have a tremendous sense of freedom (they would feel as though a great burden had been lifted from their back or as though they had been suddenly let out of prison). The listener would feel spiritually reborn.

So at that moment, that turning point in his life, what would that person say? What would be his response to the Buddha? According to those ancient Pali texts, he would say, '*Buddhaṁ saraṇaṁ gacchāmi! Dhammaṁ saraṇaṁ gacchāmi! Saṅghaṁ saraṇaṁ gacchāmi!*' which means 'To the Buddha for Refuge I go! To the Dharma for Refuge I go! To the Sangha for Refuge I go!' His response would be to go for Refuge. He would commit himself. The vision that the Buddha had shown him – the vision of truth, of existence, of human life itself in all its depth and complexity – was so great, that all he could do was give himself to that vision completely. He would want to live for that vision, if necessary to die for it.

This is how one can know who is a Buddhist. This is the criterion. A Buddhist is one who goes for Refuge in response to the Buddha and his teaching. A Buddhist is one who commits himself. He gives himself to the Three Jewels. This was the criterion in the Buddha's day and remains the criterion today.[100]

It is clear that Buddhist organizations can be run only by those who have committed themselves wholeheartedly to the Three Jewels. Furthermore, a Buddhist organization run by committed Buddhists is no longer an organization in the ordinary sense of the word. It is a spiritual movement. It is what we call a 'spiritual community': an association of committed individuals, freely working together for a common spiritual end. In this way commitment gives birth to spiritual community.

An order is different from a Buddhist organization. An order consists of those who have been ordained. In Buddhist terms, ordination means giving full formal expression to one's commitment to the Three Jewels and having that commitment recognized by others who are already committed. One can join an organization by paying the required subscription, but one can be received into an order only by committing oneself. An order is founded on the basis of commitment and spiritual community, or, in more traditional Buddhist language, Going for Refuge and Sangha. There are three factors that make it clear why a Buddhist order – a spiritual community – rather than a Buddhist organization is essential for bringing Buddhism to the West.

First of all, there is what can only be described as inertia and force of habit. Buddhism started to become known in the West (including Westernized India) not much more than a hundred years ago.[101] At that time there was a great expansion in knowledge, especially in scientific knowledge. Societies were set up for the study of many different things. (The structures of these societies included: a general membership, annual general meetings, office bearers, and entry by payment of a membership subscription.) It was inevitable that sooner or later there would be societies for the study of Buddhism, for the publication of Buddhist texts, and so on.

As long as the approach to Buddhism remains purely scientific or academic, such societies may be suitable. But they are no longer suitable when we approach Buddhism in a more practical way (a more spiritual, or even existential, way). Unfortunately people did not realize this. They thought that an organization devoted to spreading Buddhism could have the same structure as an organization devoted to the scientific study of Buddhism. Furthermore, those people who held prominent positions in Buddhist organizations of the usual type were very satisfied with things as they were. After all, the existing set-up gave them a certain amount of power and authority, which they did not want to relinquish.

The second and third reasons are more traditional. The second reason is the devaluation of the Going for Refuge. Buddhism has a long history; in the course of a thousand years Buddhism spread over practically the whole of Asia. Millions of people committed themselves to the Buddha, the Dharma, and the Sangha; they recited the Refuge formula – '*Buddhaṁ saraṇaṁ gacchāmi*' etc. Eventually, however, people started reciting the Refuge formula out of habit. They recited it not because they were real Buddhists, but simply because their parents or their grandparents had recited it. (Sometimes people consider themselves 'born Buddhists', but that is a contradiction in terms.)

This is the situation to a great extent in the Buddhist countries of Asia today. The Going for Refuge is not regarded any longer as an expression of genuine individual spiritual commitment; the recitation of the Refuges and Precepts simply shows that one belongs to a particular social and cultural group. In India, for instance, Sinhalese, and Thai, and Burmese, and Indian Buddhists recite the Refuges and Precepts on all sorts of occasions: at big public meetings; at weddings; at funerals; when performing name-giving ceremonies for children. People recite the Refuges and Precepts, but nobody bothers about their significance. They recite the Refuges and Precepts just to show that they are 'good Buddhists', or respectable citizens. There is no question of the Refuge formula being regarded as an expression of commitment to the ideals of Buddhism. This is how the Going for Refuge has been devalued – not to say degraded and debased.

The Going for Refuge is the essential act of the Buddhist life – it is what makes one a Buddhist. It is the simplest thing in Buddhism, and the most important.

The last reason for the apparent reluctance to start an order instead of yet another Buddhist organization is an overvaluation of monasticism, especially formal monasticism. If nowadays you talk to a serious-minded Eastern Buddhist, especially from South-east Asia, and you ask him who is a real Buddhist, he will, more often than not, say that the real Buddhist is the monk. He will say that if you really want to practise Buddhism you must become a monk. A layman cannot practise Buddhism or can practise it only to a very limited extent. The best thing that the layman can do is support the monks – supply them with food, clothing, shelter, and medicine. In that way the layman can earn some merit and, hopefully, be reborn in heaven after his death – or at least be reborn on earth in a rich family. Because the Going for Refuge has been devalued, monasticism has been overvalued. Being a Buddhist is no longer a question of committing oneself to the Three Jewels, but, in effect, of becoming a monk.

I most certainly do not want to undervalue monasticism – that would be going to the other extreme. But to be a Buddhist it is not necessary to be a monk. What is necessary is that one should go for Refuge. Commitment to the Three Jewels is primary; the leading of a particular life-style is secondary. For many people commitment does find expression in leading a monastic life. This was particularly the case in the Buddha's own day. But even in the Buddha's own day it was not invariably the case. According to the Pali texts, some of the Buddha's disciples attained a high level of spiritual development while continuing to live at home as laymen and laywomen. Therefore, even though a number of committed people are following the same life-style, the distinction between commitment and life-style holds good.

I have spoken of commitment finding expression in the leading of the monastic life. By this I mean the leading of a genuinely monastic life. This unfortunately is not always the case. In many parts of Asia commitment has been replaced by monasticism. More often than not this is not genuine monasticism, but formal monasticism. The laity in many parts of the Buddhist world go through the motions of Going for Refuge (they simply recite the Refuge formula on all possible occasions); in much the same way, the monks go through the motions of being monks: they recite the monastic rules at intervals, without really asking themselves what they mean. As soon as you put the emphasis on Going for Refuge, monasticism is no longer overvalued; it takes its proper place as one possible life-style (amongst others) for the committed individual Buddhist.

What Members of the Spiritual Community Do

What Members of the Spiritual Community Do – For Themselves, For One Another, and For the World.

What do members of the spiritual community do for themselves? In the first place, they all carry on with their individual spiritual practice: they continue to study; they meditate; they practise Right Livelihood;[102] they observe the Precepts.

Secondly, a member of the spiritual community relates to others on a purely – or at least on a predominantly – spiritual basis, i.e. on the basis of a common spiritual commitment to a common spiritual ideal.

We meet people all the time – at home, at the office, in the street, at the club, and so on. We relate to these people in different ways, but usually it is on the basis of our own need. Sometimes it is a sexual need; sometimes it is a psychological or an emotional need; sometimes it is an economic or a social need – but it is a *need*, and the relationship is therefore very often exploitative. (The need may be mutual, in which case the relationship is mutually exploitative.) Very often we don't care to admit that we are relating on the basis of our need; we don't like to say what it is that we really want from other people – sometimes we don't fully consciously know. This means that only too often our relationships are dishonest or at best confused. They are accompanied by a certain amount of mutual misunderstanding and rationalization.

Within the spiritual community we do not relate to others in this way. Within the spiritual community we want to develop spiritually and others want to develop spiritually; they have gone for Refuge and we have gone for Refuge. Therefore we relate on the basis of our common commitment and our common ideal: our highest common concern. If we relate to others in this way then we experience them as we do not usually experience them: we experience them as spiritual beings. Because we experience others as spiritual beings we experience ourselves too as spiritual beings. Because we each experience ourselves as spiritual beings, the pace of spiritual development is accelerated, and we experience ourselves more and more truly and intensely.

In more ordinary terms, within the context of the spiritual community we can be ourselves, that is to say, ourselves as we are at our best and our highest. (Very often when one speaks of 'being oneself' one means oneself at one's worst; one means letting out that part of oneself that one doesn't usually like to acknowledge. But being oneself can mean letting out the best in oneself. Very often it is the best rather than the worst that does not have an opportunity of expressing itself.) Within the context of the spiritual community we can be ourselves at our best, even at our worst if necessary, but be ourselves completely, wholly, perfectly.

In the context of ordinary life this is rarely possible, as most people know only too well. It is rarely possible even with our own nearest and dearest. It may be our own mother or father, our own husband or wife, our own friend, but only too often, on certain occasions or in connection with certain topics, we cannot truly be ourselves. Quite a few people go through their lives without being able to be themselves, completely and continuously, with anyone, so they find it difficult ever to experience themselves as they are.

Within the context of the spiritual community we can be ourselves even with many people. We can come where there are five or six people, ten or twelve people, and still be ourselves. (With maybe forty, fifty, sixty people present, everyone is still being themselves.) This is unprecedented within the experience of the majority of people, but it is quite possible within the spiritual community, because here one is relating on the basis of what is best and highest in each and every one.

Therefore within the spiritual community you experience great relief and great joy. There is no need to put up any defences. There is no need to pretend. There is no need for misunderstanding. You can be yourself with others who are also being themselves. There is complete clarity between people, without even the possibility – at its best – of any misunderstanding. In a situation like this you naturally develop more rapidly than would otherwise be possible. Consequently you do a great deal for yourself simply by being a member of a spiritual community, that is to say, an active member (there isn't, of course, really any other kind of member).

What do members of the spiritual community do for one another? They help one another in all possible ways. They help one another spiritually. They also help one another psychologically, economically, even in the ordinary affairs of everyday life. There are two ways in which members of the spiritual community help one another, which are particularly relevant.

Within the spiritual community one relates on the basis of a common commitment and a common ideal. This is not always easy. Many people join the spiritual community. There are people from many different backgrounds, with different outlooks and temperaments. We find some of them easy to get on with, but others not so easy. We may even discover, to our horror, that we dislike certain members of the spiritual community. What do we do? We do not want to leave the spiritual community, and we can hardly ask them to leave. The only thing we can do is work on it together. We have to recognize that what we have in common is far more important than what we do not have in common and we have to learn – even painfully learn – to relate on the basis of what we have in common. In this way members of the spiritual community help one another get over purely subjective antipathies and limitations and help one another to relate on the basis of what is common and higher.

Again, spiritual life itself is not easy. It is not easy to eradicate unskilful thoughts and develop skilful thoughts.[103] Sometimes we may feel like giving up altogether. We may feel that it is too much for us, that it is going too much against the grain, that there are too many difficulties. We may feel like leaving the spiritual community. On occasions like this members of the spiritual community support one another, encourage and inspire one another. Perhaps this is the most important thing that they can do for one another: just bear one another up when they get in this difficult and disturbing condition, when they get even quite depressed, as sometimes happens in the case of members of the spiritual community, at least until such time as they have their feet firmly on the path. When you are going through this sort of crisis it is a great comfort to have around you members of the spiritual community who sincerely wish you well and desire your spiritual welfare.

Finally, what do members of the spiritual community do for the world? First of all, I would like to make one thing clear. Members of the spiritual community are not obliged to do anything at all for the world. The operative word here is 'obliged'. Whatever they do, they do it quite freely, because they want to. They do it even as part of the process of their own spiritual development. To put it in a slightly different way, the spiritual community does not have to justify its existence to the world. It does not have to show that it brings about social and economic improvements or that it is helpful to the government. It does not have to show that it benefits the world in a worldly sense.

In general, members of the spiritual community do two things for the world. First, they keep the spiritual community itself in existence. One might say that it is a good thing for the world that such a thing as the spiritual community should simply be there, that there should be people who are dedicated to the spiritual life, who are trying to develop skilful mental states. It is good because it helps to develop a more wholesome atmosphere.

Secondly, members of the spiritual community help the world by building a bridge between the world and the spiritual community, or at least by laying down a few stepping-stones. Five or more of them get together and conduct various activities that are conducive to the development of skilful mental states and help people evolve. They conduct activities such as meditation classes, retreats, lectures, yoga classes, and courses in human communication.

Communication

Those who go for Refuge to the Sangha also necessarily go for Refuge to the Buddha and the Dharma. It is a condition precedent of your taking effective Refuge in the Sangha that you have gone for Refuge to the Buddha and the Dharma. It is possession of the common spiritual ideal, the Buddha, and the common spiritual principle and way of life, the Dharma, which makes it possible for people to come together into the spiritual community, the Sangha.

The fact that they share a common ideal and a common way of life tends naturally to draw people together, even on the social plane. So the Sangha is a congregation of all those who are taking Refuge in the Buddha and Dharma and who are in contact with one another: who are together. But 'together' does not just mean physical proximity. It may be that we quite sincerely take Refuge in the Buddha (take him for our spiritual teacher) and quite sincerely take Refuge in the Dharma (try to practise it) and are all sitting here together, but we do not, for that reason, constitute a Sangha: we haven't taken Refuge in the Sangha. We haven't even taken Refuge in the Sangha if there is agreement between us on doctrinal questions (if, for instance, your interpretation of *anātman* (Pali *anattā*) agrees with mine, or if your rather firm repudiation of theism[104] agrees with mine). Taking Refuge in the Sangha does not even depend upon the attainment of the same spiritual stages or meditation experiences. It is rather more subtle than this. Taking Refuge in the Sangha is essentially, or at least largely, a matter of communication between those who take Refuge in the Buddha and the Dharma. When there is communication between those who take Refuge in the Buddha and the Dharma, then there is taking Refuge in the Sangha.

But what, within the context of Going for Refuge, do we mean by 'communication'? To attempt a definition, we might say that communication is a matter of 'vital mutual responsiveness on the basis of a common ideal and a common principle'. We can elucidate this a little. Communication, in this context, is a common exploration of the spiritual world by people who are completely honest and in full harmony with one another. It is not an exploration by oneself alone, but with others with whom one is in communication. In fact, the communication is the exploration and the exploration is the communication.

The most common, and often the most valuable, context for communication of this kind is the relationship which develops between guru and disciple.[105] There may, however, be communication between those who don't stay in any such mutual relationship. There may be communication between those who are Kalyana Mitras, spiritual friends. When there is, on the basis of a common allegiance and devotion to the Buddha and the Dharma, an exploration by two spiritual friends of a spiritual dimension, which neither could have explored individually, then there is taking Refuge in the Sangha. (Beyond a certain point there is no question of any mutual relationship at all, whether of guru and disciple or friend and friend, because such distinctions have been transcended; in the process of communication and taking Refuge in the Sangha one as it were reaches a dimension higher than that on which these distinctions have meaning.)

In whatever context it arises, spiritual communication is very different from mere contact, which is what we usually have with people. If we look over all our acquaintances, even all our friendships, we have to admit that most of them, if not all of them, practically all the time, are quite meaningless. If you just reflect on all the people that you've known, all the people that you've talked to, all the people that you've met, how very few of them have you ever had any really meaningful communication with? Real communication hardly ever seems to take place; the contact is usually quite external. That is why we usually get very little out of these contacts. We often find them frustrating and disappointing, because no communication takes place.

Now we can begin to understand what taking Refuge in the Sangha means. In Buddhism, taking the Refuges constitutes conversion: conversion from a mundane way of life to a spiritual way of life. Taking Refuge in the Sangha represents conversion from meaningless worldly contact to meaningful spiritual communication.

Friendship

Now the Exalted One saw that brother lying where he had fallen in his own excrements, and seeing him he went towards him, came to him, and said: 'Brother, what ails you?' 'I have dysentery, Lord.' 'But is there anyone taking care of you, brother?' 'No, Lord.' 'Why is it, brother, that the brethren do not take care of you?' 'I am useless to the brethren, Lord: therefore the brethren do not care for me.'[106]

The main point of this section is contained in the sick monk's last reply to the Buddha: *'I am useless to the brethren, Lord: therefore the brethren do not care for me.'* This is a very shocking statement. It implies, sadly, that people are interested in you only so long as you are useful to them. It implies that they see you not as a person, but as a thing. (This distinction between treating a person as a person and treating a person as a thing was given currency in Western thought by the philosopher Kant.[107]) To treat a person as a thing is to treat him unethically. This is how the other monks were treating the sick monk. He was not useful to them, therefore they were not interested in him. He was left lying there in his own excrements. No one took care of him. There was no kindness between the sick monk and the other monks. There was no ordinary human friendship. Neither was there any sympathy, or sensitivity, or awareness. There could not be, because these are qualities you can experience only in relation to a person you actually see as a person. The other monks did not see the sick monk as a person. To them he was like an old worn-out broom or a broken pot. He was useless to them, so they did not care for him.

I need hardly remind you that we ourselves often behave like this. We often consider people primarily in terms of their usefulness. We do this even within the spiritual community. Sometimes we are more interested in someone's talents and capacities (as a bricklayer or accountant or lecturer) than in what someone is in themselves. If you are treated in this way, when you are no longer able or willing to employ your talents you may have the disappointing and disillusioning experience that nobody wants to know you. Nobody wants to be 'friends' any more.

We must learn therefore to see persons as persons. There must be kindness between us. There must be spiritual friendship (Kalyana Mitrata).[108] There must be sympathy, sensitivity, and awareness.

There are two principal aspects to persons treating each other as persons. These are communication and taking delight. These two are of the essence of friendship (friendship is what develops when two people start treating each other as persons).

Even in the case of ordinary friendship there is the great benefit and blessing of being able to share all our thoughts and feelings with another human being. It has been said that self-disclosure, the making of oneself known to another human being (being known by them and knowing that you are known by them), is essential to human health and happiness. If you are shut up in yourself without any possibility of communication with another person you don't stay healthy or happy long. In the case of spiritual friendship, we share our experience of the Dharma itself. We share our enthusiasm, our inspiration, and our understanding. We even share our mistakes. Communication then takes the form of confession.

The aspect of taking delight means that we not only see a person as a person, but we also like what we see. We take delight in what we see, just as with a beautiful painting or poem, except that here the painting or poem is alive, which makes it very exciting and stimulating indeed. Here we see, we like, we love, a person entirely for his own sake. This too happens in ordinary friendship to some extent and in spiritual friendship to a far greater extent. The primary meaning of *kalyāṇa* is 'beautiful', and in spiritual friendship we take delight in the spiritual beauty of our friend; we rejoice in his or her merits. Thus communication and taking delight are of the essence of friendship.

Unfailing Mutual Kindness

Brethren, ye have no mother and no father to take care of you. If ye will not take care of each other, who else, I ask, will do so? Brethren, he who would wait on me, let him wait on the sick. If he have a teacher, let his teacher take care of him so long as he is alive, and wait for his recovery. If he have a tutor or a lodger, a disciple or a fellow-lodger or a fellow-disciple, such should take care of him and await his recovery. If no one take care of him, it shall be reckoned an offence.[109]

'Brethren, ye have no mother and no father to take care of you'. Here the Buddha is asserting an absolute discontinuity between the biological family and the spiritual family, or between the 'group'[110] and the 'spiritual community'. Once you enter the spiritual community you no longer belong to the group. The Buddha does not mean that your mother and father are dead in the literal sense. He means that spiritually speaking they no longer exist. In other words, they no longer exist as your mother and father. You can therefore no longer depend on them to take care of you.

This is what is meant by the 'going forth'.[111] You go forth from the group to the spiritual community. Spiritually speaking the group no longer exists. Since it no longer exists you no longer rely on it or take refuge in it.

Once you enter the spiritual community only the spiritual community exists. You take Refuge solely in the 'Three Jewels': the Buddha, the Dharma, the Sangha. You rely only on other members of the spiritual community. That also means that other members of the spiritual community rely on you. You rely on one another. You take care of one another. You encourage one another. You inspire one another.

Suppose, however, someone is ill, or depressed, or experiencing psychological difficulties, or not finding the spiritual life very enjoyable. If that person is left, as the sick monk was left, he may drift back to the group. He may wander back to the family – to his mother or wife or girlfriend. He may go in search of comfort and consolation.

It is important that members of the spiritual community realize that they have no real Refuge except one another. They have no real friends except spiritual friends. From the group they can expect absolutely nothing – nor should they. *'Brethren, ye have no mother and no father to take care of you.'* They belong absolutely to the spiritual community; they belong absolutely to one another. They should be prepared therefore to live and to die for one another – otherwise they have not really gone for Refuge. Their future is with one another; they are one another's future; they have no future apart from one another.

The Buddha says, *'If ye will not take care of each other, who else, I ask, will do so?'* If members of a spiritual community do not love one another, who else will love them? If they do not inspire one another, who else will inspire them? If they cannot be happy with one another, who else can they be happy with? Perhaps they should enjoy one another's company more, appreciate one another more, value one another more. The Buddha certainly valued the brethren highly. He says, *'Brethren, he who would wait on me, let him wait on the sick.'* The Buddha is not being mystical or metaphysical here: he is dealing with the realities of life in the spiritual community. By 'the sick' he means sick brethren, that is to say, fellow members of the spiritual community. If one wants to wait on the Buddha one should wait on them. Thus the Buddha, in a sense, equates members of the spiritual community with himself. It would hardly be possible to value them more highly than that.

'If he have a teacher, let his teacher take care of him so long as he is alive, and wait for his recovery. If he have a tutor or a lodger, a disciple or a fellow-lodger or a fellow-disciple, such should take care of him and await his recovery.' Thus all conceivable relationships within the spiritual community are covered. Teacher should take care of pupil and pupil of teacher; fellow-disciple should take care of fellow-disciple; occupants of the same *vihāra* (the same residential spiritual community) should take care of one another. In sickness and in health there should be unfailing kindness and spiritual friendship between them.

'If no one take care of him, it shall be reckoned an offence.' 'Offence' in this connection means an unskilful action[112] which needs to be confessed. The responsibility for the care of each member rests on the whole spiritual community. Ultimately all are responsible for each and each is responsible for all, to the extent of their strength. Otherwise there can be no spiritual community, no order.

This incident, then, is not just a matter of a sick monk being neglected by the brethren. It is not just a simple case of diarrhoea. It is a case of unfailing mutual kindness; a case of personal interest; a case of harmonious and effective action; a case of treating persons as persons; a case of communication and taking delight; a case of recognizing the absolute discontinuity between the group and the spiritual community. Above all, it is a case of mutual responsibility and mutual spiritual friendship. It is not a case of something that happened in the past, 2,500 years ago; it is a case of something that is happening in the present, now. It is not a case of something that concerned the ancient brethren; it is something that concerns their modern successors.

Part **2**

Introduction

The Path of Regular Steps and the Path of Irregular Steps

The distinction between the Path of Regular Steps and the Path of Irregular Steps is a very ancient one.[113] It goes back to sixth century China, and to the great Chinese teacher Chih-i, well known as the virtual founder of one of the greatest and most important of all the schools of Chinese Buddhism, the T'ien-T'ai School[114] – a school which, though one of the greatest Buddhism has known, has so far been rather neglected by Western Buddhists. In the course of his lifetime Chih-i preached the Dharma widely, founded monasteries, and by reason of his profound spiritual attainments was able to attract an extraordinarily large number of disciples. These disciples he addressed from time to time, commenting upon the scriptures, speaking about the spiritual life, and especially, it seems, speaking about meditation. In the course of his discourses on meditation, many of which have come down to us, Chih-i spoke of Meditation by Regular Steps, of Meditation by Irregular Steps, and also of Meditation without Any Steps at All.[115]

On the present occasion we are concerned only with regular steps and irregular steps, and we are concerned with them because Chih-i's distinction between meditation by regular steps and meditation by irregular steps is applicable not only to the practice of meditation but to the practice and experience of the whole spiritual path, in all its stages and all its aspects.

What, then, is the Path of Regular Steps? What is the Path of Irregular Steps? In attempting to answer these questions I propose to be a little irregular myself and deal with the second Path first.

The Path of Irregular Steps

In order to understand what the Path of Irregular Steps is, we must first look at Buddhism as it actually exists in the Western world today, whether in Britain, in continental Europe, or in the Americas. When we look, the first thing that we see is books – hundreds of books – about Buddhism. This is the most conspicuous feature of Buddhism in the West.

If we are young and enthusiastic, and have lots of time, we start trying to read these books – all of them if possible, or at least as many as we can of the better-known ones. Usually we read quite a lot – some of us may even get around to reading the Buddhist scriptures themselves. In this way, by virtue of our miscellaneous reading, we start getting an impression of Buddhism and even start forming ideas about it. These ideas are usually very confused. They are so confused that in many cases we do not even begin to realize how confused they are until years afterwards. In some cases we may never realize it. But meanwhile, we *think* we understand Buddhism because we have read about it. We *think* we know all about it.

The position is, however, that we do not understand Buddhism *at all*. When I say 'at all' I mean this quite literally. It is not that we have a little understanding of Buddhism, that we have grasped just a portion of it. The position is that we do not understand Buddhism *at all*. But we think we do. From this a very important consequence follows.

When we understand a thing – whether we really understand it or just think we do – we become as it were superior to that thing. Understanding means appropriating; it means taking the subject of knowledge unto oneself. It means taking it *into* oneself and making it one's own, making it part of oneself. For this reason, i.e. because understanding means appropriating, we speak in terms of 'mastering' a subject. Thus we speak of mastering accountancy, or mastering mathematics. We even speak – or at least think – of mastering Buddhism. So because we have, as we think, understood Buddhism – because we have appropriated it, and made it part of ourselves – we start feeling superior to Buddhism, because we have 'mastered' it. Because we feel superior to Buddhism we do not look up to it; we do not feel towards Buddhism any real devotion or reverence. We are in fact devoid of any such feelings. We have simply 'mastered' the subject.

This kind of attitude is not new, and is by no means confined to modern Western Buddhists. It has been widespread in the Western world for quite a long time. We find the great poet and thinker Coleridge complaining about this kind of attitude – complaining, of course, within a Christian context – one hundred and fifty years ago. On 15 May 1833 he delivered himself of these sentiments:

> *There is now no reverence for anything. And the reason is that men possess conceptions only, and all their knowledge is conceptional only. Now, as to conceive is a work of the mere understanding, and as all that can be conceived may be comprehended, it is impossible that a man should reverence that to which he must always feel something in himself superior. If it were possible to conceive God in a strict sense, that is, as we conceive of a horse or a tree, even God himself could not excite any reverence…*

And reverence, Coleridge goes on to say,

> *…is only due from man and is only excitable in man towards ideal truths which are always mysteries to the understanding. For the same reason that the motion of my finger behind my back is a mystery to you now, your eyes not being made for seeing through my body.*[116]

This is what Coleridge said on the subject of lack of reverence 150 years ago. At about the same time we find in Germany an even greater poet and thinker saying much the same thing as Coleridge, though rather more briefly. In his *Maxims and Reflections* Goethe says: 'The finest achievement for men of thought is to have fathomed the fathomable, and quietly to revere the unfathomable.'[117]

It is this quiet revering of the unfathomable, of that which, in Buddhist terminology, is *atakkāvacarā* or beyond the reach of thought – beyond the reach of understanding and conception – that until recently has been so lacking among Western Buddhists. We have been much too quick to 'understand', much too ready to speak, even about the unfathomable. In fact, we have been much too ready to speak *especially* about the unfathomable.

This is not altogether our fault. To a great extent it is the result of the situation in which we find ourselves. There are so many books on Buddhism, so many translations of ancient Buddhist texts, and we have to admit that some of this material is extremely advanced. Some of it – the sūtras – is addressed to disciples of a high degree of spiritual development. The opening scene of some of the great Mahāyāna sūtras may be familiar. The Buddha is seated in the midst of a great concourse of disciples, perhaps in some heaven or archetypal realm. All around him are Arhants and great Bodhisattvas, even irreversible Bodhisattvas, that is, Bodhisattvas who cannot regress from the ideal of Supreme Buddhahood and who have, as it were, nirvāṇa in the palm of their hand, and the sublime teachings that the Buddha proceeds to give are addressed to *these* great beings – beings who exist on a very high level of spirituality, beyond all that we can conceive or imagine.

Many of these Mahāyāna sūtras have now been translated and thus, in a sense, made available to us. So we read this or that sūtra, and we think we have mastered its contents, and thinking we have mastered it we tend to adopt a cool, superior, even patronizing attitude towards Buddhism. So much is this the case that some of us may even think it unnecessary to call ourselves Buddhists at all – after all, we have 'gone beyond' all that – and may even look down somewhat on those simple-minded folk in the West who do choose to call themselves Buddhists, who actually pay their respects to images, who actually offer flowers and light candles, and who actually try to observe the Precepts. We may think our attitude more advanced, but the truth is that it is purely theoretical, purely mental, and devoid of any deep and genuine feeling of reverence and devotion.

Because of this purely theoretical and mental approach and the lack of all devotional feeling, of all 'quiet revering of the unfathomable' in Buddhism, until recently Western Buddhism has tended to be a rather shallow and superficial thing. Western Buddhists tend to pick and choose from the material available and to select *not* according to their real spiritual needs but according to quite subjective and superficial whims and fancies. Thus you find people saying 'I like this bit, but I do not like that bit. I am happy with the idea of karma, but I do not like the idea of rebirth.' Or you find people being drawn by the doctrine of *anātman* (Pali *anattā*). For some reason or other, the idea that they do not have a soul or a self seems rather to attract some people – though at the same time they find the thought of nirvāṇa rather depressing. Thus people tend to pick and choose, and to select – and of course their likes and dislikes change. For a while one may be into Zen, because one rather likes the idea that one is already a Buddha, already 'there', and that there is nothing to do. It seems to make life a lot easier: one does not have to practise anything, apparently! One does not have to give up anything. So you rather like Zen – for a while. But eventually you get rather bored with being a Buddha, so you start getting into the Tantra, and Tantra, of course, immediately conjures up visions of sex, and you start getting into the yoga of sex (theoretically, of course!). In this way the average Western Buddhist has been browsing and dabbling for all these years.

Even so, despite all these difficulties – and they are difficulties which every one of us has experienced – some Western Buddhists do get around to practising Buddhism. On the basis of my personal experience, seeing so many people coming and going, I would say that perhaps, at a liberal estimate, one in twenty Western Buddhists gets around to trying to practise Buddhism. Eventually it dawns on them that Buddhism is not just a collection of interesting ideas – not just a philosophy, not just something to think about. It dawns on them that Buddhism is something to be applied, even something to be experienced. So they start trying to practise it; start trying to put it into operation. But, unfortunately, so strong is the force of conditioning and of habit that even when they start trying to practise Buddhism the same old pattern, derived from their previous theoretical approach, persists. Their attitude is still shallow and superficial. They still tend to pick and choose.

In the first half of this century there was very little Buddhism in the West, in any form, books or otherwise. Now the situation is different. We could even say that there is too much Buddhism around. There are so many books, so many practices, so many teachers, so many schools represented! There is such a bewildering confusion and profusion of forms of Buddhism! In our excitement and greed we snatch first at this and then at that, sampling a bit here and a bit there, like a greedy child in a sweet shop. We are in the transcendental sweet shop of Buddhism, with all these beautiful spiritual goodies around us, and so we grab this and grab that: Zen, Tantra, Theravāda, Ethics, Meditation – this sort of meditation and that sort of meditation. We just grab. *That* is our attitude, very often. But we do make some progress in this way. The Path of Irregular Steps is a path and it *does* give us some experience of Buddhism.

But only up to a point. As we practise in this way – as we follow the Path of Irregular Steps – we find, sooner or later, that we are slowing down. We find, sooner or later, that we are up against an invisible obstacle. It is as though we have got into a spiritual doldrums. We are stagnating; we are not going forward. We are still going through the motions of following the Path of Irregular Steps, but nothing is happening: it has all come to a standstill. If we want to overcome this invisible obstacle – if we want to make progress and continue to make progress – there must be a radical change, and that change consists in making the transition from the Path of Irregular Steps to the Path of Regular Steps.

The Path of Regular Steps

Now why is this? What is the Path of Regular Steps? How does it differ from the Path of Irregular Steps, and why does further progress depend on our making a transition from the one to the other? These questions cannot be answered without our first understanding the nature of the path in general, that is to say, the path from that which Buddhists call the saṁsāra, or the round of mundane existence, to nirvāṇa; the path from conditioned to Unconditioned being; the path from unenlightened humanity to the Enlightened humanity of the Buddha.

This great path, which constitutes the main theme of Buddhism on the practical side, is traditionally divided into three successive stages: the stage of *śīla* (Pali *sīla*) or morality, the stage of *samādhi* (Sanskrit and Pali) or meditation, and the stage of *prajñā* (Pali *paññā*) or wisdom.

Though there are other ways of dividing, and even subdividing, the path, this threefold division remains the most important and the most fundamental.[118]

Śīla or morality is simply skilful action: action which benefits oneself, and helps one to grow and develop; and action which benefits others, too, and helps *them* to grow and develop. Not that *śīla* is a matter of external action divorced from mental attitude; *śīla* comprises mental attitude as well: it is both the mental attitude *and* the mode of behaviour in which that attitude naturally expresses itself. Thus *śīla* is skilful action in the sense that it is action arising from, or based upon, certain skilful mental states, especially states of love, generosity, and peace and contentment. *Śīla* is everything one does out of, or because of, these skilful mental states. *That*, essentially, is what morality or ethics is in Buddhism: actions expressive of skilful mental states.[119]

Samādhi or meditation comprises various things. It is a word with many different meanings, on a number of different levels. First of all it consists in the gathering together of all one's scattered energies and bringing them together into a single focus. Most of the time our energies are divided, and go in different directions; they are not unified, not integrated. So first of all we have to integrate them. This does not mean forcibly concentrating on a particular point; it means bringing together all our energies, both conscious and unconscious, and harmonizing them in a natural and spontaneous manner. Thus concentration, in the sense of the complete unification of one's psycho-spiritual energies, is the first grade or level of *samādhi*.

Next, *samādhi* consists in the experience of progressively higher states of consciousness – states extending into what are called the *dhyānas* or superconscious states. In these superconscious states we transcend the body and, eventually, transcend the mind in the sense of discursive mental activity. We also experience bliss, peace, joy, and ecstasy – but we do *not* experience Insight, since we are still within saṁsāra, still within the realm of the mundane. Finally, *samādhi* includes the development of such supernormal – though not 'supernatural' – powers of the mind as telepathy, clairvoyance, clairaudience, and the recollection of one's previous existences – powers which sometimes arise quite naturally and spontaneously in the course of meditation.[120]

Prajñā or wisdom means direct insight into the Truth or into Reality. This direct insight into, or personal contact with, Reality is at first only momentary, like a sudden flash of lightning that, on a dark night, lights up the landscape just for an instant. As the flashes of insight become more frequent, however, and more continuous, they eventually become a steady beam of light that is capable of penetrating as it were into the depths of Reality. When fully developed this wisdom or insight is what we call *bodhi* or Enlightenment – though at *that* level it is not to be spoken of in exclusively cognitive terms. At that level we also have to speak of it in terms of love and compassion or, rather, in terms of the transcendental counterpart of the emotions which we usually designate by those names.

Thus the path, which constitutes the main theme of Buddhism on the practical side, consists of the three great successive stages of *śīla*, *samādhi*, and *prajñā*. This division into three stages is not an arbitrary one. The stages are no mere chalk marks, as it were, but are inherent in the Path itself, and represent natural stages in the spiritual and transcendental growth of the individual. As such they resemble stages in the growth of a plant. First there is the seed; from the seed comes forth a little shoot; the shoot grows into a stem; then leaves are produced; and finally buds and flowers. Of course we must not push an analogy of this sort too far. The whole process of the flower's growth is unconscious. The flower does not have to decide whether to grow or not; nature 'decides' for it.

In the case of a human being, spiritual development is conscious and deliberate and by its very nature must be so. Man is dependent for his further growth on his own individual, personal effort – though this is not a matter of one-sided, egoistic willing but of the growth and development, in awareness, of the whole being. (Spiritual development can also be compared with the construction of a house or any multi-storey building. First we lay the foundation, then the first storey, then the second, and finally put on the roof, or the belfry, or the steeple. We cannot really reverse the sequence, which is determined by the nature of the structure itself.)

In Buddhism, or Dharma, as it has come down to us, there are many different teachings, and these teachings correspond to the various stages of the path. Not all teachings pertain to one and the same stage: different teachings pertain to different stages of the Path or, in other words, pertain to different stages of spiritual and transcendental development. When we practise the Dharma we should therefore practise those teachings which correspond to the stage of development which we have actually reached – reached not mentally or theoretically but with our whole being. This is the traditional method, or at least the predominant traditional method.

First we practise morality: we observe the precepts; we become thoroughly ethical individuals, both inwardly and outwardly – and this may take several years. Then, when our ethical individuality has been established relatively firmly, we take up the practice of concentration: we learn to tame the unruly wandering mind, and to concentrate at will on any object for any length of time – and this may take several more years. Then, slowly, we start raising the level of consciousness: we experience the first *dhyāna*, the second *dhyāna*, and so on, gradually training ourselves not just to touch them but even to dwell in them. Finally, perhaps after many years of endeavour, one raises one's purified and concentrated – one's elevated and sublime – mind, together with the integrated energies of one's whole being, to the contemplation of Reality itself. This is the Path of Regular Steps.

On the Path of Regular Steps progress is systematic. One consolidates an earlier stage of the path before proceeding to the next, or a later, stage. But in the Path of Irregular Steps one does not do this. In the Path of Irregular Steps what happens is that one starts with a more or less mental or theoretical idea of Buddhism, or of the Path (and a confused and incomplete idea at that!) and one then starts practising – usually, in the West, without a teacher. One does not start practising those teachings which correspond to the stage of development one has actually reached, because one does not know that anyway: one starts practising what appeals to one mentally; starts practising, perhaps, what appeals to one's vanity.

One might, for instance, start practising the Perfection of Wisdom.[121] Now even for an absolute beginner to practise the Perfection of Wisdom is not absolutely impossible. After all, the seed of Buddhahood is there, however deeply hidden. Deep down there *is* an affinity with the Perfection of Wisdom, so that it is *not* absolutely impossible, *even* for the beginner on the basis of a *purely* theoretical understanding of the subject, to start practising the Perfection of Wisdom. Such a person may *even* succeed, to a very slight extent. By sheer force of the egoistic will one may succeed in holding oneself, just for an instant, at a level of concentration where one gets a glimpse even of the Perfection of Wisdom: even of the Void (*śūnyatā*). But one will not be able to keep it up. One will slip, one will sink, one will fall, and there will even be a reaction – a reaction from the being and consciousness as a whole, which is simply not at that level and not ready to practise the Perfection of Wisdom. So one has to go back. One has to practise meditation, has to develop higher states of consciousness and, in this way, create a firm basis for the practice of the Perfection of Wisdom. Having done that, one can then go forward again.

Going Back to Go Forward

Thus following the Path of Irregular Steps usually involves forcing the process of spiritual development. It is like trying to make a plant grow by forcibly opening the tiny buds with one's fingers, or like trying to put on the upper storey of a house before the foundation is really complete. Sooner or later we discover that it cannot be done. It is no use trying forcibly to open the buds; one has to water the roots. It is no use trying to put on the upper storey; one has to strengthen the foundation. As Buddhists, the flower that we want to see blooming is the thousand-petalled lotus itself,[122] so plenty of water is needed. The tower we want to build is the tower that reaches up into the very heavens, so a firm foundation is needed. To state the matter axiomatically, we may say that a higher stage of the Path cannot be developed in its fullness, or even to a moderate extent, before a lower stage of the Path has been developed in its fullness. This is the basic principle. If we want to experience the higher stage, or higher level, with any intensity or any permanence, we must first perfect the lower stage, on the basis of which, alone, the higher stage is to be established. This is why, sooner or later, we have to make the transition from the Path of Irregular Steps to the Path of Regular Steps. This is what that transition itself means. It means going back in order to go forward.

But how far back do we have to go? One could say 'Back to morality': that is quite a popular slogan nowadays! Or one could say 'Back to the Hīnayāna': after all, Buddhism is thought of as consisting, historically and spiritually, of three great phases of development (Hīnayāna, Mahāyāna, and Vajrayāna), so one could say: back to the Hīnayāna or basic Buddhism, back to the Theravāda. But in fact we have to go back even further than that. We have to go back to something even more basic and fundamental than morality, even more basic and fundamental than the Hīnayāna – *we have to go back to the Three Jewels.* We have to go down on our knees, as it were, and go for Refuge saying '*Buddhaṁ saraṇaṁ gacchāmi, Dhammaṁ saraṇaṁ gacchāmi, Saṅghaṁ saraṇaṁ gacchāmi.* To the Buddha for Refuge I go, To the Dharma for Refuge I go, To the Sangha for Refuge I go.' This is where Buddhism really begins. This is the root, the foundation, the absolute bedrock of our spiritual life. This is how we really start practising the path – by Going for Refuge.

Morality

The Criterion of Ethics

In retrospect it seems that Western ethics started off rather on the wrong foot. Our ethical tradition is a very composite thing, not to say mixed. There are elements deriving from the classical, i.e. Greek and Roman, tradition; there are Judaeo-Christian elements, and, especially in some of the northern European countries, there are elements of Germanic paganism. But though our Western ethical tradition is made up of many interwoven strands, it is the Judaeo-Christian element which predominates. This is the 'official' ethic, to which, at least in the past, everybody claimed to subscribe, whatever their private practice or preference may have been.

In this Judaeo-Christian ethic we find that morality is traditionally conceived very much in terms of Law. A moral obligation or moral rule is something laid upon man by God. This is well illustrated by the biblical account of the origin of the Ten Commandments.[123] Moses goes up Mount Sinai and there, amidst thunder and lightning, he receives the Ten Commandments from God. On coming down from Mount Sinai with – according to Christian art – the two stone tablets on which they were inscribed tucked under his arm like a couple of tombstones, Moses in turn gives the Ten Commandments to the Children of Israel. This illustrates the idea of ethics as something imposed on man, almost against his will, by a power or an authority external to himself. According to the Old Testament, God has created man, has formed him out of the dust of the earth, and breathed life into his nostrils. So man is God's creature, almost God's slave, and his duty is to obey. To disobey is a sin.

This attitude is again illustrated by the story of the Fall.[124] Adam and Eve were punished, as we all know, for disobeying an apparently arbitrary order. God said, '... of the tree of the knowledge of good and evil, thou shalt not eat of it',[125] but he did not give them any reason for the prohibition. Nowadays we know that stories of this sort are myths, but though few people any longer believe them to be literally true the attitudes which they represent still persist. The word 'commandment' itself is significant. It is significant that a moral law or moral rule should be a *commandment*, i.e. something you are commanded to do, obliged to do, almost coerced into doing, by some power or authority external to yourself.

These two illustrations are both from the Old Testament, and Christianity certainly goes beyond this conception of ethics; but it does not go much beyond it, and even then only in a rather imperfect manner. The sources of specifically Christian ethics are, of course, to be found in Christ's teaching as contained in the Four Gospels, but according to Christian tradition Christ is God, so when God himself tells you to do something the order obviously comes with a tremendous weight of authority behind it. Thus one does something not so much because it is good to do it but because one is asked to do it, even commanded to do it, by one in whom reposes all power and all authority in heaven and upon earth. Even within the context of Christian ethics, therefore, there is, generally speaking, this same idea of ethics as something obligatory, as something imposed upon one from without to which one must conform. This is our traditional heritage. This is the mode of thought by which, consciously or unconsciously, we are all influenced when we think in terms of ethics.

Nowadays the majority of people still do tend to think of morality, of ethics, in this way, i.e. as an obligation laid upon them from without, a command which they are obliged to obey. We can perhaps summarize the position of traditional ethics today by saying that it consists in not doing what we want to do and doing what we don't want to do, because, for reasons which we don't understand, we have been told so by someone in whose existence we no longer believe. So no wonder we are confused. No wonder we have no ethical signposts and therefore have to try to muddle through somehow or other. But though we try to make some sort of sense of our lives, try to discover some sort of pattern in events, where ethics is concerned the picture is mostly one of chaos.

Ethics in the Buddhist Tradition

I don't want to exaggerate, or to make the contrast seem too abrupt or dramatic, as between black and white, but the Buddhist tradition is quite different from this. In fact,

Moses comes down from Mount Sinai

the whole Eastern tradition, especially the Far Eastern tradition, is quite different. According to the Buddha's teaching, as preserved in the traditions of whatsoever sect or school, actions are right or wrong, perfect or imperfect, according to the state of mind with which they are performed. In other words the criterion of ethics is not theological but psychological. It is true that in the West we are not unacquainted with this idea, even within the context of Christianity, but so far as Buddhist ethics is concerned – indeed so far as Far Eastern ethics is concerned, whether Buddhist, Taoist, or Confucian – this criterion is the only one. It is a criterion which is universally applied and rigorously carried through to the end.

According to Buddhist tradition there are two kinds of action, *kauśalya* (Pali *kusala*) or skilful, and *akauśalya* (Pali *akusala*) or unskilful. This is significant because the terms 'skilful' and 'unskilful', unlike the terms 'good' and 'bad', suggest that morality is very much a matter of intelligence. You cannot be skilful unless you can understand things, unless you can see possibilities and explore them. Hence morality, according to Buddhism, is as much a matter of intelligence and insight as one of good intentions and good feelings. After all, we have been told that the path to hell is paved with good intentions, but you could hardly say that the path to hell is paved with skilfulness. It just doesn't fit.

Unskilful actions are defined as those which are rooted in craving or selfish desire, in hatred or aversion, and in mental confusion or bewilderment, i.e. in a state of spiritual obfuscation or ignorance. Skilful actions are those which are free from craving, free from hatred, free from mental confusion, and which are, positively speaking, motivated instead by generosity, or the impulse to share and to give, by love and compassion, and by understanding. This very simple distinction at once places the whole question of morality in a very different light. The moral life becomes a question of acting from what is best within us: acting from our deepest understanding and insight, our widest and most comprehensive love and compassion.

Observing the Precepts

By this time serious students of Buddhism may well be wondering how the 'Five' or the 'Ten *Śīlas*' (Pali *Sīlas*) or Precepts fit into the picture. Are these not lists of moral rules which have been laid down by the Buddha himself and to which we must conform? In reply it may be said that while the *Śīlas* or sets of Precepts have certainly been taught, certainly been recommended, by the Buddha, they have not been laid down authoritatively, as the Ten Commandments were by God. What the Buddha says, in effect, is that one who is Enlightened, or who has attained Buddhahood, thereby realizing the plenitude of Wisdom and the fullness of Compassion, will inevitably behave in a certain way, because it is in the nature of an Enlightened being to behave in that way. Furthermore, to the extent that you are Enlightened, to that extent you too will behave in that way. If you are *not* Enlightened, or to the extent that you are not Enlightened, then the observance of the *Śīlas* or Precepts will help you to experience for yourself the state of mind of which they are, normally, the expression.

An example may make this point clear. We may say that an Enlightened person, one who is a Buddha, is free from (let us say) craving or selfish desire. We ourselves are full of craving. We crave, for example, food of various kinds; we have a special liking for this or for that. Suppose, as an experiment, we stop eating some of our favourite foodstuffs, whatever they may be. We give them up; we decide we won't take them any more. Very regretfully, very sorrowfully, we close the larder door. We resist the temptation, whatever it may be – say plum cake. (I knew a Buddhist monk who was wonderfully addicted to plum cake. It was said you could get anything out of him if you offered him sufficient plum cake!) What happens is that we may suffer for a while, and may not have an easy time at all. In fact, it may be quite hard going. But if we stick it out, if we banish those visions of plum cake, craving is gradually reduced and eventually we shall reach a happy state where there is no craving at all, and where we never even think of that particular thing. Our abstention from plum cake is now no longer a disciplinary measure, but has become a genuine expression of the state of non-craving to which we have attained.

In any case the *Śīlas* or Precepts are not just lists of rules, though when you come across them in books on Buddhism they may indeed read like that. Only too often the Buddha is represented as telling people all the things they should *not* do, and the impression is created that Buddhism is a dreary and negative business. But the *Śīlas* are, in reality, just patterns of ethical behaviour. They are the natural expression of certain skilful mental states. Since they are the natural expression of skilful mental states we can find out to what extent we have developed those states by checking our behaviour against the *Śīlas*.

The Five Precepts

The best-known pattern of ethical behaviour is that of the 'Five *Śīlas*', generally known as the Five Precepts. The Five Precepts, as usually transmitted, are negative in form. They tell us what not to do. In the case of each Precept, however, there is a positive counterpart. It is significant that in modern Buddhist teaching the positive counterpart is far less widely known than the negative formulation. Many will have heard of the Five *Śīlas* who have never heard of the 'Five *Dharmas*', as the five positive counterparts are called. In this context, the Five *Dharmas* may be translated as the 'Five Ethical Principles'. We shall briefly consider both the Five Precepts and the Five *Dharmas*, one by one, examining first the negative and then the positive formulation. This will give us a balanced picture of this particular pattern of Buddhist ethics.

The first of the Five Precepts is abstention from harming living beings. This is the literal translation. Although sometimes rendered as 'not to kill', it is really abstention not only from killing but from harming in any way. It conveys the meaning of abstention from all forms of violence, all forms of oppression, all forms of injury. Violence is wrong because ultimately it is based, directly or indirectly, on an unskilful mental state, i.e. on the state of hatred or aversion, and if we indulge in violence this unskilful mental state, of which violence is the natural expression, will become stronger and more powerful than it is already.

The positive counterpart of abstention from violence is, of course, the practice of *maitrī* (Pali *mettā*), love or friendliness. Here, *maitrī* is not just an emotion or a feeling, but *maitrī* as embodied in deeds – as put into actual practice. It is not enough simply to *feel* goodwill towards others. It must be expressed in action. Otherwise, if we simply gloat over it in our own mind, thinking how much we love everybody and how kind we are, it becomes a sort of emotional self-indulgence – not to say something worse. So we should watch ourselves in this respect. We often consider we love other people. At least, we consider we love *some* other people. But if we examine ourselves, we find we never really express our love: we take it for granted that it is understood.

A familiar example is that of the couple who have been married for twenty or thirty years, and the husband never bothers to bring the wife so much as a bunch of flowers or a box of chocolates. If someone was to ask him, 'Don't you love your wife? You never take her so much as a bunch of flowers or a box of chocolates,' the average husband would reply, 'What's the need? Of course I love her, but she should know that after all these years!'

This is very bad psychology. People should not have to take it for granted, or just imagine, that we do have feelings towards them. It should be quite obvious from our words and actions. Indeed, we should actually take steps to keep alive the spirit of love and friendship. That is why in all social life, and in Buddhist social life especially, such things as the exchanging of gifts, and the extending of invitations, are very much emphasized. It is not enough to sit in your own room, or even in your own cell, radiating thoughts of love. Good and wonderful though that may be, it must come down to some concrete expression. Only then will such thoughts be reciprocated in a tangible way by other people.

The second of the Five Precepts is abstention from taking the not-given. This, again, is a literal translation. It is not just abstention from theft. *That* would be too easy to evade or to circumvent. The second Precept involves abstention from any kind of dishonesty, any kind of misappropriation or exploitation, because all these things are expressions of craving, or selfish desire. The positive counterpart of abstention from taking the not-given is, of course, *dāna*, or generosity. Here, again, it is not simply the generous feeling, the will to give, that is meant, but the generous act itself. *Dāna* is something which all those who have contact with living Buddhism for any length of time quickly come to understand.

Thirdly, abstention from sexual misconduct. In the sūtras the Buddha makes it clear that, in the context of the Five Precepts, sexual misconduct comprises rape, abduction, and adultery. All three are unskilful because they are expressions, simultaneously, of both craving and violence. In the case of rape and abduction, which in the comparatively unorganized society of the Buddha's day seem to have been fairly common, violence is committed not only against the woman herself but also, if she happens to be a minor, against her parents or guardians. In the case of adultery, the violence is committed against the woman's husband, inasmuch as his domestic life is deliberately disrupted. It should also be noted that in Buddhism marriage is a purely civil contract, not a sacrament. Moreover, divorce is permitted and from a religious point of view monogamy is not compulsory. In some parts of the Buddhist world there are communities which practise polygamy and this is not considered as amounting to sexual misconduct.

The positive counterpart of abstention from sexual misconduct is *saṁtushti* (Pali *santuṭṭhi*), or contentment. In the case of the unmarried, contentment means contentment with the single state; in the case of the married, it means contentment with one's recognized, socially accepted sexual partner. Here contentment is not just passive acceptance of the status quo. In modern psychological terms, it means a positive state of freedom from using sex to satisfy neurotic needs in general and, in particular, using it to satisfy the neurotic need for change.

Fourthly, abstention from false speech. False speech is that which is rooted in craving, hatred, or fear. If you tell a lie, it is either because you want something, or because you wish to harm or hurt someone, or because for one reason or another you are afraid of telling the truth. Untruthfulness, therefore, is rooted in unskilful mental states. This requires no demonstration. The positive counterpart of abstention from false speech is *satya* (Pali *sacca*), or truthfulness.

Fifthly, abstention from drink and drugs the taking of which results in loss of awareness. There is a certain amount of disagreement about the interpretation of this Precept. In some Buddhist countries it is interpreted as requiring strict teetotalism, i.e. total abstinence; in other Buddhist countries it is interpreted as requiring moderation in the use of anything which, taken in excess, is likely to result in intoxication. One is free to take one's choice between these two interpretations. The positive counterpart of the Precept is, of course, *smṛti* (Pali *sati*), mindfulness or awareness. This is the real criterion. If you can drink without impairing your mindfulness (it might be said), then drink; but if you can't, then don't. However, one must be quite honest with oneself, and not pretend that one is mindful when one is merely merry. Thus even if the fifth Precept is interpreted as requiring simply moderation, in the light of its positive counterpart total abstinence will still be required in the vast majority of cases.

The Principle of Non-Violence

Though there can be no world peace without the abolition of nuclear weapons, abolition of nuclear weapons is far from being synonymous with world peace in the full sense of the term. Nuclear weapons are not the only weapons in the arsenals of the sovereign nation-states. There are many others, some of them hardly less horrible than nuclear weapons themselves, and even if nuclear war ceases to be a possibility these could still do irreparable damage to civilization and inflict untold suffering on mankind. If peace in the full sense of the term is to be achieved we shall therefore have to work not only for the abolition of nuclear weapons but for the abolition of conventional weapons too. We do not want to abolish nuclear weapons only to find ourselves in the same kind of situation that we are in today, minus nuclear weapons. Neither do we want to abolish them only to find ourselves in the same kind of situation that we were in yesterday, or even the day before yesterday. Though it will undoubtedly be an unspeakable blessing to mankind, and an infinite relief, the abolition of nuclear weapons is by no means enough. Even the abolition of both nuclear and non-nuclear weapons is by no means enough. Peace in the full sense of the term will be achieved only when disputes between sovereign nation-states, as well as between smaller groups and between individuals, are settled entirely by non-violent means.

In order to achieve peace – world peace – in this fuller sense, we shall have to deepen our realization of the indivisibility of humanity, and act on that realization with even greater consistency. We shall have to regard ourselves as citizens of the world in a more concrete sense than before, and rid ourselves of even the faintest vestige of nationalism. We shall have to identify ourselves more closely with all living things, and love them with a more ardent and selfless love. We shall have to be a louder and clearer voice of sanity and compassion in the world. We shall also have to bring to bear on the governments and peoples of the world, and on ourselves, the same kind of pressure that was required for the abolition of nuclear weapons but to an even greater extent. Above all, we shall have to intensify our commitment to the great ethical and spiritual principle of non-violence, in respect to relations between both individuals and groups.

Ever since the dawn of history – perhaps from the very beginning of the present cosmic cycle itself – two great principles have been at work in the world: the principle of violence and the principle of non-violence or, as we may also call it, the principle of love – though love in the sense of *agape* rather than in the sense of *eros*.[126]

The principle of violence finds expression in force and fraud, as well as in such things as oppression, exploitation, intimidation, and blackmail. The principle of non-violence finds expression in friendliness and openness, as well as in such things as gentleness and helpfulness, and the giving of encouragement, sympathy, and appreciation. The principle of violence is reactive, and ultimately destructive; the principle of non-violence is creative. The principle of violence is a principle of Darkness, the principle of non-violence a principle of Light. Whereas to live in accordance with the principle of violence is to be either an animal or a devil or combination of the two, to live in accordance with the principle of non-violence is to be a human being in the full sense of the term, or even an angel.

So far, of course, people have lived in accordance with the principle of violence rather than in accordance with the principle of non-violence. They could do this because it was possible them to live in accordance with the principle of violence without destroying themselves completely. But this is no longer the case. Owing to the emergence of superpowers armed with nuclear weapons it is now virtually impossible for us to live in accordance with the principle of violence without, sooner or later, annihilating ourselves. We are therefore faced with the necessity of either learning to live in accordance with the principle of non-violence or not living at all. Thus the possibility of nuclear holocaust has not only enabled us to realize the true nature of violence, by showing us what the consequences of violence on the biggest conceivable scale would be, but it has also given us a much deeper appreciation of the real value of non-violence.

The Principle of Non-Exploitation

The significance of the principle of non-exploitation extends far beyond the field of economics. It has its ramifications in the psychological and even in the spiritual fields. In fact, the principle of non-exploitation can be extended to cover the whole field of personal relationships, especially the closer and more intimate personal relationships.

Let us imagine, for instance, that we meet someone whom after a short while we start to like. The question arises: why do we like them? The answer is: we like them because they satisfy a need in us. This need may be conscious but most often it is unconscious. (When the need is unconscious we start to like a person but we do not quite know why we like them.) If the need is unconscious we may, if we try, become conscious of it. Usually, however, we do not try. Instead we rationalize the situation and say, 'I like them because they are kind and considerate,' or, 'I like them because they love animals as I do,' or, 'I like them because they are interested in Buddhism as I am.' Whatever it is that we say, the real source of the liking is, in most cases, something quite different. That particular person, whom we say we like for such and such a reason, satisfies a certain need – perhaps a very deep need – in us. They may, for instance, satisfy our need for attention. If we get the attention from someone which psychologically we need, then we naturally start speaking in terms of liking that person.

If someone has started to satisfy a need of ours of this sort, then we shall want our relationship with that person to continue; so long as our need continues, we shall continue to want it satisfied. The best way for us to ensure that someone continues satisfying our need is to find out what that person needs and then satisfy that. This is what we usually do, whether consciously or unconsciously. The other person may, for instance, have a need for appreciation. Suppose they have painted a picture, but feel that they are not sufficiently appreciated – no one recognizes their artistic talent. We latch on to this and say, 'What a beautiful picture!' We give them the appreciation and encouragement that they feel they need.

In this way they become dependent upon us for the satisfaction of their need, just as we have become dependent upon them for the satisfaction of our need. We depend upon them for attention; they depend upon us for appreciation. Thus there arises mutual dependence and mutual exploitation, which together form the basis of most human relationships. It is as if a mutual but largely unconscious bargain is struck between two people, each person as it were saying to the other, 'You give me what I need and I will give you what you need.' Neither person, neither party to the bargain, questions whether either need is a real need which ought to be satisfied or is an artificial need which were better not satisfied – the whole process is more or less unconscious.

At this point someone might well ask, 'Should we, then, never take what we need from another person?' The answer to this question is found in the verse from the *Dhammapada*:

> *Let the silent sage live [literally, 'fare'] in the village as the bee goes taking honey from the flower without harming colour or fragrance.*[127]

We may take what we need from another person, whether what we need is material, psychological, or spiritual, but we must take it like the bee, without harming the flower, i.e. without harming the person from whom we take it. In other words, we must take non-exploitatively.

We may say that there are two kinds of relationship: one based on exploitation, the other free from exploitation. We usually find that a relationship which is based on exploitation, or rather mutual exploitation, either terminates catastrophically (when one person, for whatever reason, is no longer prepared to meet the need of the other) or settles down into a routine of ever-increasing boredom (if two people are involved in a relationship in which they are each giving to the other because the other is giving to them, then for some time the mutual need is satisfied and they each continue to honour the 'bargain' between them, but eventually this becomes very repetitious and boring indeed). On the other hand, a relationship in which the satisfaction of need is more conscious, more aware, and which is not based upon any sort of bargain or exchange but upon what we may call a full and free mutual giving without any thought of return, can go on continually deepening, becoming more and more meaningful.

The relationship between parents and children, at its best, is an example of this sort of relationship. The parents give freely to the children without thinking that the children are going to give back to them later on – they just give because that is right and natural. In the same way the children also give to the parents, to the best of their capacity. They do not give thinking that they are giving in return for what their good parents have done but simply because they love their parents. In this way the parents give and the children give: the giving is mutual. The giving is mutual, but there is no giving *because* you are given to; there is nothing exploitative, nothing of the nature of a bargain.

The Buddha's philosophy of personal relationships, therefore, whether in the life of religion, or in the field of economics, or even in the more intimate personal relationships, is that personal relationships should be based on the principle of non-exploitation.

Contentment

It will help us to understand the third Precept, especially in its positive form as Contentment, if we can see it within the context of traditional Buddhist cosmology. That cosmology reveals to us what may be described as a three-tiered universe. Mundane existence is divided into three horizontal layers, as it were, the second of which is higher than the first, in the sense of being more refined, positive, blissful, and luminous, and the third higher than the second. These three 'layers' are the planes, worlds, or spheres – the terminology varies – of sensuous desire (*kāmaloka*), of archetypal form (*rūpaloka*), and of no archetypal form (*arūpaloka*). The plane of sensuous desire comprises (in ascending order) the hell world, the world of hungry ghosts, the world of *asuras* or anti-gods, the animal world, the human world, and the world of the (lower) gods, from the four great kings (or gods of the four directions of space, as they are also called) up to the gods who control the creations of others.[128] The plane of archetypal form comprises altogether sixteen sub-planes, from the heaven of the gods belonging to the company of Brahmā, up to and including the five 'pure abodes', which are inhabited by Non-Returners, i.e. those great spiritual beings who have developed transcendental insight to such an extent as to break the five fetters binding them to the plane of sensuous desire, so that they will no more be reborn there.[129] The third plane, the plane of no archetypal form, comprises four sub-planes, all of which are inhabited by Brahmās, a class of spiritual beings superior even to the gods (though sometimes spoken of as such).

Much could be said about these three planes of conditioned existence. All that concerns us at the moment is the fact that on the planes of archetypal form there is no such thing as sexual dimorphism, i.e. no separation into male and female, the inhabitants of these planes all being what we would call, from the human point of view, androgynous. Sexual dimorphism, or separation into male and female, is found only on the plane of sensuous desire, including, of course, the human world. Since spiritual life consists, in objective or cosmological terms, in a progression from lower to higher planes and worlds, spiritual life also consists in a progression from a state of biological and psychological sexual dimorphism to a state of spiritual androgyny. Moreover, since a state of sexual dimorphism is a state of polarization, tension, and projection, it is also a state of discontent. The state of spiritual androgyny, on the contrary, is a state of harmony, relaxation, and content. Observance of the third Precept, therefore, does not consist simply in abstention from the various well-known forms of sexual misconduct, but also, and more importantly, in the experience of Contentment, the 'vertical' as distinct from the 'horizontal' counterpart of such abstention.

In meditation the state of sexual dimorphism is transcended. In meditation one ceases, for the time being, to be either male or female. This is because in meditation, in the sense of *śamathā-bhāvanā* or 'development of calm' one progresses through the *dhyānas* or states of higher consciousness, as they may be called, and these states of higher consciousness are the subjective, psychological counterparts of the different sub-planes of the planes of archetypal form and no archetypal form. While meditating, in the sense of actually experiencing the *dhyānas*, one is therefore a *deva* or Brahmā. In terms of the Western spiritual tradition, one is an angel and leading an angelic life – angels of course being by nature androgynous. It is thus no accident of language that the Sanskrit word for what we call celibacy or, more correctly, chastity, is *brahmacarya* (Pali *brahmacariya*), which literally means faring, practising, or living like Brahmā, i.e. not merely abstaining from sexual activity but transcending the sexual dimorphism on which sexual activity and sexual desire are based.

This is why Vajraloka, our meditation and retreat centre in North Wales, is dedicated not only to meditation (*dhyāna*) but also to celibacy (*brahmacarya*). Meditation and celibacy go together: they mutually reinforce each other. For the same reason, we encourage single-sex situations of every kind. This is not simply in order to curtail the opportunities for sexual misconduct, but also, more positively, to give both men and women some respite from the tensions of sexual polarization and to provide them with an opportunity of transcending, for a few moments, the state of sexual polarization and being simply a human being and – to some extent – a true individual. For those who wish to develop as individuals, and to progress on the path to Enlightenment, meditation and all kinds of single-sex situations are, in the absence of transcendental insight, absolutely indispensable.

From all this it also follows not only that abstention from sexual misconduct is not enough, not only that one must experience contentment, but that one should not think of oneself as being either a man or a woman in any absolute or exclusive sense. After all, according to traditional Buddhist teaching, in the course of the beginningless series of one's existences one has been both a man and a woman many times. One has even, perhaps, been a god – an androgynous being. Within a perspective of this kind it would seem quite ridiculous to think and to feel that, just because one happened to be a man or a woman in this existence, one was a man or a woman for ever and ever, world without end, amen.

To the extent that one ceases to think of oneself as being a man or a woman in any absolute and exclusive sense, to that extent one will cease to speak and act as though one was a man and nothing but a man or a woman and nothing but a woman, i.e. one will cease to behave in that sexually ultra-polarized fashion which for Buddhism is exemplified by the figures of the male and female *asuras*. Male *asuras* are fierce, aggressive and very ugly, rather like the orcs in *The Lord of the Rings*.[130] The female *asuras* are voluptuous, seductive, and very beautiful, and eat any human males who are so unfortunate as to fall into their clutches. What the male *asuras* do to human females we are not told, though no doubt it can be imagined.

This does not mean that sexual differences can be simply 'ironed out' or ignored, or that it is possible to pretend that they do not exist. A feeble and colourless unisexuality, which merely seeks to negate sexual differences on their own level, is not to be confused with the ideal of spiritual androgyny. A castrate is not an angel, certain representations of angels in Christian art notwithstanding. Here as elsewhere in the spiritual life what is needed is not negation but transformation, not evasion but progression. So far as the Third Precept is concerned, especially in its positive formulation as Contentment, this progression is from an absolute identification with one psycho-physical sex to a relative and provisional identification with it, and from a relative and provisional identification with it to no identification at all. If we can only see this, whether with or without the help of traditional Buddhist cosmology, we shall understand the Third Precept more deeply, and because we understand it more deeply we shall observe it with greater confidence. Theory and practice will both be clear.

Levels of Communication

Better than a collection of a thousand meaningless words is one word full of meaning, on hearing which one becomes peaceful.

This verse comes from the eighth chapter of the *Dhammapada*, the 'Chapter of Thousands'.[131] In each of the verses of this chapter a thousand (sometimes a hundred) things of lesser value are contrasted with one thing of greater value. In other words, this chapter gives expression to the contrast – even the conflict – between quality on the one hand (the one thing of greater value) and quantity on the other (the many things of lesser value). The whole chapter may be viewed as an exhortation to us to discriminate between quality and quantity and to prefer the former to the latter.

In the verse above the Buddha applies this principle to the question of speech and contrasts 'one word full of meaning' with 'a thousand meaningless words'. There is a touch of irony here on the part of the Buddha. He suggests that our speech is usually meaningless and delicately hints that the ratio of meaningless to meaningful words is about a thousand to one.

Meaningful speech corresponds to what elsewhere is called 'right speech', and meaningless speech corresponds to 'wrong speech'. Right speech, or perfect speech, is the third step of the Buddha's 'Noble Eightfold Path'.[132] Abstention from false speech is the fourth Precept out of the list of 'Five Precepts' which it is incumbent upon every professing follower of the Buddha to observe. From these facts we can understand the importance which the Buddha attached to speech. In fact we find in Buddhism that a very important place is given to the principle of speech – or to the principle of communication.

But what exactly is right speech? Usually in Buddhism right speech is described as speech which is truthful, speech which is affectionate (or kind), speech which is useful (or helpful), and speech which promotes concord. Wrong speech, on the other hand, is the opposite of these things: it is speech which is untruthful, harsh, useless, and which promotes discord. If we look at most contemporary expositions of right speech, we find that it is usually understood in a rather superficial, not to say moralistic, manner; no attempt is made to penetrate what we may describe as the psychological and spiritual depths of the subject and to explore what 'right speech' really means. (This, I think, is true of our approach to the Buddha's teaching as a whole. Sometimes we are misled by the simplicity of the Buddha's teaching and, rather than going into its depths, we are content to remain on the surface of it, thinking that we have mastered it.)

Those who write on the subject usually think that truthfulness, kindliness, helpfulness, and promoting concord are four separate qualities or attributes of right speech, as if to say that right speech is such and such and it has 'stuck on' to it these different attributes – that it is truthful, that it is affectionate, that it is useful, and so on. But this isn't so. This isn't going nearly deep enough. Truthfulness, kindliness, and so on, really represent four successive levels of speech, each level deeper than the preceding one. We may even describe them as four progressive stages of communication. We will look at each of the four in this light, and then we shall be in a position to appreciate what the Buddha meant by that very rare and precious thing, a meaningful word.

Truthful Speech

First of all, right speech is truthful. We take it for granted that we know what this means. But do we *really* know what is meant by speaking the truth? The first thing that is required if we are to speak the truth is factual accuracy. But factual accuracy is something which one can expect of very few people. Very few people are content, for example, to describe something exactly as it happened. They usually embroider, exaggerate a little, to make it look a little better – or a little worse. We all have this tendency to exaggerate or minimize. We find it extremely difficult to be truly factually accurate.

I remember, in this connection, how some years ago in Kalimpong I attended a Buddhist Wesak celebration. It was a nice little meeting; about a hundred people attended. I was rather surprised therefore when about a month later I saw a report of this Wesak celebration in a Buddhist magazine, which described it as 'a mammoth meeting'. You can hardly describe a hundred people as 'a mammoth meeting', but this was the description that was given. No doubt whoever wrote the report thought that it would increase people's faith and devotion if they heard that in Kalimpong there was a mammoth meeting on the anniversary of the Buddha's Enlightenment, and so did not hesitate to depart from strict factual accuracy. This is the sort of thing that people usually do: if it's two they make it three, if it's four they make it five, if it's big they make it a bit bigger, if it's small they make it a bit smaller; but they don't present a thing exactly as it is.

Factual accuracy is the first thing we must train ourselves in, but speaking the truth involves much more than factual accuracy. We must speak the truth not only with factual accuracy, but, as it were, with psychological and spiritual accuracy. In order to speak the truth in this way, we have to speak with honesty and sincerity. We have to say what we *really* think and what we *really* know. Here, however, the very relevant question arises: do we know what we think? One cannot really speak the truth unless one knows what one thinks, unless one knows what it is that one wants to express. Most people, we have to recognize, live in a state of what can only be described as chronic mental confusion. They are not able to speak the truth because they don't really know what they think. They may *think* that they think, but they don't *know* what they think.

Most of the time when we speak – even when we think we are speaking – the truth, we are only repeating something that we have heard or read, but which we haven't really understood. We haven't really made it our own; we don't really know that it is so: we simply reproduce it at second-hand. In these circumstances how can we really be said to be speaking the truth? It isn't possible. If we want to speak the truth in this fuller sense – with psychological and spiritual accuracy – we must know what we think and why we think it. We must also know what we don't think. This means that we must clarify our ideas – we must think more clearly. We must be much more intensely aware of ourselves – aware of what it is that we know, what it is that we don't know, and so on. We must be much more honest with ourselves. In other words, we must know ourselves. We cannot speak the truth in this fuller sense unless we know ourselves.

By now it should be clear that speaking the truth is by no means an easy matter; it is very difficult indeed to speak the truth. Most of the time we fall very far short of the truth. We may not speak a positive lie, but it is certainly not a pure white truth – it is all sorts of shades of grey, merging sometimes almost into black. We may go so far as to say that some people, unfortunately, seem to go through the whole of life without even once being able to speak the truth.

If you just survey your relationships with other people, you realize that there are very few people to whom you can speak the truth in the fullest sense, to whom you can really speak your mind. Very often it happens that, even to those who are supposedly nearest and dearest to you, you cannot say what you really think. Very often you cannot speak the truth to your own mother or father, to your own son or daughter, to your own husband or to your own wife, to your own friend, to your employer or employee – something holds you back. There is something which you cannot say. It may be something which you feel it is not proper to say, or something which you feel you dare not say, or something which you think you had better not say because it might hurt the other person. In one or other of these ways the truth is so often held back.

We cannot speak the truth until we know it, but even when we know it we often hold back and don't speak it, or at least don't speak it in its fullness. When you go into the witness box in court you swear (if you are a Buddhist you will affirm and not take an oath) to speak the truth, the whole truth, and nothing but the truth. Very few people find it possible to speak that, and then only *to* very few people.

If therefore it ever does happen, in any of the relationships of life, that we, at least for once, 'break through' and speak the truth in its fullness, if we say what we really know and think, then this comes as a great relief. It sometimes happens that we are worried about something – it may be something to do with our health, or our finances, or somebody about whom we are concerned. And perhaps we have been thinking about this thing, turning it over in our mind, for a long time, yet without being able to talk about it to anyone. If this happens, whatever it is that we are worried about seems to become a heavier and heavier burden. But if, one day, we *are* able just to speak out and say what so far we have kept to ourselves, if we are able just to tell someone – maybe a friend, maybe a doctor, maybe of course the psychoanalyst – we find that it is as though a great weight had been lifted from us and we feel free.

We may go so far as to say that only when we are speaking the truth in the fullest sense are we really and truly being ourselves. In other words, *then* we are giving expression to what we are – and what also we know we are – not to what we appear to be or would like to appear to be. So this is speaking the truth, which is the first 'level' of communication but is difficult enough in itself to achieve.

Affectionate Speech

The truth is never spoken in a vacuum, as it were. You may have some truth to speak but you don't go out into the garden and just speak the truth among the trees and the flowers – that is not psychologically possible, apparently. The truth is always spoken *to someone*. This brings us to the second level of right speech, which is that right speech is affectionate, or is loving. This does not mean that it is affectionate in the ordinary sense, in the gushing sentimental sense. If someone calls you 'dear' or 'darling', it is not necessarily affectionate. There are many definitions of love, but in this context we may say that love is the awareness of the being of another person. When we say then that right speech, or the truth, should be loving, should be affectionate, we mean that the truth should be spoken in full awareness of the person to whom one is speaking.

But how many people can do this? How often do people speak the truth, or even speak at all, with full awareness of the person to whom they are speaking? If we just reflect, we will recollect – perhaps even to our horror – that usually when we speak to someone, or even when they speak to us, we don't even look at them. We either look down a bit, or a little to the side, or a little above their head. We don't look *at* the person to whom we are speaking. Because we don't even *look* at them, we can't really be aware of them.

If we are aware, or conscious, of them to any extent, we tend to see them in terms of our own emotional reactions to them. This is just like our attitude to the weather. If we want to go out, and the sun is shining, we say 'It is a lovely day'; but if the farmer wants rain for his crops, and it is raining heavily, he too says 'It is a lovely day.' Our judgements, in this way, are subjective.

In just the same way with people, we see them in terms of our own emotional reactions to them: if they do or say what we like we say how good they are, how kind they are, and so on. Usually we never get to the core of the person himself or herself, because we are never aware of them, never know them, never see them as they are. If we communicate at all, we communicate only with what we project on to that person. This is why there are so many misunderstandings between people. This is why so often we are disappointed by people we meet – even by people that we have known for a long time. We are not really in communication with, or aware of, *them*, but only with and of our own mental and emotional projections.

Useful Speech

If we *are* really aware of someone, if we do really know the person to whom we are speaking, we shall know what it is that they need. This brings us to the third level of right speech: we should speak what is useful. In this context 'what is useful' means what promotes the growth, especially the spiritual growth, of the person to whom we are speaking; it means what helps them – in the words of the *Dhammapada* – to become peaceful.[133] This useful speech does not necessarily consist in specifically spiritual instruction: it does not mean that you have to be talking about nirvāṇa, or about right means of livelihood, or about anything of that sort. The ostensible subject of your conversation can be anything you like – it hardly matters – but through your awareness of that other person, through your appreciation of their needs, you speak in such a way that they are stimulated and their growth is promoted. By 'speaking what is useful' we really mean speaking to people in such a way that they are raised in the scale of being and consciousness, and not lowered; in other words, we mean speaking in such a way that the people to whom we speak become more alive.

We may not be able to inspire people spiritually, but at least we can be positive and appreciative, not negative and critical. Some people you meet have a very depressing effect upon you: whatever you want to do they have a reason for not doing it; they always dampen your enthusiasm. We should watch ourselves in this way and try to be positive, appreciative, and constructive. Some time ago I was talking to someone about Lama Govinda.[134] While I was speaking, it occurred to me that in the course of the time that I have known him I think I can say that I cannot remember an occasion on which Lama Govinda was negative, or when he really disapproved of anything, or even criticized anything. Whenever he commented upon anything, he always did so in a very positive, constructive, and appreciative way. Even if confronted by a rather unpromising situation, he would still manage somehow to be quite positive about it. This is a very rare quality, and it is one which we should do our utmost to cultivate. Even if we cannot speak usefully to anyone in the full sense of stimulating and promoting their spiritual growth, at least we can be positive, constructive, appreciative, and even creative.

If, in addition to this, we are able actually to give some spiritual guidance (in Buddhism this is called 'giving the gift of the Dharma'), so much the better. But even here there is no question of giving it in the abstract, as a form of cold words, but only in the preceding contexts of truthfulness and love, because it is only then that the guidance becomes really effective.

Harmonious Speech

If we are aware of, and are concerned to provide for, another person's needs, we will think about that other person. Thinking about that other person, we will tend to think less about ourselves, we will tend to forget about ourselves, just as, for example, a mother does when she is caring for her baby. This brings us to the fourth and the deepest level of right speech: right speech promotes concord, or harmony. 'Concord' in this context does not mean just intellectual agreement: it is not just sharing the same ideas, following the same religion, accepting the same philosophy, belonging to the same political party. It is much more than this. It really means what we may describe as mutual helpfulness leading to mutual self-transcendence.

A situation arises in which you think about somebody else's needs so much that you forget yourself; that person, on the other hand, is at the same time thinking about your needs so much that he or she forgets, transcends, himself or herself. Each person is preoccupied with the needs of the other, while forgetting about themselves. There is a reciprocity of services and helpfulness, but within a context of continually decreasing selfishness and continually increasing selflessness. When, therefore, we speak of right speech promoting concord, we really mean speech bringing people closer together by making them transcend themselves in mutual helpfulness.

Awareness

We usually think of the spiritual life in terms of growth, progress, development, evolution. We think of it as something slow and steady, as something which proceeds by continuous regular steps. Thinking of the spiritual life in terms of gradual evolution is perfectly valid, in fact very helpful. But we can think of it in another way also: in terms of breaking through.

There are certain advantages in thinking of the spiritual life in this way. If we think in terms of breaking through – or even bursting through – it makes it clear that spiritual life consists, in part at least, in an abrupt transition from one level or dimension of experience, or from one mode of being, to another. It draws attention to the fact that the spiritual life involves not just effort – we are all familiar with that idea – but even violence. This is not a popular conception, that the spiritual life involves violence, but involve violence it does. It does not, of course, involve violence to others, but violence to oneself, or to certain aspects of oneself which constitute obstacles to one's growth.

Breaking through any aspect of conditioned existence is accomplished mainly through the cultivation of awareness. Awareness, mindfulness, recollection,[135] is the great dissolver of negative emotions, also of psychological conditionings, in fact of *every* aspect of the conditioned within us. So much is this the case that we can even say that there is *no* spiritual life without awareness. To the extent that there is awareness there is spiritual life. If we wanted to be paradoxical, we might even say it is better to steal with real awareness than to do a *pūjā* without any awareness.

An action, a thought, a feeling, is spiritual to the extent that it is accompanied by awareness. If we do anything with awareness, that awareness, if it is maintained, will sooner or later eat away anything negative – anything that smacks of the conditioned – in what we are doing. Awareness is of paramount importance in the spiritual life: no spiritual life without awareness; no breakthrough – no *breaking through* – without awareness.

Meditation

A System of Meditation

Buddhism grew out of meditation; it grew out of the Buddha's meditation under the Bodhi tree, 2,500 years ago. It grew therefore out of meditation in the highest sense: not simply meditation in the sense of concentration, nor even the experience of higher states of consciousness, but out of meditation in the sense of contemplation – a direct, total, all-comprehending vision and experience of ultimate Reality. It is out of this that Buddhism grew, and out of this that it has continually refreshed itself down through the ages.

Of the many methods of meditation developed within the Buddhist tradition, in my own teaching I have taken a few to form what can be called, perhaps a trifle ambitiously, a system: an organic, living system, not a dead, mechanical, artificially-created system. These more important and well-known methods of meditation are: the Mindfulness of Breathing; the Metta Bhavana, or the development of universal loving-kindness; the Just Sitting practice; the visualization practice (the visualization of a Buddha or a Bodhisattva, together with the recitation of the mantra of that Buddha or Bodhisattva); the recollection of the six elements; and the recollection of the *nidāna* chain.

There is also the arrangement of the five basic methods of meditation which appears in *Meditation, Systematic and Practical*.[136] In this arrangement each of the five basic methods of meditation is the antidote to a particular Mental Poison. Meditation on impurity (the 'corpse meditation') is the antidote to craving. The Metta Bhavana is the antidote to hatred. Mindfulness, whether of the breathing process or of any other physical or mental function, is the antidote to doubt and distraction of mind. Recollection of the *nidāna* chain is the antidote to ignorance. Recollection of the six elements is the antidote to conceit. If you get rid of these 'Five Mental Poisons', then you are well on your way indeed; you are, in fact, quite close to Enlightenment. In this arrangement, however, the relationship between the practices is, as it were, spatial (they are all on the same level, arranged like a sort of pentad), not progressive (you do not progress from one method to another). What we need is a progressive arrangement of the methods of meditation, a definite cumulative sequence that takes us forward step by step.

The Mindfulness of Breathing

In such a series, first comes the Mindfulness of Breathing. This probably constituted, for many of you, your first introduction to meditation; this is usually the first method of meditation that we teach in the FWBO.

There are various reasons we teach this meditation first. This is a 'psychological' method, in the sense that the newcomer can look at it psychologically; one does not need to know any distinctively Buddhist teaching to practise it.

It is a very important practice, inasmuch as it is the starting point for the development of mindfulness in general – mindfulness with regard to all the activities of life. We start by being mindful of our breath, but that is only the beginning. We have to try to extend this until we are aware of all our bodily movements and aware of exactly what we are doing. We must become aware of the world around us and aware of other people. We must become aware, ultimately, of Reality itself. But we start with the Mindfulness of Breathing.

The development of mindfulness is also important because it is the key to psychical integration. This is the real reason the Mindfulness of Breathing is usually the first practice to be taught to people at our centres. When we come to our first meditation class, we do not have any real individuality. We are usually just a bundle of conflicting desires, even conflicting selves, loosely tied together with the thread of a name and an address. These desires and selves are both conscious and unconscious. Even the limited mindfulness that we practise when we practise the Mindfulness of Breathing helps to bind them together; it at least tightens the string a little bit, so that they are not so loose in the middle; it makes more of a recognizable, identifiable bundle of these different desires and selves.

If we carry it a bit further, the practice of mindfulness helps to create real unity and real harmony between the different aspects (as they have now become) of ourself.

In other words, it is through mindfulness that we begin to create true individuality. Individuality is essentially integrated; an unintegrated individuality is a contradiction in terms. Unless we become integrated, unless we are really individuals (which means integrated), there is no real progress. There is no real progress because there is no commitment, and you cannot commit yourself unless there is just one individuality to commit itself. Only an integrated person can commit himself, because all his energies are flowing in the same direction; one energy, one interest, one desire, is not in conflict with another. Awareness, mindfulness, at so many different levels, is therefore of crucial importance – it is the key to the whole thing.

But there is a danger. There are in fact dangers at every step, but here, at this step, there is a particularly big danger. The danger is that in the course of our practice of awareness we develop what I have come to term 'alienated awareness', which is not true awareness. Alienated awareness arises when we are aware of ourselves without actually experiencing ourselves. Therefore, as well as practising awareness, mindfulness, it is very important that we establish contact with our emotions, whatever they are. Ideally we will establish contact with our positive emotions – if we have any or can develop any. For the time being, we may have to establish contact with our negative emotions. It is better to establish real, living contact with our negative emotions (which means acknowledging them and experiencing them but not indulging them) than to remain in that alienated state and not experience our emotions at all.

The Metta Bhavana

It is here that the Metta Bhavana and similar practices come in: not just *maitrī* (Pali *mettā*), loving-kindness, by itself, but also the other *brahma-vihāras*: *karuṇā*, *muditā*, and *upekṣā* (Pali *upekkhā*) (compassion, sympathetic joy, and equanimity respectively), as well as *śraddhā* (Pali *saddhā*), faith.[137] All of these are based on *mettā*; *mettā*, loving-kindness, friendliness (in a deep and positive sense), is the fundamental positive emotion. As the years go by, as I come into contact with more and more Order members, Mitras, and Friends, and even people outside the Movement, I see more and more clearly the importance of positive emotions in our lives – whether spiritual lives or worldly lives. I would say that the development of positive emotions, the development of friendliness, joy, peace, faith, serenity, etc., is absolutely crucial for our development as individuals. It is, after all, our emotions which keep us going; we are not kept going by abstract ideas. It is our positive emotions which keep us going on the spiritual path, giving us inspiration, enthusiasm, and so on, until such time as we can develop Perfect Vision and be motivated by that.

Unless we have positive emotions, unless we have plenty of *mettā*, *karuṇā*, *muditā*, *upekṣā*, *śraddhā*, then there will not be any real life in the Order. Positive emotion, in the quite ordinary sense, is the life-blood of the Order. If there is no positive emotion in the Order, there is no life in it at all, and no life, therefore, in the Movement. So the development of positive emotion in each one of us, and in all of us in association with one another, is absolutely crucial. Therefore the Metta Bhavana, as the practice for developing the basic positive emotion of *mettā*, is absolutely crucial.

The Six-Element Practice

But suppose you have developed mindfulness, and suppose you have developed all these positive emotions, suppose you are a very aware, positive, responsible person, even a true individual, at least psychologically speaking, then what is the next step? The next step is death! The happy, healthy individual which you now are – or were – must die. In other words, the subject–object distinction itself must be transcended; the mundane individuality, pure and perfect though it may be, must be broken up. Here the key practice is the recollection of the six elements. (The six elements are earth, water, fire, air, ether or space, and consciousness.)

There are other practices also which help us to break up our present (even aware, even emotionally positive) mundane individuality: the recollection of impermanence, the recollection of death, also the *śūnyatā* meditations,[138] including the meditation on the *nidāna* chain. But the *śūnyatā* meditations can become rather abstract, not to say intellectual. The recollection of the six elements – involving the giving back of the earth, water, fire etc. elements in us to the earth, water, fire etc. elements in the universe, relinquishing in turn earth, water, fire, air, space, even our individualized consciousness – is the most concrete and most practical way of practising at this particular stage. This is the key practice for breaking up our sense of relative individuality.

We can even say that the six-element practice is itself a *śūnyatā* meditation, because it helps us to realize the voidness of our own mundane individuality – it helps us to die. There are many translations for the word *śūnyatā*. Sometimes it is translated 'voidness', sometimes 'relativity'; Guenther renders it 'nothingness'. But *śūnyatā* could well be rendered 'death', because it is the death of everything conditioned. It is only when the conditioned individuality dies that the unconditioned Individuality – as we can call it – begins to emerge. In meditation, as we go deeper and deeper, we often experience a great fear. Sometimes people shy away from this fear, but it is good to allow oneself to experience it. The fear occurs when we feel what may be called the touch of *śūnyatā*, the touch of Reality, on the conditioned self. The touch of *śūnyatā* feels like death. In fact, for the conditioned self it *is* death. So the conditioned self feels – *we* feel – afraid. The recollection of the six elements and the other *śūnyatā* meditations are *vipaśyanā* (Pali *vipassanā*) or insight meditations, whereas the Mindfulness of Breathing and the Metta Bhavana are *śamathā* (Pali *samatha*) or pacification-type meditations. *Śamathā* develops and refines our conditioned individuality, but *vipaśyanā* breaks down that individuality, or rather it enables us to see right through it.[139]

Visualization

When the mundane self has died, what happens next? In not very traditional language, out of the experience of the death of the mundane self the transcendental self arises. The transcendental self arises in the midst of the sky – in the midst of the Void – where we see a lotus flower. On the lotus flower there is a seed in the form of a letter. This letter is what we call a *bīja* mantra. This *bīja* mantra is transformed into a particular Buddha or Bodhisattva-figure. Here, obviously, we have come on to the visualization practices.

The visualized figure before you, the figure of a Buddha or Bodhisattva, sublime and glorious though it may be, is, in fact, you: is the new you – you as you will be if only you allow yourself to die. When we do the full visualization practice, at least in certain forms, we recite and meditate first of all upon the *śūnyatā* mantra: *oṁ svabhāvaśuddhah sarvadharmah svabhāvaśuddho'haṁ*, which means '*oṁ*, all things are pure by nature; I too am pure by nature'. Here pure means Void, means pure of all concepts, pure of all conditionality, because we cannot be reborn without passing through death. To be a little elliptical, there is no Vajrayāna without Mahā yāna, and Mahāyāna is the *yāna* of *śūnyatā*, the experience of *śūnyatā*. This is why my old friend and teacher, Mr Chen, the Ch'an hermit in Kalimpong, used to say, 'Without the realization of *śūnyatā*, the visualizations of the Vajrayāna are only vulgar magic.'

There are many different kinds of visualization practice; there are many different levels of practice; there are many different Buddhas, Bodhisattvas, *ḍākas*, *ḍākinīs*, *dharmapālas*[140] which one can visualize. The particular practices most widely current in the Order pertain to Śākyamuni, Amitābha, Padmasambhava, Avalokiteśvara, Tārā, Manjughoṣa, Vajrapāṇi, Vajrasattva, and Prajñāpāramitā. Every Order member has his or her own individual visualization practice, together with the mantra pertaining to it, which they received at the time of ordination. I would personally like all the more experienced Order members to be thoroughly familiar with at least two or three different kinds of visualization practice.

The general significance of visualization practice comes out with particular clarity in the Vajrasattva *sādhana*. Vajrasattva is a Buddha appearing in

Bodhisattva form. He is white in colour: white for purification. Here the purification consists in the realization that in the ultimate sense you have never become impure: you are pure from the beginning, pure from the beginningless beginning, pure by nature, pure essentially; in the depths of your being you are pure of all conditionality, or rather you are pure of the very distinction between conditioned and Unconditioned, and hence are Void. For anyone brought up in a guilt-ridden culture like ours in the West, this sort of statement must surely come as a great revelation – a great, positive shock.

Vajrasattva is also associated with death: not only with spiritual death, but also with physical death. There is a connection here with the *Tibetan Book of the Dead*.[141] In Tibetan, the (so-called) 'Book of the Dead' is called the *Bardo Thödol*, which means 'liberation by hearing in the intermediate state' (that is to say, by hearing the instruction of the Lama seated by your erstwhile body and explaining to you what is happening to you in the intermediate state after your death). The intermediate state is intermediate between physical death and physical rebirth. But meditation itself is also an intermediate state, because when we meditate – in the true sense – we die. In the same way, physical death is a meditative state, a state of enforced meditation, enforced *samādhi*. In both intermediate states – the one between death and rebirth and the one which occurs in meditation – we can see Buddhas and Bodhisattvas, even mandalas of Buddhas and Bodhisattvas. These are not outside us; they are the manifestation of our own True Mind, the manifestation of the *dharmakāya*, and we can, as it were, identify with them and thus be spiritually reborn, reborn, as it were, in a transcendental mode of existence. If we do not succeed in identifying in this way, then we are simply reborn in the ordinary sense – we fall back into the old conditioned self.

The Four stages

I hope that we can now begin to see the whole system of meditation, at least in outline. There are four great stages, which I will briefly recapitulate. The first great stage is the stage of integration. That is the first thing you must do in connection with meditation. Integration is achieved mainly through practice of the Mindfulness of Breathing, as well as with the help of mindfulness and awareness in general. Here, in this stage, we develop an integrated self.

The second great stage is the stage of emotional positivity. This is achieved mainly through the development of *mettā, karuṇā, muditā*, and so on. Here the integrated self is raised to a higher, more refined, at the same time more powerful level, symbolized by the beautiful blooming white lotus flower.

Then there is the third great stage of spiritual death, achieved mainly through the recollection of the six elements, but also through the recollection of impermanence, the recollection of death, and the *śūnyatā* meditations. Here the refined self is seen through, and we experience the Void, experience *śūnyatā*, experience spiritual death.

And then, fourthly, there is the stage of spiritual rebirth. This is achieved through the visualization and mantra recitation practice. Abstract visualization (the visualization of geometric forms and letters) also helps. This, in broad outline, is the system of meditation.

But perhaps you are wondering: Where does ordination fit in? Where does the arising of the Bodhicitta fit in? What about the Just Sitting practice? I will deal briefly with each of these questions.

Firstly, where does ordination fit in? Ordination means Going for Refuge. Going for Refuge means commitment. Commitment is possible on different levels. Theoretically speaking, one could be ordained without ever having practised meditation; practically, however, I would say that it is highly unlikely – as far as I know, it has not happened yet. One cannot commit oneself – which is what ordination means – unless one is reasonably integrated. Otherwise you commit yourself to that today, but tomorrow you withdraw the commitment, because the total being was not involved. You also cannot commit yourself unless you have a certain amount of emotional positivity, otherwise you have nothing to keep you going. For commitment, there should also be a faint

glimmer of Perfect Vision, or at least the reflection of a glimmer of Perfect Vision. That glimmer – or reflection of a glimmer – will not be nearly enough to make you a Stream-Entrant, but nevertheless it is something of that nature that is necessary. Ordination would therefore seem to come somewhere in between the second and the third of the main stages of meditation. One might say that it comes when one has just begun to enter on the third stage, the stage of spiritual death, or when one is at least open to the possibility of experiencing that spiritual death. (This, of course, is according to the Path of Regular Steps; we know that there is also a Path of Irregular Steps.[142])

Secondly, where does the arising of the Bodhicitta fit in? Bodhicitta means 'Will to Enlightenment'. It is not an egoistic will; it is more of the nature of a supra-individual aspiration. It arises only when the individuality (in the ordinary sense) has to some extent been seen through. The Bodhicitta is the aspiration to gain Enlightenment for the benefit of all – that is how it is usually popularly phrased. Not that there is a 'real individual' seeking to gain Enlightenment for the sake of 'real others'. The Bodhicitta arises beyond self and beyond others – though not without self and others. It arises when the mundane self is seen through, but before the transcendental self has really emerged. It arises when one is no longer seeking Enlightenment for the (so-called) self, but has not yet fully dedicated oneself to gaining it for the (so-called) others. The Bodhicitta therefore arises in between the third and the fourth stages, between the stage of spiritual death and the stage of spiritual rebirth. The Bodhicitta is the seed of spiritual rebirth. There is an anticipation of this at the time of the private ordination when one receives the mantra. On this occasion the mantra is the seed of the seed of the Bodhicitta. After all, when one is ordained one has gone forth; one's ordination is a going forth; one has gone forth from the group, at least psychologically if not physically; one has died to the group: one aspires after Enlightenment. And surely one aspires not just for one's own sake but for the sake, ultimately, of all. It is not surprising, therefore, that at that time some faint reflection of the Bodhicitta should arise, at least in some cases.

Thirdly, what about the Just Sitting practice? It is difficult to say much more about this than 'when one just sits, one just sits'. But at least one can say that there are times when one just sits and times also when one does not just sit. A time when one does not just sit is when one is practising other meditations. One does not just sit when one is practising the Mindfulness of Breathing, the Metta Bhavana, the recollection of the six elements, etc. In all these other meditations, conscious effort is required. But one must be careful that this conscious effort does not become too willed, even too wilful, and in order to counteract this tendency we can practise Just Sitting. In other words, we practise Just Sitting in between the other methods. There is a period of activity (during which you are practising, say, the Mindfulness of Breathing or the Metta Bhavana) and then a period of, as it were, passivity, a period of receptivity. In this way we go on: activity – passivity – activity – passivity – and so on; Mindfulness of Breathing – Just Sitting – Metta Bhavana – Just Sitting – recollection of the six elements – Just Sitting – visualization – Just Sitting. We can go on in this way all the time, having a perfect rhythm and balance in our meditation practice: there is taking hold of and letting go; there is grasping and opening up; there is action and non-action. Thus we achieve a perfectly balanced practice of meditation, and the whole system of meditation becomes complete.

The Five Basic Methods of Meditation

In the Buddhist tradition there are five basic meditation exercises, each of which is an antidote to one or another of the 'Five Poisons' (distraction, anger, craving, conceit, and ignorance).

Distraction

First of all, the Poison of distraction, or the tendency of the mind to jump about from this to that. We speak of people having a 'grasshopper mind', or a 'butterfly mind', by which we mean that they are unable to settle on one thing for any length of time. It's a matter of being – in T.S. Eliot's famous line – 'distracted from distraction by distraction'.[143] That just about summarizes modern life; it is a constant process – every day, every week – of being 'distracted from distraction by distraction'. The antidote to this, at least as a mental state, is the Mindfulness of Breathing. One-pointed concentration on the breathing process is the antidote to all our distractions.

Anger

The second of the Five Poisons is anger. The antidote to anger is again quite simple. It's the Metta Bhavana, the development of universal loving-kindness, the beautiful practice which so many of us find extremely difficult. And many people do know from their own experience, at least from time to time, that this particular negative emotion of anger can be dispelled through this particular practice – the deliberate, mindful development of love and good will towards all living beings. Thus one eradicates the Poison of anger through developing universal loving-kindness.

Craving

Thirdly, we come to craving. In a sense this is the Poison *par excellence.* It is not just 'desire' but what we may describe as 'neurotic desire'. Take, for instance, the case of food – just ordinary food. We all have a desire for food and enjoy eating it – this is quite normal and healthy. But the desire for food becomes neurotic when we try to use food as a substitute satisfaction for some other need, whether mental or emotional. Only last night I was reading a report by a writer for girls' magazines to the effect that many girls who read the magazines wrote in to say that when faced by emotional problems they felt an uncontrollable urge to eat sweets. This is a neurotic desire. In other words, it's a craving.

As we can see, only too easily, craving is quite a problem, especially in modern times. There is a whole vast industry geared to the stimulation of our craving and to nothing else. This is, of course, the industry – or whatever you like to call it – of advertising. It is geared to persuading us, with or without our knowledge, that we 'must' have this, that, or the other. In fact, we may say that advertising is one of the most unethical of all the professions.

Craving can be eradicated by various practices. You can see how big the problem is from the number of antidotes. Some of them are quite drastic. For instance, contemplation of the ten stages of decomposition of a corpse. This is still quite a popular practice in some Buddhist countries. It is said to be especially good as an antidote for sexual craving, in other words for neurotic sexual desire.

If one can't go the whole hog there is a milder version of this practice: meditating in a cremation ground. In India, as you probably know, they usually cremate rather than bury, and a special area called a cremation ground or a burning ground is set aside for this purpose – often on the banks of a river. One is advised to go there at night, alone, and to sit and meditate. I can assure you that these cremation grounds are not always very pretty places, at least by day. There are fragments of charred bone and charred cloth lying about, and usually there is quite a stench of burning human flesh in the air. But it can be a very beneficial and interesting, and even I would say exhilarating, practice.

I had an experience of this myself many years ago, on the banks of the River Ganges, not far from Lucknow. There was a beautiful stretch of silver sand that was used as a cremation ground, and it was the night of the full moon. Everything was completely silvered over, and one could just make out the low mounds here and there on the sand where cremations had been held. Little bits of bone and pieces of skull lay scattered around. It was very quiet and peaceful, and one really felt quite away from the world. There was nothing depressing about the experience at all; one can only say that it was exhilarating. One felt, as I say, away from it all, almost as though one's own cremation had already taken place. In this connection it is interesting that when a Hindu becomes an orthodox sannyasin he performs his own funeral service, going through the motions of cremating himself. The idea is that when one becomes a sannyasin, and gives up the world, one is civilly dead and no longer exists so far as the world is concerned. This is the last thing he does before donning his yellow robe. This association of death with renunciation and the eradication of all worldly cravings represents the same sort of idea.

If even an occasional visit to the graveyard is too much (it may be too much for quite a lot of people), and one wants a still milder form of the same kind of practice, one can simply meditate on death: that death is inevitable, that it comes to everybody in due course, and that none can escape it. Since it must come, why not make the best possible use of one's life? Why devote one's life to unworthy ends? Why indulge in miserable cravings which don't bring any satisfaction and happiness in the long run? In this way one meditates upon the idea of death. This is an antidote for craving in general, whether for possessions or success or pleasure.

One can also meditate upon impermanence: that everything is impermanent, that nothing lasts (whether it is the solar system or your own breath); from instant to instant everything is changing. One remembers that everything is going to pass away just like clouds drifting through the sky. This meditation has the same general effect as the other practices I have mentioned. One can't hang on very determinedly to things when one knows that sooner or later one is going to have to give them up.

There is another kind of practice. This consists in what is known as the contemplation of the loathsomeness of food. I'm not going into the details of this practice either, because they are rather unpleasant and have been made so quite deliberately. But this practice is very good for young ladies who are neurotically addicted to sweets.

Out of the various antidotes to craving one should select the exercise suited to one's need. If one feels that craving is very strong, and really has one in its grip, then by all means just grit your teeth and go off to the cremation ground and, if you can find a corpse or something reminiscent of death, even if it's only a bone or two, dwell upon the idea of death. Some people familiarize themselves with this idea by keeping skulls and bones around them.

After all, what is there to be afraid of? In my flat at Highgate I have a highly polished old skull-cup. One day a lady came to tea, and was asking about my Tibetan things. She told me she loved everything Tibetan, so I said to her, 'Would you like to see *this*?' and put it into her hand. She nearly dropped it, as though it had been a live coal. She said, 'Oh, but it's a skull!' I said, 'Of course it is: the Tibetans are always using them.' Tibetans, I would say, are very fond of these things. They're very fond of anything made out of human bone or a human skull. They like rosaries made out of bits of human bone; they like thighbone trumpets; and they like skull-cups. This is because they take a quite natural, common-sense view of death. They don't think there is anything morbid or macabre in it as we do. Many people have been brought up in the Christian tradition in which the word 'death' sends a shiver down one's spine. But this isn't the Buddhist way of looking at it. Death is something just as natural as life. I often quote, in this connection, those beautiful words of the great modern Bengali poet, Tagore: 'I know I shall love death because I have loved life.'[144] He sees life and death as two facets of the same thing, so that if you love life you will love death. This is paradoxical but true.

Conceit

The fourth of the Poisons is conceit. The original term is sometimes translated as 'pride' but I think 'conceit' is better. We all know about conceit from our own experience and I need not say very much about it. Conceit may be described as one's experience of oneself as separate, not only separate but isolated, not only isolated but *superior*.

The antidote for this Poison of conceit is meditation on the Six Elements. The six elements are earth, water, fire, air, ether or space (*ākāśa* in Sanskrit), and consciousness.

How does one do this meditation? First one meditates upon earth. One reflects, 'In my physical body there is the solid element, earth, in the form of flesh, bone, and so on. And where does this come from? It comes from the earth element in the universe, from the solid matter in the universe. When I die, what is going to happen? My flesh, bone, and so on are going to disintegrate and go back to the earth element in the universe: "Ashes to ashes, dust to dust!"' One thinks and reflects in this way – though this is just an outline of the meditation, which is much more elaborate.

Then one takes up the water element in one's physical body, thinking, 'In me there is blood, sweat, tears, and so on. This is the water element. Where does this water element in me come from? It is not my own; it doesn't really belong to me. It came from the water around: from the rain, from the seas, from the streams. One day I shall have to render it back. One day the liquid element in me will flow back into the liquid element in the universe.'

Then one meditates upon the element fire (still more subtle). One reflects, 'In me there is heat, there is warmth. Where does this come from? What is the great source of heat for the whole solar system? It is the sun. Without the sun the entire solar system would be cold and dark. So the warmth in me comes from *that* source. And when I die, what will happen? Heat – which is one of the last things to leave the body – will withdraw from my limbs until in the end there is just a little hot spot at the top of the head. When *that* disappears I shall be dead. The heat element in me will have returned to the reservoir of heat and light for the whole universe.' This is how one meditates on the element of fire, reflecting that that too has been borrowed for a while and must be rendered back.

Then one thinks of air. 'What is the air element in me? It's the air in my lungs. I'm taking it in and giving it back every instant. It doesn't *really* belong to me. None of the elements belongs to me, but in the case of the breath I have it only for a few instants at a time. One day I'm going to breathe in and breathe out, breathe in and breathe out ... and then not breathe in again any more. I will have given my breath back finally. I will be dead. My breath won't belong to me then, so it doesn't really belong to me even now.'

Then one meditates upon ether or space. One reflects, 'My physical body occupies a certain space. But when that body disintegrates what becomes of the limited space it formerly occupied? It merges with the infinite space around or, in other words, disappears.'

And then, what about consciousness? You reflect, 'At present my consciousness is associated with the physical body, and with the space occupied by that body. When that body ceases to exist, and the space it formerly occupied merges with infinite space, what will become of that limited consciousness? It will become unlimited. It will become free. When I die physically I will experience, just for an instant, that unlimited consciousness. When I die spiritually my consciousness will finally transcend all limitations whatsoever and I will experience complete freedom.' In this way one meditates upon consciousness.

This is only a summary, but it may give you some idea of how one meditates upon the six elements of earth, water, fire, air, ether, and consciousness. Meditating in this way one applies the antidote to the Poison of conceit. One progressively dissociates oneself from the material body made up of the gross elements, from the space occupied by that body, and from the limited consciousness associated with that body and that space. Thus one becomes totally free: one becomes Enlightened.

Ignorance

The fifth Poison is that of ignorance. Here is meant spiritual ignorance, or unawareness of Reality – in a sense, the basic defilement. The antidote for this is meditation on the 'Links' (*nidānas*) of Conditioned Co-production. There are twenty-four of these, twelve worldly, pertaining to the cyclical order of existence, and twelve spiritual, pertaining to the spiral order of existence. While the first twelve represent the Wheel of Life, the second twelve represent the stages of the path. One set corresponds to the reactive mind, the other to the creative mind.

These are the five basic meditations: Mindfulness of Breathing, which is the antidote to the Poison of distraction; development of universal loving-kindness, which is the antidote to the Poison of anger; various forms of meditation on impermanence, death, impurity, and so on, all of which are antidotes to the Poison of craving; meditation on the six elements, the antidote to conceit; and meditation on the *nidānas*, the antidote to spiritual ignorance.

Alienated Awareness and Integrated Awareness

What is alienated awareness? What is it alienated from? What is integrated awareness? What is it integrated with? If we can answer these questions the nature of the distinction between alienated awareness and integrated awareness will be clear.

Briefly, we may say that alienated awareness is awareness of ourselves, without actually experiencing ourselves, especially without experiencing our feelings and emotions. In its extreme form alienated awareness is awareness of one's own non-experience of oneself, even awareness that one is 'not there', paradoxical as that may seem. Obviously this is a quite dangerous state to be in. Alienated awareness may be accompanied by various physical symptoms, especially by severe – even excruciating – pains in the head. This is more likely to occur when one is deliberately increasing alienated awareness under the erroneous impression that one is thereby practising mindfulness. (I am not, of course, saying that *all* pains in the head encountered in the course of meditation are due to alienated awareness.)

Integrated awareness, on the other hand, is awareness of ourselves, while at the same time actually experiencing ourselves. Our experience of ourselves may be either positive or negative; we may be in either a positive or a negative mental state. But if it is a negative state that we are in, the negativity will eventually be resolved by the fact that besides allowing ourselves to experience it we are also aware of it.

Alienated awareness is therefore that awareness which is alienated *from* the experience of self, especially from the experience of the emotions; integrated awareness is that awareness which is integrated *with* the experience of self, especially with the experience of the emotions. From this the nature of the distinction between alienated awareness and integrated awareness should be at least conceptually clear.

The Three Levels of Experience and Awareness

Perhaps, however, it is still difficult for some of us to recognize the distinction in a way that accords with our actual experience. So let us approach the matter in a somewhat different way, thinking in terms of three levels, or three grades. The first level is the level of experience without awareness. This is what we have most of the time. We feel happy or sad, experience pain or joy, love or hate, but we don't really know, we are not really aware, that we are experiencing these things. There is no awareness, just the bare sensation, or feeling. We are lost in the experience. We 'forget ourselves', as when, for example, we become very angry. After we have been angry, when we recover and survey the damage, we say, 'I didn't know what I was doing. I wasn't myself. I forgot myself.' In other words, while we were identified with, even 'possessed' by, that emotion, there was no awareness. At this first level there is experience – no lack of it at all – but no awareness alongside the experience.

The second level is the level of awareness without experience. This is alienated awareness. We as it were stand back from our experience. It is as though it is not *our* experience – it is going on 'out there'. So we are not really experiencing it. We are not really feeling our feelings: we love but we don't *really* love, we hate but we don't *really* hate. We stand back and look at our experience with this alienated awareness.

The third level is that of experience plus awareness. This is integrated awareness. Here, by very virtue of the fact that we are now experiencing integrated awareness, the emotional experience tends to be a positive rather than a negative one. Here we have the experience, but also, saturating the experience, identical even with the experience, we have awareness. The awareness and the experience have come together. We might say that the awareness gives clarity to the experience, while the experience gives substance to the awareness. The awareness and the experience coalesce, without it being really possible to draw a line between the two, isolating the experience on this side and the awareness on that side. You are fully immersed in the emotion, in the sense of actually experiencing it, but at the same time, together with it, without being different from it, there is the awareness. This is a much higher state, a state that it is difficult for us to have any idea about if we have not experienced it ourselves. It is not so much an awareness *of* experience but an awareness *with* experience. It is an awareness *in* experience, even an awareness *in the midst of* experience.

These three levels therefore are: (1) experience without awareness, which is our usual state; (2) awareness without experience, or relatively without experience, which is our state when sometimes we get on to the spiritual path and go a little astray; and (3) awareness with experience, experience with awareness, the two beautifully blended together.

How does alienated awareness arise? How do we come not to experience ourselves? We may say that to some extent it is due to the nature of the times in which we live, especially here in the West. We are often told that we are living in an age of transition. This is very true. Sometimes we do not realize how abrupt, how violent even, yet also how potentially valuable, the transition is. Many of the old values are breaking up. We are no longer so sure what is right and what is wrong. We no longer know how we ought to live, what role in life to adopt. Our sense of identity is weakened in this way, and as a result there is a widespread feeling of anxiety.

I do not want to attach too much importance to this factor of the times in which we live; I want to look more closely at some of the more immediate factors that give rise to alienated awareness. I have spoken elsewhere of three levels of awareness of self: awareness of the body, awareness of feelings and emotions, and awareness of thoughts. We can speak in the same way of three levels of experience of self and even of three levels of non-experience of self.

The Three Levels of Experience and Non-Experience of Self

First of all, there is non-experience of the body. There are several reasons for this. One of the most important is the refusal actually to experience bodily sensations, especially sensations connected with sex. Such refusal is often connected with wrong training early in life. One finds, for instance, that people are brought up with the idea, or with the vague feeling, that the body is somehow shameful, or at least that it is not so noble, or so respectable, as the mind. Similarly some people have been indoctrinated with the idea that sexual feelings are sinful. All these sorts of ideas and feelings are legacies from Christianity. Though in many ways we might have outgrown Christianity, at least outgrown Christian dogma and ecclesiastical supervision, these attitudes are very widespread and still do quite a lot of harm. We may say that it is one of the great merits of Wilhelm Reich that he went into this whole subject so very thoroughly, and showed quite clearly how inhibition in infancy of pleasurable bodily sensations can lead ultimately to a crippling negation on the part of the adult of his or her whole life force.[145]

Secondly, there is non-experience of feelings and emotions. This also comes about in various ways. For instance, we have been brought up to believe that certain emotions, especially negative emotions, are wrong and should not be indulged in. We may have been taught that it is wrong to get angry. Having been taught in this way, we feel guilty if for any reason we happen to become angry. Even when we *are* angry, we sometimes try to pretend that we are not. We refuse to recognize that we are angry. In other words, we repress the feeling: we refuse to experience it, and it goes underground.

Then again we experience an emotion but we are told by someone in an authoritative position that we do *not* in fact experience that emotion. Perhaps as a small child we don't like our little sister – a common family situation. Our mother or father, however, says, 'Of course you like her. You like her because she is your little sister.' In this situation we don't know where we stand: we experience a feeling but we are told that we don't experience it. It is not even that we are told we *ought not* to experience the feeling. We are told that we *do not* experience it.

To take another example, mother tells the small boy that he is not afraid of the dark 'because,' she says, 'brave little boys are never afraid of the dark.' Wanting, of course, to be considered a brave little boy, the child tries to push his fear out of sight – it gets repressed. He ceases to experience his fear consciously, but it may, of course, come out in dreams or nightmares. Again, the little boy sometimes blurts out, 'I want to kill daddy.' But mother says, 'No, you don't. No one would ever want to kill daddy.' Or the little boy or little girl doesn't like brown bread, but mother says, 'Of course you like brown bread. You like it because it's good for you.' In each of these cases there is confusion and repression, and the child becomes alienated from his or her own feelings.

The effects of this may continue throughout life. In fact they may not only continue but be powerfully reinforced from other sources. When we are a bit older, maybe when we are adolescent, we perhaps discover that we dislike going to parties, but we convince ourselves that we do like going, because everybody – so we tell ourselves – likes going to parties. On another level, we may discover that we are not in the least bit moved by the work of a certain famous artist – his work just leaves us cold. But we find that all our most intelligent friends are much moved by his work. In fact they are highly excited about it. So we, though we may privately think his work even deplorable, have to be highly excited too. We need not multiply examples here. The end result is that we become alienated, to a greater or lesser degree, from our own feelings and emotions.

Thirdly, there is non-experience of thoughts. Here it is not so much that we fail to experience our thoughts, but that we fail to have any thoughts at all. This is because nowadays so many agencies – parents, teachers, the various media, etc. – are telling us what to think. This is not just a case of feeding us with information, with facts – that is quite a different thing. These various agencies impart value judgements too: they tell us that 'this is right' and 'that is wrong', that 'this is good' and 'that is bad', and so on. The newspapers, radio, television give us very selective, slanted information. They make up our minds for us about all sorts of things, but we are rarely conscious of how they are doing this or even that they *are* doing this.

Having made this little survey, we can begin to see what sort of state most of us are in, at least to some extent. We are alienated from ourselves: alienated from our physical bodies, from our feelings and emotions, and from our thoughts. The world, the age, society, our parents and teachers, finally we ourselves – continuing the good work – have got us into this state. We do not experience ourselves. This is something that we really have to recognize, accept, and come to terms with. We can think in terms of an iceberg. Only the tip of an iceberg protrudes above the surface of the waves, while the greater part lies below. Similarly, our self is relatively extensive, just like the iceberg continuing underneath the water, but that part of our self which we experience, which we allow ourselves to experience, which we are allowed to experience, like the tip of the iceberg, is relatively small – in some cases it is infinitesimal.

While in this state of alienation, some of us now come into contact with Buddhism. We start learning about all sorts of wonderful things, including mindfulness. What we are taught about mindfulness seems to suggest that what we have to do is stand aloof from ourselves, especially from our negative emotions, and not experience anything; we have to just watch ourselves, as though we were watching another person. Of course, we are much impressed by this teaching because, in our alienated state, we cannot help thinking that this is just the thing for us. So we start practising mindfulness – or what we think is mindfulness. We stand back from our thoughts, back from our feelings; we push them 'out there' and just look at them. The result of this, in nine cases out of ten, is that we simply succeed in intensifying our experience of alienated awareness.

We learn other good things from Buddhism. We learn that desire, anger, and fear are unskilful states. (We are told that we must call them 'unskilful states' not 'sins' because in Buddhism there are no sins, though they seem to be just as bad as sins, if not much worse.) We learn that we have to get rid of these unskilful states. We *think* we are glad to hear this – at this stage we can't really *feel* glad. We think we are glad because this means we can continue sweeping all these emotions under the carpet, pretending that they are not really there. This too increases our alienated awareness.

Later on still, when we start reading books about

Buddhism, we come across the *anātman* (Pali *anattā*) doctrine, the doctrine of no-self. At this stage, if we are lucky, some smiling Eastern monk tells us that, according to Buddhism, there is no self, that the self is pure illusion. He says that if we could only see clearly, we would see that the self is just not there. He tells us that it is our big mistake that we think we have a self. We rather like the sound of this teaching too. This appeals to us because, as a result of practising so-called mindfulness, we have begun to feel rather unreal. To us, in our experience of our unreality, it seems as though we have begun to realize the truth of *anātman*. In other words, we start thinking that we have developed Transcendental Insight. The same smiling Eastern monk, because he does not know anything about the mistakes that Western people can make, may encourage us to continue thinking this. The result again is that we get more and more alienated. Here the trouble is not that the teaching itself is wrong, but that we apply it wrongly, or, we may say, sometimes Eastern teachers, even in the West, unacquainted with Western psychology, apply it wrongly. The teaching is metaphysically true: in a metaphysical sense there is no individual self. We, however, don't take this metaphysically. We take it psychologically; in this way all the harm is done.

So a strange pseudo-spirituality develops in some Buddhist circles. The people there are on the whole quite mindful: they shut the door silently; if it's a rainy day they wipe their feet before they come into the house. They don't get angry – or at least they don't show it. They are very controlled and very quiet. But everything seems a bit dead; they don't seem really alive. They have repressed their life-principle and have developed a cold alienated awareness. They have not developed the true integrated awareness, in which one's awareness and one's life-principle, one's aliveness, are 'merged'.

Developing Integrated Awareness

Another question now arises: how can integrated awareness be developed? In order to develop integrated awareness, we have, first of all, to understand, at least theoretically, what has happened; we have to understand the distinction between alienated awareness and integrated awareness. We have to retrace our steps and undo the harm that we have done – or that has been done to us. We have to allow ourselves to experience ourselves. If we have once taken that wrong turning, if alienated awareness has developed to any serious degree, then we have to go back to square one and learn to experience ourselves. We have to learn to experience our own body, to experience our own repressed feelings and emotions, have to learn to think – to insist on thinking – our own thoughts.

This will not be easy, especially for those who are comparatively advanced in life, because some feelings are very deeply buried and are therefore very difficult to recover. We may even need professional help in the matter. We may even sometimes have to act out our feelings, express them externally. This does not mean that we indulge them, but that slowly and mindfully we start letting them out: we allow ourselves to experience our feelings, remaining aware of them as we are actually experiencing them.

If we do this and other things of the same nature, we shall begin to experience ourselves all over again. We shall begin to experience the whole of ourselves, ourselves in our totality: we shall experience the so-called good and the so-called bad, the so-called noble and the so-called ignoble, all as one living whole which is ourself. When we have done this, when we really experience ourselves in this way, fully and vividly, we can begin to practise mindfulness, because then when we practise mindfulness, it will be the real thing: it will be integrated – or integral – awareness.

The Four Brahma-Vihāras

Maitrī

The first of the 'Four *Brahma-vihāras*' is *maitrī* (Pali *mettā*), or love. The Sanskrit word *maitrī* is derived from *mitra*, which means friend. According to the Buddhist texts, *maitrī* is that love which one feels for a near and dear, very intimate, friend. The English words 'friend' and 'friendship' nowadays have a rather tepid connotation, and friendship is regarded as a rather feeble emotion. But it is not like that in the East. There *maitrī* or friendship is a powerful and positive emotion, being usually defined as an overwhelming desire for the happiness and well-being of the other person – not just in the material sense but in the spiritual sense too.

Again and again one is exhorted, in Buddhist literature and Buddhist teaching, to develop this feeling of friendship which we have for a near and dear friend towards all living beings. This feeling is summed up in the phrase *sabbe sattā sukhī hontu* or 'May all beings be happy!' which represents the heartfelt wish of all Buddhists. If we really do have this feeling in a heartfelt way, not just thinking about the feeling but experiencing the feeling itself, then we have *maitrī*.

In Buddhism the development of *maitrī* is not just left to chance. Some people indeed think that either you have got love for others or you haven't, and that if you haven't that's just too bad, because there's nothing you can do about it. But Buddhism does not look at it like this. In Buddhism there are definite exercises, definite practices, for the development of *maitrī* or love: what we call *maitrī-bhāvanā*. As some of those who have tried to practise them will know, they are not very easy. We do not find it very easy to develop love, but if we persist, and if we succeed, we find the experience a very rewarding one.

Karuṇā

Secondly, *karuṇā* (Sanskrit and Pali), or compassion. Compassion is of course closely connected with love. Love, we are told, changes into compassion when confronted by the suffering of a loved person. If you love someone, and you then suddenly see them suffering, your love is all at once transformed into an overwhelming feeling of compassion. According to Buddhism *karuṇā*, or compassion, is the most spiritual of all the emotions, and is the emotion that particularly characterizes all the Buddhas and Bodhisattvas.

Certain Bodhisattvas, however, especially embody Compassion; for instance Avalokiteśvara, 'The Lord Who Looks Down (in Compassion)', who among the Bodhisattvas is the principal 'incarnation' of Compassion, or the Compassion archetype. There are many different forms of Avalokiteśvara. One of the most interesting of these is the eleven-headed and thousand-armed form which, though it may look rather bizarre to us, from a symbolical point of view is very impressive. The eleven heads represent the fact that Compassion looks in all eleven directions of space, i.e. in all possible directions, while the thousand arms represent his ceaseless compassionate activity.

There is an interesting story[146] about how this particular form arose – a story that is not just 'mythology' but based upon the facts of spiritual psychology. Once upon a time, it is said, Avalokiteśvara was contemplating the sorrows of sentient beings. As he looked out over the world, he saw people suffering in so many ways; some dying untimely deaths by fire, shipwreck, and execution, others suffering the pangs of bereavement, loss, illness, hunger, thirst, and starvation. So a tremendous Compassion welled up in his heart, becoming so unbearably intense that his head shivered into pieces. It shivered, in fact, into eleven pieces, which became the eleven heads looking in the eleven directions of space, and a thousand arms were manifested to help all those beings who were suffering. Thus this very beautiful conception of the eleven-headed and thousand-armed Avalokiteśvara is an attempt to express the essence of Compassion, or to show how the compassionate heart feels for the sorrows and suffering of the world.

Another beautiful Bodhisattva-figure embodying Compassion, this time in feminine form, is Tārā, whose name means 'The Saviouress' or 'The Star'. A beautiful legend relates how she was born from the tears of Avalokiteśvara as he wept over the sorrows and miseries of the world.[147]

We may think of these legends as being just stories, and the sophisticated may even smile at them a little, but they are not just stories – not even illustrative stories. They are of real, deep, symbolical, even archetypal significance and represent, embodied in very concrete form, the nature of Compassion.

In the Mahāyāna form of Buddhism, that is to say in the teaching of the 'Great Way', the greatest possible importance is attached to Compassion. In one of the Mahāyāna sūtras, in fact, the Buddha is represented as saying that the Bodhisattva, i.e. the one who aspires to be a Buddha, should not be taught too many things. If he is taught only Compassion, learns only Compassion, this is quite enough. No need for him to know about Conditioned Co-production, or about the Mādhyamika, or the Yogācāra, or the Abhidharma – or even the Eightfold Path. If the Bodhisattva knows only Compassion, has a heart filled with nothing but Compassion, that is enough. In other texts the Buddha says that if one only has compassion for the sufferings of other living beings, then in due course all other virtues, all other spiritual qualities and attainments, even Enlightenment itself, will follow.

This is illustrated by a moving story from modern Japan. We are told there was a young man who was a great wastrel. After running through all his money, and having a good time, he became thoroughly disgusted and fed up with everything, including himself. In this mood he decided there was only one thing left for him to do, and that was to enter the Zen monastery and become a monk. This was his last resort. He didn't really *want* to become a monk, but there was just nothing else left for him to do. So along to the Zen monastery he went. I suppose he knelt outside in the snow for three days, in the way that we are told applicants have to kneel. But in the end the abbot agreed to see him. The abbot was a grim old soul. He listened to what the young man had to say, not saying very much, but when the young man had told him everything, he said, 'Hmm, well ... is there *anything* you are good at?' The young man thought, and finally said, 'Yes, I'm not so bad at chess.' So the abbot called his attendant and told him to fetch a certain monk. The monk came. He was an old man, and had been a monk for many years. Then the abbot said to the attendant, 'Bring my sword'. So the sword was brought and placed before the abbot. The abbot then said to the young man and the old monk, 'You two will now play a game of chess. Whoever loses, I will cut off his head with this sword.' They looked at him, and they saw that he meant it. So the young man made his first move. The old monk, who wasn't a bad player, made his. The young man made his next move. The old monk made his. After a little while the young man felt the perspiration pouring down his back and trickling over his heels. So he concentrated; he put everything he had into that game, and managed to beat back the old monk's attack. Then he drew a great breath of relief, 'Ah, the game isn't going too badly!' But just then, when he was sure he would win, he looked up and saw the face of that old monk. As I have said, he was an old man, and had been a monk for many years – maybe twenty or thirty, or even forty years. He had undergone much suffering, had performed many austerities. He had meditated very much. His face was thin and worn and austere. The young man suddenly thought, 'I've been an absolute wastrel! My life is no use to anybody. This monk has led such a good life, and he's going to have to die.' So a great wave of compassion came up. He felt intensely sorry for the old monk, just sitting there and playing this game in obedience to the abbot's command, and now being beaten and going to have to die. So a tremendous compassion welled up in the young man's heart, and he thought, 'I can't allow this.' So he deliberately made a false move. The monk made a move. The young man deliberately made another false move, and it was clear that he was losing, and was unable to retrieve his position. But suddenly the abbot upset the board, saying, 'No one has won, and no one has lost.' Then to the young man he said, 'You've learned two things today: concentration and compassion. Since you've learned compassion – *you'll do.*'

Like the Mahāyāna sūtras, this story teaches that all that is needed is Compassion. The young man had led

such a wretched, wasteful life, yet since he was capable of compassion there was still hope for him. He was even ready to give up his own life rather than let the monk sacrifice his – there was so much compassion deep down in the heart of this apparently worthless man. The abbot saw all this. He thought, 'We've got a budding Bodhisattva here,' and acted accordingly.

Muditā

Thirdly, *muditā* (Sanskrit and Pali), or sympathetic joy. This is the happiness we feel in other people's happiness. If we see other people happy, we should feel happy too, but unfortunately this is not always the case. A cynic has said that we feel a secret satisfaction in the misfortunes of our friends.[148] This is often only too true. Next time someone tells you of a stroke of bad luck that they have had, just watch your own reaction. You will usually see, if only for an instant, that little quiver of satisfaction; after which, of course, the conventional reaction comes and smothers your first, *real* reaction. This is the sort of thing that happens. It can be eliminated with the help of awareness, and also by means of a positive effort to share in other people's happiness. Speaking generally, we may say that joy is a characteristically Buddhist emotion. If you are not really happy and joyful, at least on some occasions, you can hardly be a Buddhist.

Upekṣā

The fourth *brahma-vihāra* is *upekṣā* (Pali *upekkhā*). *Upekṣā* is tranquillity or, more simply, peace. We usually think of peace as something negative, as just the absence of noise or disturbance, as when we say, 'I wish they would leave me in peace.' But really peace is a very positive thing. It is no less positive than love, compassion, or joy – indeed even more so, according to Buddhist tradition. *Upekṣā* is not simply the absence of something else, but a quality and a state in its own right. It is a positive, vibrant state which is much nearer to the state of bliss than it is to our usual conception of peace.

The Dhyānas

The Sanskrit word *dhyāna* (Pali *jhāna*) is derived from the verbal root *dhyai* which means 'to think of', 'imagine', 'contemplate', 'meditate on', 'call to mind', 'recollect'. The term later developed quite a different meaning, and I think Dr Marion Matics put his finger on it when he said that the goal of *dhyāna* is 'to pass through the door of the mind to other regions of experience than those provided by the common faculties of thought and sense perception'.[149] This is a good general definition. Two of the secondary meanings of *dhyāna* are 'insensibility' or 'dullness' – insensibility with regard especially to the sense perceptions, what Christian mysticism sometimes calls Holy Insensibility – and the mental representation of the personal attributes of a deity, as in visualization.

We can consider *dhyāna* as comprising two things: higher or supernormal states of consciousness – states of consciousness above and beyond those of our ordinary everyday waking minds – and the various practices leading to the experience of those higher states of consciousness.

In the Buddhist tradition there are quite a number of lists which describe the different levels within, or different dimensions of, the higher consciousness. Here we are going to look at two lists, comprising the 'Four *Dhyānas* of the World of Form' and the 'Four Formless *Dhyānas*'.

The Four Dhyānas of the World of Form

Usually four *dhyānas* are enumerated, but sometimes five. This reminds us that one should not take these classifications too literally. The Four *Dhyānas* represent successively higher stages of psychic and spiritual development, which in reality are one continuous, ever unfolding process.

Traditionally there are two ways of describing these Four *Dhyānas*. One way is in terms of psychological analysis – trying to understand what psychological factors are present in each of these higher states of consciousness. The other way is in terms of images. Here therefore we will first describe the Four *Dhyānas* in terms of psychological analysis and then in terms of images.

In terms of psychological analysis, the experience of the first *dhyāna* is characterized by an absence of negative emotions, such as lust, ill-will, sloth and torpor, restlessness and anxiety, and doubt – in other words, the 'Five Mental Hindrances'. Unless all negative emotions are inhibited, are suppressed, are suspended, unless the mind is clear not only of the Five Mental Hindrances but of fear, anger, jealousy, anxiety, remorse, guilt, at least for the time being, there is no entry into higher states of consciousness. It is quite clear therefore that if we want to practise meditation seriously, our first task must be to learn to be able to inhibit, at least temporarily, the grosser manifestations – at least – of all these negative emotions.

Dhyāna, in the sense of the experience of superconscious states, is a natural thing. Ideally, as soon as one sits down to meditate, as soon as one closes one's eyes, one should go straight into *dhyāna*. It should be as simple and natural as that. If we led a truly human life, this would happen. In our practice we have to strive, struggle, and sweat, not to meditate, not to get into the *dhyāna* states, but to remove the obstacles which prevent us assuming those states. If we could only remove these obstacles, we would go sailing into the first *dhyāna*.

On the positive side, the first *dhyāna* is characterized by a concentration and unification of all our psychophysical energies. Our energies are usually scattered, dispersed over a multiplicity of objects; our energies leak away in various directions and are wasted; our energies are blocked. But when we take up the practice of meditation all our energies are brought together: those energies which were blocked are unblocked; those which were being wasted are not wasted any longer. Our energies come together – they are concentrated, they are unified, they flow together. This flowing together of energy, this heightening of energy, is characteristic of the first *dhyāna* (it is in fact characteristic, in increasing degrees, of all four *dhyānas*).

This concentration and unification of the energies of our total being is experienced in the first *dhyāna* as something intensely pleasurable, even blissful. These pleasurable sensations are of two kinds: there is a purely mental aspect and there is a physical aspect. The physical aspect is often described as rapture (Sanskrit *prīti*). It manifests in various ways. It may manifest for instance in the experience of one's hair standing on end. Some people when they practise meditation may find themselves weeping violently. This also is a manifestation of rapture on the physical level, and it is a good, healthy, and positive manifestation, though it does pass away after some time.

The first *dhyāna* is also characterized by a certain amount of discursive mental activity. One can enter upon the first *dhyāna* having suspended all negative emotions, having unified one's energies, having also experienced various pleasurable sensations mentally and physically, but with some vestige of discursive mental activity – if only about the meditation experience itself – still remaining, though it will not be enough to disturb one's concentration. After a while it may seem as though this discursive mental activity recedes to the fringes of one's experience, but is still present.

In the second *dhyāna* the discursive mental activity disappears. It fades away with increased concentration. The second *dhyāna* is therefore a state of no thought. When one speaks in terms of no thought, people often become a little afraid. They imagine that when there is no thought one almost ceases to exist – perhaps one goes into a sort of trance, or even into a sort of coma. It must be emphasized that in the second *dhyāna* there is simply no *discursive* mental activity: one is, at the same time, fully awake, one is aware, one is conscious. In fact, if anything, one's whole consciousness, one's whole being, is heightened: you are more alert, more awake, more aware, than you normally are. Even though the discursive mental activity fades away, even though the mind is no longer active in that sense, still a clear, pure, bright state of awareness is experienced.

In the second *dhyāna* one's psychic energies become still more concentrated and unified, with the result that the pleasurable sensations (both mental and physical) of the first *dhyāna* persist.

In passing from the first *dhyāna* to the second *dhyāna* discursive mental activity is eliminated. In passing from the second *dhyāna* to the third *dhyāna* it is the pleasurable physical sensations that disappear. The mind is blissful, but consciousness is increasingly withdrawn from the body and these pleasurable, even blissful, sensations are no longer experienced in the body or with the body. In fact in this stage bodily consciousness may be very peripheral indeed. It is as though you are conscious of your body a great way away, right on the periphery of your experience – not right at the centre of it, as is usually the case. The other factors in the third *dhyāna* remain as before except that they are further intensified.

In the fourth *dhyāna* even the mental experience of happiness disappears. Not, of course, that one becomes unhappy or uneasy in any way, but rather the mind passes beyond pleasure and pain. This is something which is rather difficult for us to understand; we cannot help thinking of such a state – which is neither pleasure nor pain – as being a neutral grey state, rather lower than either pleasure or pain. But it is not like that. In the fourth *dhyāna* the mind passes beyond pleasure, beyond pain, beyond even the mental bliss of the previous *dhyānas*, and enters a state of equanimity. To be paradoxical, one may say that the state of equanimity is even more pleasant than the pleasant state itself. (It is not true to say, however, that it is also more painful than the painful state.) In the fourth *dhyāna* all one's energies are fully integrated, so that this fourth *dhyāna* is a state of perfect mental, perfect spiritual, harmony, balance, and equilibrium.

These four *dhyānas* are illustrated in the Buddha's teaching by four appropriate and even delightful similes:

As an expert bath attendant, or bath attendant's apprentice, puts soap powder into a dish, soaks it with water, mixes and dissolves it in such a manner that its foam is completely permeated, saturated within and without with moisture, leaving none over, even so the monk suffuses, pervades, fills, and permeates his body with the pleasure and joy arising from seclusion, and there is nothing in all his body untouched by the pleasure and joy arising from seclusion....

As a lake with a subterranean spring, into which

II.
III.
I.
IV.

there flows no rivulet from east or from west, from north or from south, nor do the clouds pour their rain into it, but only the fresh spring at the bottom wells up and completely suffuses, pervades, fills, and permeates it, so that not the smallest part of the lake is left unsaturated with fresh water, even so the monk ... permeates his body with the pleasure and joy arising from concentration....

As in a lake with lotus plants some lotus flowers are born in the water, develop in the water, remain below the surface of the water, and draw their nourishment from the depths of the water, and their blooms and roots are suffused, pervaded, filled, and permeated with fresh water, even so the monk ... permeates his body with pleasure without joy....

As a man might cloak himself from head to foot in a white mantle, so that not the smallest part of his body was left uncovered by the white mantle, even so the monk sits having covered his body with a state of extreme equanimity and concentration....[150]

One can see from these four similes that there is a definite progression as one passes from one *dhyāna* to the next. In the first simile there is water and there is soap powder, in other words there is a duality; but there is a resolution of that duality in their being kneaded together. In the first *dhyāna* there is a complete unification of the energies of the conscious mind on the conscious level.

The second simile describes the trickling in, the percolating through, perhaps finally the pouring in, as a source of inspiration, of the superconscious energies, once one's energies have been unified on the level of the conscious mind.

The third simile of the lotuses permeated by water describes the energies of the conscious mind permeated and transformed by the superconscious energies.

The fourth simile of the man covered by a white mantle describes the superconscious energies not only permeating, but dominating, enclosing, and enfolding the energies of the conscious mind. In the second *dhyāna*, the superconscious energies in the form of the water flowing in from the subterranean spring are contained within the unified conscious mind (the lake). In the fourth *dhyāna*, it is the conscious mind which is contained within the superconscious energies (the white mantle). The situation has been completely reversed.

The Four Formless Dhyānas

The Four Formless *Dhyānas* consist of the experience of objects of ever-increasing degrees of subtlety and refinement.

The first of these four states of higher consciousness associated with the formless world is known as the Sphere of Infinite Space, or the Experience of Infinite Space. Here one's experience is devoid of all objects. One may recollect that by the time one reaches the fourth *dhyāna* of the world of form one leaves behind the body consciousness. If one abstracts oneself from the senses through which objects in space are perceived, one is left with the experience of infinite space – space extending infinitely in all directions, all of which is everywhere. It is not just a sort of visual experience of looking out into infinite space from a certain point *in* space; it is a feeling of freedom and expansion, an experience of one's whole being expanding indefinitely.

The second formless *dhyāna* is known as the Sphere of Infinite Consciousness. One reaches this by 'reflecting' that one has experienced infinite space; in that experience there was a consciousness of infinite space. That means that, conterminous with the infinity of space, there is an infinity of consciousness: the subjective correlative of that objective state or experience. Abstracting or subtracting from the experience of space and concentrating on the experience of consciousness, the infinity of consciousness, one experiences infinite consciousness, once again extending in all directions, but not from any one particular point – consciousness which is all present everywhere.

The third formless *dhyāna* is even more rarefied – though still mundane. This state of superconsciousness is known as the Sphere of No-thingness, the Sphere of Non-particularity. In this experience one cannot pick out any one thing in particular as distinct from any other thing. In our ordinary everyday consciousness we can pick out a flower as distinct from a tree, or a man as distinct from a house, but in this state there is no particular thingness of things. One cannot identify this as 'this' and that as 'that'. It is not as though they are confused and mixed up together, but the possibility of picking out does not exist. This is not a state of nothingness but of no-thingness.

The fourth formless *dhyāna* is the Sphere of Neither Perception nor Non-perception. One has passed from the infinite object to the infinite subject, and now one goes beyond both. One reaches a state in which one cannot say – because in a sense there is no one to say – whether one is perceiving anything or whether one is not perceiving anything. One is not fully beyond subject and object, but one can no longer think or experience in terms of subject and object.

The Symbolism of the Five Elements in the Stupa

The symbolism of the five elements was incorporated into the structure of the stupa[151] during the Vajrayāna (the Tantric) phase of the development of Buddhism in India.[152]

The five elements are earth, water, fire, air, and space. The first four of these are the 'material' elements, which together make up the 'material' universe. In Buddhist thought of all schools these four elements are collectively known as *rūpa*. (*Rūpa* in turn is the first of the 'Five *Skandhas*', the 'Five Aggregates', into which the whole of conditioned, phenomenal existence is divided.)

Early translators of Buddhist texts into Western languages used to translate *rūpa* as 'matter', matter as opposed to mind; but this is in fact quite wrong (in Buddhism there is no mind–matter dualism, least of all in the Tantra). *Rūpa* literally means 'form'. It represents what Western philosophers call the objective content of the perceptual situation. We shall see what this means. We have an experience; perception takes place. For instance, we see a flower or hear a melody. That is a perceptual situation. In it we can distinguish two elements. Firstly there is what we ourselves contribute to it. There is, for instance, a sensation of colour (say, red or white) – we contribute that. Or there is a sensation of sweetness or harshness of sound – we contribute that. There is a feeling of pleasure – we also contribute that. Secondly, in the perceptual situation there is something that we ourselves do not contribute: there is something which the experience seems to be an experience *of*, something to which the perceptual situation seems to refer, or to which it seems to point. This something, as yet unknown and unidentified, is what we call technically the objective content of that perceptual situation. It is this objective content that Buddhism calls *rūpa*.

Rūpa, as the objective content of the perceptual situation, is not only perceived, but is perceived as possessing certain qualities. There are four principal qualities, technically known as *mahābhūtas*. *Rūpa* is perceived as something solid and resistant, as something fluid and cohesive, as possessing a certain temperature, and as light and moving. These four qualities of *rūpa* are symbolized in Buddhist thought, tradition, and art by the four material elements: earth, water, fire, and air. These elements are not 'things' (earth does not mean a lump of earth, and water does not mean the water we get out of the tap) but symbols for these main qualities of *rūpa*. In other words, whatever there is of solidity and resistance in a particular perceptual situation is symbolized by earth; whatever there is of fluidity and cohesiveness in that situation is symbolized by water; whatever in that situation possesses temperature is symbolized by fire; whatever possesses lightness and mobility is symbolized by air.

Mahābhūtas literally means 'great elements' or 'primary elements'. (They are so called because all the other secondary elements of *rūpa* derive from these four primary ones.) But that is just the most obvious meaning of the word; the word has other interesting meanings. *Mahābhūta* also means a great magical transformation, such as a magician performs when he makes you see one thing as another. It also means a great ghost, in the sense of some horrible haunting spirit. A magician, who transforms clay into gold, makes you perceive clay as gold. In the same way we perceive *rūpa*, the objective content of the perceptual situation, as earth (as solidity), as water, as fire, as air. But what *rūpa* is in itself, if it is in fact anything at all, we do not know and do not experience. We do not, as it were, experience the clay – we do not even know whether there is any clay there; we only experience the gold.

Similarly, we are told, the great ghost, which is here a *yakṣiṇī*, a terrible female sprite, appears one dark night as a beautiful maiden. You do not know that it is a terrible female sprite who might gobble you up the next morning; you think it is a beautiful maiden. You experience just the beautiful maiden; you do not experience the ghost reality underneath. So it is the same in this case too: what *rūpa* is in itself we do not know and do not experience; we only experience, through our five senses, these four great elements, these four primary qualities.

Space, the fifth element in this context, is that which contains the other four elements. In a sense, space is what makes earth, water, fire, and air possible; it is the possibility of their existence. Or we may say that space is that which supports, which makes possible the existence of, the whole material universe. In a sense, therefore, in Buddhist thought space is regarded as somewhat more real, more ultimate, than the four material elements.

Each of these five elements is associated with a particular colour and a particular geometrical form. Earth is associated with yellow and the cube; water with white and the sphere, or sometimes the hemisphere; fire with red and the cone, or a pyramidal form; air with pale green and a sort of hemisphere (its flat surface uppermost), or sometimes a bowl-like shape; space with blue and the flaming drop.

The Structure of the Stupa

After this preliminary survey we can now begin to see how the Tantra incorporated the five-element symbolism into the structure of the stupa. What the Tantra did was very simple and rather drastic. The Tantra placed the geometrical forms – the cube, the sphere, the cone, the inverted hemisphere, and the flaming drop – one on top of the other, and then came to regard the stupa as a whole as consisting essentially of them, as built up out of them. In other words, the Tantra came to regard the stupa as an architectural symbol of the whole material universe as existing in space.

Having done this the Tantra went further. It gave the symbolism of the five elements, and the symbolism of the stupa itself, an even more deeply Tantric significance. The order in which the Tantra placed the geometrical forms on top of each other was not arbitrary. The symbols are arranged in the order of the increasing subtlety of the elements which they represent, with the grossest at the bottom and the subtlest at the top. Water is subtler and more refined than earth; fire is subtler and more refined than water; air is subtler and more refined than fire; and space, right at the top, is the subtlest and most refined of all. This suggested to the Tantric sages that what was true of the material world was true also of the world of mind. In the material world some elements are grosser, coarser, while others are more refined, more subtle. It is just the same in the mental world; mind too, spirit too, has its levels – lower, grosser, coarser levels and higher, subtler, more refined levels. Transposing the symbolism – transposing the stupa itself – from the material plane to the mental and spiritual plane, these mental and spiritual levels could also be symbolized by the five elements. In this way, for the Tantra, the stupa came to be a symbol not only of the material world, but of the world of the mind, the world of successive levels of consciousness, or rather of successively higher stages in the transformation of psycho-spiritual energy.

The Energy of the Five Elements

Let us go into this a little, remembering that we are now in the mental and spiritual world, and that the five elements now symbolize different stages in the transformation of psycho-spiritual energy. We are now in the world within, not the world without.

Earth, in this world, represents static energy, energy which is potential rather than actual, even energy which is blocked, obstructed. Many people, unfortunately, are very familiar with this state. You feel that you have got energy somewhere inside you, but it is blocked. The energy is shut up like fire in a sealed volcano; there is no way out for it; there is no channel through which and by which it can express itself. Perhaps the energy is not only blocked, but even repressed. If energies are pressed down and not allowed to come out, eventually they *cannot* come out.

Sometimes this whole process of blocking, obstructing, suppressing, and repressing goes on for years. Then all that energy starts congealing. It congeals only too often into a hard, solid, cold lump. The person in whom energy congeals in this way himself hardens into a hard, solid, cold lump. Such a person becomes progressively more and more petrified, more and more unresponsive, uncommunicative, unexpressive, less and less alive, more and more dead. Occasionally, just to relieve the tedium, there may be an explosion. Little bits of rock – bits of rather hard substance – go flying in all directions.

But usually this does not do much good. Afterwards it is practically the same as ever it was.

Even if they are not actually blocked, even if there is no actual suppression, nor repression, the majority of people, unfortunately, are able to utilize only a small fraction of their potential energy. (This is something that most people do not realize.) We remain in the state of earth: our energy is static energy – potential rather than actual.

The state of water is a state of slightly freed energy. Water, unlike earth or rock, moves; it flows from side to side on approximately the same plane; it can flow down but it cannot (under its own power) flow up. In this state of water, in much the same way, there is a small amount of energy that gets free and goes backwards and forwards; it never gets far, but goes a certain distance and then returns to the first point. In other words, this energy, this water state, moves between pairs of opposites: it flows between love and hate, attraction and repulsion, hope and fear, pleasure and pain. Energy at this level is very reactive in a very limited sphere. It is a little free, but only within certain definite limits. It is like a goat tethered to a post. The goat can eat the grass up to a certain point, but not beyond that. When the grass on one side is finished, the goat has to eat on the other side.

Fire is energy which is moving upwards. In this state energy is being liberated in ever greater and greater quantities, and because of this regular liberation of energy the level of one's whole being and consciousness is steadily rising. You may experience overwhelming joy, ecstasy, bliss, and so on. When the fire is blazing, when energy is soaring upwards, then mental conflicts are resolved, problems are transcended – they become like wisps of smoke flowing in all directions, or little sparks. This is also a state of continuous creativity: something higher and ever higher is being produced all the time. The state of fire is the state of higher and ever higher spiritual experience. It is the state of the true artist and the mystic, not in their ordinary everyday lives, but at their peak, when they are creating, when they are reaching out to that which is beyond, when the flame is soaring right up into the sky.

Whereas fire represented energy freed upwards, air represents energy freed in all directions. Air is energy which radiates from a central point in all directions at once. Air is energy which is pouring from an inexhaustible central fountain, just as light and heat in our universe pour from the sun. There is no limitation whatsoever. It is pouring in all directions, at the same time, for ever.

And then we have space. Here energy is in a state almost beyond words and thought. It has gone, as it were, into another dimension – a fourth, a fifth, a sixth dimension. We can say that space is the state in which energy, having propagated itself in all directions to infinity, remains eternally propagating itself.

These are the five elements in this psycho-spiritual sense. These are the successive stages in the transformation of psycho-spiritual energy as symbolized by the Tantric stupa.

Let me give a simile for what an individual is like in each of these successive states – in the state of earth, in the state of water, in the state of fire, and so on.

In the state of earth he is like a prisoner bound tightly hand and foot. I am sure that most people have felt like this at some time. He cannot move, cannot stir. He may be blindfolded too and cannot even blink his eyes. There is nothing he can do; he cannot make any movement whatsoever. His energy is completely blocked. This is what someone is like in the state of earth.

But then someone comes along and cuts his bonds and takes the bandage from his eyes. The prisoner finds himself in a little cell about six feet across. He finds he can move: he can lift his arm, he can raise his leg. He finds he can actually walk, walk in fact all day long if he likes, *but* only in his little cell – six feet this way, six feet that way. In other words, there is a little energy moving about within a very circumscribed space: it can go up to the wall in this direction and up to the wall in that direction, but that is all. This is the state of water, of energy feebly oscillating between pairs of opposites – sometimes this state is even called 'freedom'.

In the state of fire the prisoner succeeds in making a hole in the roof and, like a Tibetan yogi, goes floating up through the hole, up and up, right into the clouds.

In the state of air he discovers that he does not have to go merely up, but can go in other directions as well: he can go sideways; he can go down and come up again; he can go to any of the points of the compass. Here I am afraid our analogy breaks down, because in the state of air he can travel in all directions simultaneously. One can perhaps imagine him as a magician, or a yogi with even greater occult powers, multiplying himself: there are millions of him, and they are all travelling in different directions from this central point, all over the universe into infinity for ever.

Beyond that there is space. I am not even going to try to extend the analogy to space. Here words simply break down and one is left to one's own imagination.

These are the successive stages in the transformation of psycho-spiritual energy: from earth to water, from water to fire, from fire to air, from air to space. These are the stages of the Tantric path to Enlightenment, stages symbolized by the five elements as incorporated into the Tantric symbolism of the stupa.

The Stupa Visualization Practice

The central problem of the spiritual life is the conservation and unification of our energies. Most of the time our energies are not available for the spiritual life: they are blocked, repressed, or draining away. Therefore we often find it difficult to get deeply into meditation. The stupa visualization practice is intended to release, stimulate, and purify psycho-spiritual energy.

When one takes up a practice of this kind, one may at first see only an undifferentiated patch of colour; in time the colour will assume a certain definite form. To see the colour, and more than this, to 'feel' the colour, is of the utmost importance. It is the colour that gives one the feel, the inner feeling, of the particular aspect visualized, i.e. earth, water, fire, air, or space. This inner feeling is something that is very subtle and indefinable. One experiences the colour as a colour and as more than a colour, as a symbol. The colour becomes a vehicle for the experience of a spiritual quality, a spiritual state, which the colour symbolizes. Through the form and colour symbol one can experience the spiritual principle which the symbol embodies.

Visualization of the Stupa

1. Visualize an infinite, clear blue sky.
2. Appearing within the clear blue sky visualize a yellow cube, symbol of the element earth.
3. Above the yellow cube visualize a white sphere, symbol of the element water.
4. Above the white sphere visualize a red cone, symbol of the element fire.
5. Above the red cone visualize a pale green hemisphere, symbol of the element air.
6. Above the pale green hemisphere visualize an iridescent, rainbow-scintillating flaming drop, symbol of the element space.
7. The flaming drop is slowly dissolved into the pale green hemisphere.
8. The pale green hemisphere is slowly dissolved into the red cone.
9. The red cone is slowly dissolved into the white sphere.
10. The white sphere is slowly dissolved into the yellow cube.
11. The yellow cube is slowly dissolved into the blue sky.
12. Finally one allows the blue sky to fade away, thus bringing the practice to a close.

Wisdom

The Three Characteristics of Existence

Reality is rather a big word. It is not only rather big, it is very abstract, even a trifle vague. Buddhism, on the whole, is not very fond of abstract or vague terminology. If we take the example of Tibetan Buddhism, we find that far from dealing in abstractions it prefers concrete images. Tibetan Buddhism, in fact, is not only concrete, it is almost materialistic. If one can have a contradiction in terms, it is a materialistic spirituality. In the same spirit, Zen, another great school of Buddhism, also avoids, as far as possible, abstractions and vague generalities. In some ways Zen goes much further than Tibetan Buddhism. Rather than indulge in abstractions Zen will utter a piercing shriek or give you thirty blows.

'Reality' in any case is not really a Buddhist word. In Buddhism we have got the words *śūnyatā*, *tathatā*,[153] *dharmakāya*, but we have not got any true semantic equivalent of the word 'Reality'. So when we use this word 'Reality' in speaking about Buddhism, we use it in a very provisional way. It is not to be taken too literally, and all the connotations which attach to it when it is used in the general, Western, philosophical and religious context do not quite apply when it is used in the Buddhist context.

The Texture of Reality

'Texture' is not an abstract word, it is remarkably concrete. We speak of the texture of a piece of cloth – cotton, silk, or wool all have different textures which you can feel quite easily with your fingers. We also speak of the texture of a piece of stone – if you pass your fingers over a piece of marble and over a piece of granite the textures of the two stones are quite different. Texture is something concrete, whereas Reality is something which seems rather abstract, but it seems appropriate to use this more concrete expression to speak of Reality because it implies that Reality is something to be 'felt', even something to be 'handled', something to be experienced. Buddhism is above all else practical: it comprises ethics, religion, and spiritual tradition; it is not just a system of philosophy in the Western academic sense.

Continuing to use this word 'Reality' provisionally, we may say that in Buddhism, broadly speaking, Reality is of two kinds. There is conditioned reality and Unconditioned Reality. More simply we can speak in terms of the conditioned and the Unconditioned. This distinction is absolutely basic to Buddhist thought. 'Conditioned' in the original Sanskrit is *saṁskṛta*. *Saṁskṛta* literally means put together or compounded (*saṁ* is 'together', *skṛta* is 'made' or 'put'). 'Unconditioned' is *asaṁskṛta*, meaning that which is not put together, not compounded: that which is simple in the philosophical sense.

In the *Ariya-pariyesana-sutta*[154] the Buddha speaks of two quests, the ignoble quest (*anariyapariyesana*) and the noble quest (*ariyapariyesana*). *Esana* is a very strong word; it means 'quest', 'search', 'will', 'desire', 'urge', 'aspiration'. The ignoble quest is when the conditioned goes in search of the conditioned, the mortal pursues the mortal; the noble quest is when the conditioned goes in search of the Unconditioned, the mortal pursues the immortal. The ignoble quest corresponds to the round of existence, the Wheel of Life, within which we all go round and round from one life to the next indefinitely. The noble quest corresponds to the path (the 'Eightfold Path', the 'Sevenfold Path', the 'Path of the Bodhisattva'), leading from the Wheel of Life, up through the Spiral, to the goal of Enlightenment.

The Three Lakṣaṇas

You may say at this point, 'It's all very well to talk of the noble quest, to speak of giving up the conditioned and going in search of the Unconditioned, but that is rather vague and abstract. What exactly does one mean by the conditioned? How can we recognize the conditioned? How are we to know it?' The answer which the Buddhist tradition gives to this question is that we recognize the conditioned by means of the three characteristics (Sanskrit *lakṣaṇas*, Pali *lakkhaṇas*) which it invariably bears.

The Three *Lakṣaṇas* are *duḥkha*, *anitya*, and *anātman*. These may be rendered as 'the unsatisfactory', 'the impermanent', and 'the devoid of self'. All conditioned things whatsoever in this universe possess all these three characteristics. They are all unsatisfactory, all impermanent, all devoid of self.

Types of Suffering

Duḥkha (Pali *dukkha*) is one of the best known Buddhist words. It is usually translated as 'suffering', but I personally feel that 'unsatisfactoriness', though a bit cumbersome perhaps, is better.

The Buddha usually speaks of seven different kinds of suffering or unsatisfactoriness.[155] First the Buddha says that birth is suffering. I remember that Oscar Wilde in one of his writings says that at the birth of a child or a star there is pain. That is a bit poetic, perhaps, but it does express a spiritual truth. It is rather significant that our life begins with suffering. The event of birth is certainly physically painful for the mother and the infant. For the infant it is, we are told, a traumatic experience to be suddenly thrust into this cold world – to be slapped and beaten perhaps. It is not a very welcoming experience.

Then the Buddha says that decay in the sense of old age is suffering. Old age has quite a number of disadvantages. There is physical weakness: you cannot get about as you used to; you cannot dash up those stairs or climb those mountains as you used to. There is also loss of memory: you cannot remember names or where you put things. Sometimes it is quite tragic to see this in old people. There is also senility. Sometimes you see people who are advanced in age and who have quite evidently started losing their senses. And last, and perhaps most painful of all, when one is very old one is dependent upon others: one cannot do much for oneself; one might even have to be physically looked after by a nurse or relations. All this makes the time of old age, especially extreme old age, despite all modern comforts and amenities, very often a time of suffering.

Then sickness is suffering. No sickness is pleasant, whether it is a little toothache or a terrible disease like cancer.

Death is suffering. Death is often suffering because people do not want to go. They want to hang on to life. They are very sorry to leave. But even if they do want to go, even if they are happy to pass on to a new life – or into they know not what – very often the physical process of dissolution is quite painful. There is much mental suffering connected with it. Sometimes on their deathbeds people are stricken with remorse: they remember the wrongs they have done certain individuals in the past. Very often people experience fears and apprehensions for the future. All this makes death for many people a terrible experience and one which before it comes they try their best not to think about.

There are other forms of suffering. To be joined with what one dislikes is suffering. We all have this sort of experience. Sometimes it happens that even in our own family there are people that we don't like. This is very tragic. It is not always second cousins and such distant relations with whom we don't get on, sometimes it is even our own brothers and sisters, even our parents, even our children. But because the tie of blood is there, we have to be joined with them to a certain extent. Then with regard to, say, our jobs, many of us do not like our jobs – if we have got jobs. Many people would rather do something else, but they were pushed into their job when they were fifteen or sixteen and cannot get out. They have to do things which they do not want to do, come into contact with people with whom they do not like coming into contact. All that is suffering. There are environmental conditions which are unpleasant, like the English climate. One would prefer to go to the sunny south, Italy, Greece, Yugoslavia, Tunisia, but it is not always possible.

So very often one is joined to what one dislikes, whether people, places, or things. There seems to be no way of escaping – certainly no way of escaping entirely. You just have to go around indefinitely with these people, places, and things that you don't like. Sometimes it feels almost like being tied to a corpse from which you cannot get away.

On the other hand, the Buddha says that to be separated from what one likes is suffering. It often happens that in the course of life we are separated from relations or friends. There are people we would like to be with, people that we would like to meet more often, but circumstances interpose and it becomes simply impossible. It happens very often in time of war that families are broken up. I remember during World War II when I was in the army out in the East that many of my friends used to get letters from home, from their families and friends, regularly, every week or every two weeks. Then a time would come when the letters would stop. They did not know what had happened. They knew that there were bombs falling in England, so sometimes, after one week, after two weeks, they would start thinking that the worst must have happened. Then perhaps they would get the news, either from another relation or officially, that either their wife and children, or their parents, or brothers and sisters, had been killed in an aerial bombardment. For them of course there was the permanent separation through death. Many people brood over these sorts of losses for years and years.

Not to get what one wants is suffering. We all know this very well because we all like to get what we want. If we cannot get what we want we feel upset, disturbed, troubled. The stronger the desire is, the more the suffering. There is no need to elaborate on that because it is something with which we are acquainted almost every day, if not every hour.

The Buddha on those many occasions when he spoke about suffering, trying to get people to see it in perspective, summed up his discourse by saying, in short, that the 'Five Aggregates' (Sanskrit *skandhas*) (form, feeling, perceptions, volitions, and consciousness), which make up the totality of conditioned sentient existence, themselves are suffering.

Most people, if you ask them, certainly if you press them, are prepared to admit that birth is painful and, yes, sickness is painful, and old age, and death. Yes, they admit that all these things are painful, but at the same time they are reluctant to accept the conclusion which follows from all this that conditioned existence itself is suffering. It is as though they admit all the digits in the sum, but will not accept the total to which those digits all add up. They think that to say that conditioned existence itself is suffering is going just a bit too far. They say, 'Yes, there is a certain amount of suffering in the world, but on the whole it is not a bad place.' And they say that when Buddhism says that conditioned existence as such is suffering it is being rather pessimistic, if not morbid. 'Surely,' they say, 'there is some little gleam of happiness somewhere in the world.'

Concealed Suffering

Buddhism, of course, does not deny that there may be pleasant experiences in life as well as painful ones. But Buddhism does say that even the pleasant experiences are at bottom painful. The pleasant experiences themselves are really only concealed suffering, suffering 'glossed over', the 'honey on the razor's edge'. The extent to which we can see the suffering behind the pleasure, the extent to which we can see, to borrow a metaphor from classical mythology, the skulls and bones behind the banks of flowers in the sirens' caves,[156] depends on our spiritual maturity. Dr Edward Conze gives four interesting examples of concealed suffering.[157]

Firstly, something which is pleasant for oneself but which involves suffering for other people or for other beings. Usually we do not think of this. If *we* are 'all right' we do not bother too much about others. To take the common example of meat eating, many people enjoy eating meat and do not bother much about the sufferings of the cow, or the pig, or the lamb, or the chicken, or whatever other unfortunate animal it happens to be. Most of the time the conscious mind just ignores all that: it goes on merrily plying knife and fork without thinking about the suffering of the animals at all.

But the unconscious mind is aware. Very often the unconscious mind is wiser than the conscious mind. You cannot deceive the unconscious mind. You can shut some unpleasant fact out from the conscious mind, but then it only sinks down into the unconscious: it is there all the time. Because of this unconscious knowledge (in the depths of ourselves we know that our pleasure has been bought at the expense of the suffering of other living beings) there is an unconscious feeling of guilt.

This sort of guilt is the source of a great deal of

uneasiness, anxiety, and suffering. Dr Conze gives a quite common example, the example of wealth. He says that he has known quite a few wealthy people, nearly all of whom have been afraid of becoming poor. Strange as it may seem, a poor person is not afraid of dying of starvation or anything like that. (I know people in India who sometimes do not know where their next day's meal is coming from, but you do not find them worrying about it: they are perfectly cheerful, sometimes even quite happy.) But wealthy people, so Dr Conze says, are often afraid of losing their wealth and becoming poor. This, he says, is because unconsciously they feel that they do not deserve to have it – the unconscious says, 'It ought to be taken away from you,' and the conscious mind worries, saying, 'Perhaps it *will* be taken away from you.' Unconscious guilt feelings are often there in the mind of the wealthy person because he knows, however much his conscious mind may deny it, that he has acquired his wealth in various dishonest ways, by causing suffering to other people, directly or indirectly. He often feels a need for self-justification. He says, 'Well, if I'm rich and other people are poor it's because I work harder – others are lazy, good for nothing.'

Sometimes the feelings of guilt become very strong indeed. Then drastic measures are required to relieve it. The measures may consist even in giving away some of the wealth. The wealthy person gives some of it away in the form of donations. Often he will give money to hospitals, which is rather significant, because hospitals relieve suffering, and it suggests he is compensating for the suffering he has caused in acquiring the wealth, by giving some of it to alleviate some of the suffering in hospitals. This sort of donation is what is called 'conscience money'. If one has anything to do with religious organizations, one quickly learns how common a thing conscience money is. Sometimes it is just put through the letter box in an envelope simply inscribed 'from an anonymous donor'. Then you know that someone's conscience is really biting them.

The second example of concealed suffering that Dr Conze gives is: something is pleasant, but it is tied up with anxiety because we are afraid of losing it. A good example of this is political power. It is very sweet, so people say, to have power over other people, but all the time you are afraid of losing it. You are especially afraid if you are a dictator: if your political power has been wrested by force and other people are ready to seize it from you, then you may not have a single easy night's rest. It must be terrible to be surrounded by guards, to be always suspicious, not even able to trust your best friend, always worrying who is going to make the next move against you. Buddhist texts give a good illustration. They say, suppose there is a hawk. The hawk seizes a piece of meat and flies off with it in its claws. But then hundreds of other hawks fly after it and try to seize that piece of meat. Some peck and stab at the first hawk's body, some at his eyes, some at his head, trying to tear away the meat. So many so-called pleasures, like that of possessing political power, are rather like that, especially in the highly competitive world of today's society.

The third example of concealed suffering is: something is pleasant, but it binds us to something else which brings about suffering. He gives the simple example of the body. Through the body we experience all sorts of pleasurable sensations. Because of these pleasurable sensations we become attached to the body, the body being the source of these sensations. But the body is also the source of unpleasant sensations. So by being attached to that which provides us with the pleasant sensations we become no less attached to that which provides us with the unpleasant sensations. We cannot have them separately.

Lastly, Dr Conze says that pleasures derived from the experience of conditioned things cannot satisfy the deepest longings of the heart. In each one of us there is something which is Unconditioned, something which is 'not of this world', something transcendental, the Buddha-nature. Whatever you choose to call it, its distinctive characteristic is that it cannot be satisfied by anything conditioned: it can be satisfied only by the Unconditioned. Therefore, to come back to the Buddha's conclusion, all conditioned things, whether actually or potentially, are unsatisfactory. That unsatisfactoriness is a basic characteristic of all forms of conditioned existence, especially sentient conditioned existence.

Impermanence

The second *lakṣaṇa* is *anitya* (Pali *anicca*). *Anitya* means 'impermanent' (*nitya* is 'permanent', 'eternal' and *'a'* is the negative prefix, so *anitya* is 'impermanent', 'non-eternal'). This characteristic will not detain us as long as *duḥkha* because it is comparatively easy to understand, at least intellectually. It asserts that all conditioned things, all compounded things, are constantly changing. (Conditioned things, by their very definition, in Sanskrit and Pali, are compounded, i.e. made up of parts.) What is compounded can also be uncompounded (the parts can be separated). This is happening of course all the time. Perhaps it is easier for us to understand this truth nowadays than it was before. We know now from science that there is no such thing as hard solid matter – scattered in lumps throughout space. We know that what we think of as matter is in reality only energy in various forms.

The same truth of impermanence applies to the mind. In the mental life there is nothing unchanging; there is no unchanging permanent immortal soul: there is only a constant succession of mental states. The mind changes even more quickly than the physical body. We cannot usually see the physical body changing, but we can see our own mind changing, if we are a little observant. That is why the Buddha said that it is more reprehensible to identify oneself with the mind than with the body: to think that I am the mind is more reprehensible than to think that I am the body because the body at least possesses a certain relative stability, whereas the mind does not possess any stability at all.

To put it very broadly, the characteristic of *anitya* shows us that the whole universe, from top to bottom, in all its immensity, in all its grandeur, is just one vast congeries of processes of different types, taking place at different levels, and all interrelated; nothing is standing still, nothing is immobile, not even for an instant. It is easy to forget this. We think that the sky and the mountains are always there (the 'everlasting hills'); we think that our bodies are relatively permanent. It is only when increments of change add up to a great change, add up perhaps to a catastrophe, or when something breaks or comes to an end, or when we die, that we realize the truth of impermanence.

Non-self

The third and last *lakṣaṇa* is *anātman* (Pali *anattā*) (literally, the 'no-self', or the 'non-self'). This teaches us that all conditioned things are devoid of a permanent unchanging selfhood. I remember that my own teacher, who was an Indian Buddhist monk, used to say that one cannot possibly understand what the Buddha meant by *anātman* unless one has first understood the contemporary conception of *ātman*, that is to say, what the Hinduism of the Buddha's day meant by *ātman*. There are many conceptions of *ātman* mentioned in the Upanishads. Some Upanishads say that the *ātman* is the physical body; others say that the *ātman* is just as big as the thumb, is material, and abides in the heart. There are many different views, but the most common one in the Buddha's day, the one that he appears to have been most concerned with, asserted that the *ātman*, the self, was immaterial, conscious, unchanging, individual (as I am I and you are you), sovereign (in the sense of exercising complete control over its own destiny), and blissful.

The Buddha maintained that there was no such entity. He appealed to experience. If we look within, if we look at our own mental life, we see that there are only the Five Aggregates (form, feelings, perceptions, volitions, and acts of consciousness), all of which are constantly changing – there is nothing permanent. We see that the Five Aggregates all arise in dependence on conditions – there is nothing sovereign. We see that they are all riddled with suffering in one way or another – there is nothing (ultimately) blissful. So there is no self, *ātman*. The Five Aggregates are *anātman*; the Five Aggregates do not constitute any such self as the Hindus of the Buddha's day had in mind; the *ātman* neither exists in the Five Aggregates, nor outside of them, nor associated with them in some other way.

All conditioned things, without exception, are suffering (*duḥkha*), impermanent (*anitya*), and devoid of self (*anātman*). These are the three characteristics of conditioned existence. They are of central importance, not just in Buddhist philosophy, but in the Buddhist spiritual life. According to the Buddha, we do not really see conditioned existence until we learn to see it in these terms. If we see anything else, that is just an illusion, a projection. Once we start seeing the conditioned in these terms, then little by little we get a glimpse of the Unconditioned, and that glimpse guides us on our way.

The Bodhicitta

A Bodhisattva – as the term itself suggests – is one who seeks to gain Enlightenment, one whose whole being, in fact, is oriented towards Enlightenment. A Bodhisattva is further defined as 'one who seeks to gain Enlightenment not for his own sake only, but for the sake of all sentient beings'.[158]

A most important, practical question is: how does one become a Bodhisattva? In other words, how does one embark upon the actual realization of this sublime spiritual ideal? The traditional answer to this question is quite short and straightforward, but it demands considerable explanation. It is that one becomes a Bodhisattva upon the arising of the Bodhicitta.[159]

Let us go back for a moment to the original Sanskrit term, which is *bodhicitta-utpāda. Bodhi* means 'spiritual Enlightenment' or 'spiritual Awakening' and it consists in the seeing of Reality face to face. *Citta* means 'mind', 'thought', 'consciousness', or 'heart'. *Utpāda* means simply 'arising' or, more poetically, 'awakening'.

Bodhicitta-utpāda is one of the most important terms in the whole field of Buddhism, certainly in the field of the Mahāyāna. It is usually translated into English as 'the arising of the thought of Enlightenment', but this is exactly what it is not. In a sense you could hardly have a worse translation. It is not a 'thought' *about* Enlightenment at all. We can think about Enlightenment as much as we like. We can think about it, read about it, talk about it – we glibly say what Enlightenment is or is not and think we know all about it. We are perhaps thinking about Enlightenment even now. The thought about Enlightenment has undoubtedly arisen in our minds as we sit here, but the Bodhicitta has not arisen – we haven't become transformed into Bodhisattvas.

The Bodhicitta is something very much more than a thought about Enlightenment. Guenther translates it as 'Enlightened Attitude'.[160] I personally sometimes translate it as 'Will to Enlightenment' or as 'Bodhi Heart'. Although all these alternative translations are considerably better than 'thought of Enlightenment', none of them is really satisfactory. This is not altogether the fault of the English language. It is perhaps the fault of language itself. We might say that 'Bodhicitta' is a very unsatisfactory term for the Bodhicitta.

The Bodhicitta is, in fact, not a mental state (or mental activity, or mental function) at all. It is certainly not a 'thought' (not a thought which you or I can entertain). If we think of Enlightenment, that is not the Bodhicitta. The Bodhicitta has nothing to do with thought. It is not even an 'act of will', if by that I mean my personal will. It is not even 'being conscious', if by that I mean my being conscious, or your being conscious, of the fact that there is such a thing as 'Enlightenment'. The Bodhicitta is none of these things.

The Bodhicitta basically represents the manifestation, even the irruption, within us, of something transcendental. In traditional terms – I am thinking of Nāgārjuna's exposition of the Bodhicitta in a short but profound work which he wrote on the subject[161] – the Bodhicitta is said to be not included in the 'Five *Skandhas*'. This is a very significant statement indeed. It gives us a tremendous clue to the nature of the Bodhicitta. Nāgārjuna's statement, representing the best Mahāyāna tradition, requires a great deal of pondering.

The Five Skandhas

Skandha is another of those untranslatable terms. It is usually translated as 'aggregate', or 'confection', or something equally unsatisfactory. It is really untranslatable. It literally means 'the trunk of a tree', but that doesn't get us far. However, the Five *Skandhas* are one of the basic doctrinal categories of Buddhism. Whether it's Pali, Sanskrit, Tibetan, or Chinese literature, over and over again there are references to the Five *Skandhas*, the 'Five Aggregates', or, as Dr Conze delights to translate the term, the 'Five Heaps', which again doesn't help us much. Let us refer back to these Five *Skandhas*, so that we are quite sure what we are trying to ponder on.

The first of the Five *Skandhas* is *rūpa*. *Rūpa* means 'bodily form'; it means anything perceived through the senses. Secondly, there is *vedanā*, which means 'feeling' or 'emotion' – positive or negative. Thirdly, there is *saṁjñā*, which is, very roughly, 'perception' (sometimes it is translated as 'sensation', but 'sensation' is really a more suitable translation for *vedanā*). *Saṁjñā* is the recognition of something as 'that particular thing'. When you say, 'that's a clock,' that is *saṁjñā*. You've recognized it as that particular thing. You've identified it, pointed it out, labelled it. Fourthly, the *saṁskāras*. This term is more difficult still to translate. By some German scholars it is translated as 'steering forces'. We may translate it, very roughly indeed, as 'volitional activities', i.e. acts of will. Fifthly, *vijñāna*, which is 'consciousness'. This is consciousness through the five physical senses and through the mind at various levels.

These are the Five *Skandhas: rūpa* (material form), *vedanā* (feeling or emotion), *saṁjñā* (perception), *saṁskāras* (volitional activities), and *vijñāna* (consciousness). If you want to make anything of Buddhist metaphysics and philosophy, you must know these Five *Skandhas* inside out: you must be able to reel them off and know what you are talking about.

In Buddhist thought the Five *Skandhas* are regarded as exhausting our entire psychophysical existence. In the entire range of our psychophysical existence, on all levels, there's nothing – no thought, no feeling, no aspect of our physical existence – which is not included under one or another of the Five *Skandhas*. This is why, at the beginning of the *Heart Sūtra*,[162] the text says that the Bodhisattva Avalokiteśvara, coursing in the profound Perfection of Wisdom, looked down on the world (on conditioned existence) and saw Five Heaps (Five *Skandhas*). That is what he saw. He saw no more than that. He saw that the whole of psychophysical conditioned existence consists of these five things alone; nothing occurs, nothing exists, on the conditioned level of existence (the *saṁskṛta* level) which cannot be included under one or another of the Five *Skandhas*.

The Awakening of the Bodhi Heart

But the Bodhicitta is not included in the Five *Skandhas*. As the Five *Skandhas* comprise all that is of this world, and the Bodhicitta is not included in the Five *Skandhas*, it means that the Bodhicitta is something altogether out of this world, something transcendental. It is not a thought, nor a volition, nor an idea, nor a concept, but – if we must use words at all – a profound, spiritual (read 'Transcendental') experience, an experience which re-orients our entire being.

Perhaps I can make this rather obscure matter clearer with the help of a comparison – it is *only* a comparison – from the Christian tradition. You can imagine someone in a Christian context talking about 'thinking of God'. When you talk about 'thinking of God', even if you are a pious church-going person, it doesn't mean very much – you just think about God. You might think of God as a beautiful old gentleman seated in the clouds or as Pure Being, but 'thinking about God' would be just thinking about God. You wouldn't describe it as a spiritual experience, or as a profound experience of any sort. Suppose, however, you were to speak of 'the descent of the Holy Spirit', this would be a very different matter. Thinking about God is one thing, but having the Holy Spirit descend upon you, and into you, so that you are filled by the Holy Spirit, is a quite different thing.

It is just the same in the case of 'thinking about Enlightenment', or the 'thought of Enlightenment', on the one hand, and the actual arising of the Bodhicitta on the other. If the thought of Enlightenment is analogous to thinking about God, the arising of the Bodhicitta is analogous to the descent upon one – in full force, as it were – of the Holy Spirit. This comparison is just for the purpose of illustration – if possible, illumination. There's no question of equating these two different sets of doctrinal and spiritual concepts. I am concerned only to try to make clear the nature of the difference between thinking about Enlightenment and the arising of the Bodhicitta. The Bodhicitta is not just a thought about Enlightenment, but a profound spiritual experience, even a profound, spiritual, transcendental 'entity'.

Not only is the Bodhicitta transcendental, but the Bodhicitta is not individual. This is another point that Nāgārjuna makes. We speak of the Bodhicitta as arising in this person or that person, and one might therefore think that there were in existence a number of Bodhicittas

– apparently a glorious plurality of Bodhicittas – arising in different people, making them all Bodhisattvas. In fact, it isn't so at all. Different thoughts (even if they are thoughts of the same thing) may arise in different people. But just as the Bodhicitta is not a 'thought' of Enlightenment, it is not an individual thing, is not anybody's individually, so there is no plurality of Bodhicittas arising in different people. *Your* thought of Enlightenment is *your* thought of Enlightenment, *my* thought of Enlightenment is *my* thought of Enlightenment; there are many thoughts. But *your* Bodhicitta is *my* Bodhicitta, and *my* Bodhicitta is *your* Bodhicitta; there is only one Bodhicitta.

The Bodhicitta is only one, and individuals in whom the Bodhicitta is said to have arisen participate in that one Bodhicitta, or manifest that one Bodhicitta, in varying degrees. The Mahāyāna writers bring in that well-worn but still beautiful illustration of the moon. In this illustration the Bodhicitta is likened to the moon. The Bodhicitta is reflected, as it were, in different people (i.e. it arises in different people) just as the moon is reflected variously in different bodies of water. There are many reflections, but only one moon; in the same way, many manifestations, but one Bodhicitta.

Though I have used the expression 'reflection', which is a bit static, we are not to think of the Bodhicitta in purely static terms. What is known in the Mahāyāna tradition as the 'Absolute Bodhicitta' – the Bodhicitta outside space and time – is identical with Reality itself. Being identical with Reality, the Absolute Bodhicitta is beyond change or, rather, is beyond the opposition between change and non-change. But this doesn't hold good with what is known in the tradition as the 'relative Bodhicitta'. The relative Bodhicitta is, as it were, an active force at work. This is why I prefer personally, if I have to translate the term Bodhicitta, to translate it as 'Will to Enlightenment' (bearing in mind that one is speaking of the relative, as distinct from the Absolute, Bodhicitta).

This Will to Enlightenment, though, is not an act of will of any individual. The Bodhicitta is not something which *I* will. Just as it is not *my* thought, it's not *my* will. The Bodhicitta is no more an act of anybody's individual will than it is anybody's individual thought. We might in fact – here we have rather to grope for words – think of the Bodhicitta as a sort of 'cosmic will' (I don't like to use this word 'will', but there's really no other). We might think of the Bodhicitta as a sort of cosmic will at work in the universe, in the direction of what we can only think of as universal redemption: the liberation, the Enlightenment, ultimately, of all sentient beings.

We might even think of the Bodhicitta as a sort of 'spirit of Enlightenment', immanent in the world, and leading individuals to higher and ever higher degrees of spiritual perfection. This being the case, it is clear that individuals do not possess the Bodhicitta. If you possess it, it's not the Bodhicitta. It's something else – your own thought or idea perhaps. The transcendental, non-individual, cosmic Bodhicitta you have missed. Individuals do not possess the Bodhicitta. We may say that it is the Bodhicitta that possesses individuals. Those of whom the Bodhicitta 'takes possession' (in whom the Bodhicitta arises) become Bodhisattvas. They live for the sake of Enlightenment; they strive to actualize, for the benefit of all, the highest potentialities that the universe contains.

How the Bodhicitta Arises

The Bodhicitta is said to arise as a result of a coalescence between two trends of experience which are generally considered to be contradictory. (In ordinary experience they are in fact contradictory, in the sense that you can't pursue both of them simultaneously.) We may describe these as the trend of withdrawal and the trend of involvement.

Reflection on the Faults of Conditioned Existence

The first trend represents the movement of total withdrawal from mundane things, which is renunciation in the extreme sense. One withdraws from the world: from worldly activities, worldly thoughts, worldly associations. This movement of withdrawal is said to be aided by a particular practice, which is called 'reflection on the faults of conditioned existence'. You reflect that conditioned existence, life within the round of existence, is not only not very satisfactory, it is profoundly unsatisfactory. It entails all sorts of experiences of an unpleasant nature: things one wants but can't get, people one likes whom one is separated from, things one doesn't want to do which one has to do. There is the whole wretched business of earning a living. There is attending to the physical body – feeding it, doctoring it when it gets sick. There is looking after one's family – husband, wife, children, relations. You feel that all this is too much and you have to get away from it all, out of it all. You desire to escape from the round of existence into nirvāṇa, into a state where you don't have all these things. You wish to get away from all the fluctuations and vicissitudes of this mundane life into the peace and rest of the Eternal.

Reflection on the Sufferings of Sentient Beings

The second trend, the trend of involvement, represents concern for living beings. One thinks, 'Yes, I would like to get out. That would be all right for *me*. But what about other people? What would happen to *them*? There are some who can't stand it even as well as I can. If I abandon them, how will *they* get out?' This trend is aided by 'reflection on the sufferings of sentient beings'. In the trend of withdrawal, you reflect on the faults of conditioned existence only so far as they affect you, but here you reflect on them as they affect other living beings. You reflect, therefore, on the sufferings of living beings.

You just have to look around at the people you know – all your friends and acquaintances – and reflect on all the troubles which they have. There may be someone who has lost their job and doesn't know what to do. Another person's marriage has broken up. Someone else has perhaps had a nervous breakdown. Someone has been bereaved, may have lost their husband or wife or their child. If you reflect, you realize that there is not a single person you know who is not suffering in some way. Even if they are happy (in the quite ordinary sense), there are still things that they have to bear: separation, illness, the weakness and tiredness of old age, and finally death, which they certainly don't want.

If you cast your gaze wider, you can reflect on how much suffering there is in so many parts of the world. There are wars. There are catastrophes of various kinds, such as floods or famines. People sometimes die in very horrible ways – you need only think about World War II and of people dying in concentration camps. You can cast your eye further still and think of animals, how they suffer, not only at the hands of other animals but at the hands of man. You can thus see that the whole world of living beings is involved in suffering – so much of it! When one reflects on the sufferings of sentient beings in this way, one thinks, 'How can I think simply in terms of getting out of it all? How can I think of getting away myself to some private nirvāṇa, which may be very satisfactory to me personally, but which doesn't help them?'

One thus experiences a sort of conflict – if one's nature is big enough to embrace the possibilities of such a conflict. On the one hand, one wants to get out; on the other, one wants to stay here. The trend of withdrawal is there; the trend of involvement is there. To choose *either* alternative is easy: it is easy either to withdraw into spiritual individualism or to remain involved in a worldly way. Many people do in fact take the easy solution, some choosing to get out, others choosing to remain in. Some get out into spiritual individualism, private spiritual experience. Others remain in the world, but in a purely secular sense, without much of a spiritual outlook.

Recollection of the Buddha

The point of what we are trying to explain here is that though contradictory, *both* of these trends – the trend of withdrawal and also the trend of involvement – must be developed in the spiritual life. We might say that the trend of withdrawal embodies the Wisdom aspect of the spiritual life, *prajñā*, and the trend of involvement embodies the Compassion aspect, *karuṇā*. Both of these are to be developed. That joint development is helped by what is known as 'Recollection of the Buddha'. One constantly bears in mind the ideal of unsurpassed, Perfect Enlightenment, Enlightenment for the benefit of all sentient beings, as exemplified most perfectly by Gautama the Buddha himself, the human and historical teacher.

What one has to do is not allow the tension between these two trends to relax. If one does that, then in a sense one is lost. Even though they are contradictory, one has to pursue both simultaneously. One has to get out and stay in, see the faults of conditioned existence while at the same time feeling the sufferings of sentient beings, develop both Wisdom and Compassion.

As one pursues both of these trends simultaneously, the tension builds up and up (it is, of course, not a psychological tension but a spiritual tension). It is built up until a point is reached when one can't go any further. When one reaches that point, something happens. What happens is difficult to describe, but we may provisionally describe it as an explosion. This means that as the result of the tension which has been generated by following these two contradictory trends simultaneously, there occurs a breakthrough into a higher dimension of spiritual consciousness, where the two trends – of withdrawal and involvement – are no longer two, not because they have been artificially amalgamated into one but because the plane on which their duality existed, or on which it was possible for them to be two things, has been transcended.

When one breaks through one has the experience of being simultaneously withdrawn and involved, 'out' of it and 'in' it at the same time. Now Wisdom and Compassion have become non-dual (one can say 'one' if one likes, but it is not an arithmetical 'one'). When the explosion occurs, when for the first time one is both withdrawn and involved, having both Wisdom and Compassion not as two things 'side by side' but as 'one' thing, then one may say that the Bodhicitta has arisen.

The Four Great Vows

According to the Buddhist tradition, one gives expression to this experience in the form of the 'Four Great Vows' of the Bodhisattva. Firstly, the Bodhisattva vows that he will deliver all beings from difficulties (this means difficulties not only of a spiritual nature, but even of a mundane nature). Secondly, he vows that he will destroy within his own mind and, through his advice, within the minds of other living beings, all spiritual defilements. Thirdly, he vows that he will learn the Dharma in all its aspects, practise it, realize it, and teach it to others. Fourthly, he vows that in all possible ways he will help to lead all beings in the direction of unsurpassed, Perfect Enlightenment.

Enlightenment, Eternity, and Time

We know, even from our ordinary experience of life, that there are many different angles, or points of view, from which we can look at the same thing. We can also look at one and the same object from different levels of existence, or reality. For instance, we can look at something from the standpoint of time and also from the standpoint of what we may call 'Eternity', above and beyond time, disconnected from time altogether. In the first case, when we see things in terms of space and time, we see them as processes. In the second case, when we see things in the dimension of Eternity, we see them as unchanging realities. (In using the word 'unchanging' I do not mean that those particular phenomena remain unchanged within the temporal process, but that they are outside time, above and beyond time, in a different dimension altogether.)

We are familiar with the main details of the life of the Buddha. We know that the Buddha was born in the Lumbini garden, we know about his education and how he left home. We know how he gained Enlightenment at the age of thirty-five, how he taught the Dharma, and how finally he passed away. But we don't always bear in mind one fact about the biography of the Buddha, which is that it deals, in a sense, with two quite different people (we may call them 'Siddhartha' and 'the Buddha'), who are divided from each other by the event of the Enlightenment.

The Buddha's Enlightenment was the central event of his life. But how do we think of this? We usually think – graphically – of the Enlightenment as a peak in the Buddha's life, of his life before the Enlightenment as a gentle slope up to the peak (his going forth, his meditation in the jungle, etc. mark stages on the ascent), and of his life after the Enlightenment perhaps as a gentle slope down from the peak. We think that after his Enlightenment the Buddha was more or less the same as he was before – except of course that he was Enlightened.

Had we ourselves been with the Buddha a few months before and a few months after he was Enlightened, we almost certainly would not have been able to perceive any difference in him. After all, we would have seen the same physical body, and probably the same clothes; he would have been speaking the same language and had the same general characteristics.

Therefore we tend to regard Enlightenment as a last finishing touch to a process which has been going on for a very long time, as the hair that turns the scale – that little difference that makes all the difference. But really it is not like that at all.

Enlightenment – the Buddha's or anybody else's – represents the point of intersection of time and Eternity. Strictly speaking, it is only a line which can intersect another line, and though we can represent time as a line, we can't represent Eternity as a line, so we can't really speak of Eternity intersecting time. We should perhaps rather think of time as a line which, instead of propagating itself indefinitely, at a given point just stops. At this 'point of intersection' the first line, time, is not intersected by another line but just stops. Or it disappears into a new dimension. We may compare time disappearing into the new dimension of Eternity to a river flowing into the ocean. This simile is rather hackneyed, but if one doesn't take it too literally it is still useful. We can possibly improve on it by imagining that the ocean is just over the horizon and therefore just out of sight. Then it seems as though the river just stops (at the horizon) or flows into nothingness. So time just comes to an end at Eternity, is succeeded by Eternity. And this is what we mean by Enlightenment. From the standpoint of time, Siddhartha becomes the Buddha, evolves into the Buddha. *But* from the standpoint of Eternity, Siddhartha ceases to exist, disappears – just like the river disappearing at the horizon – and the Buddha takes his place, or simply is there, because of course he has been there all the time.

The Story of Aṅgulimāla

The story of Aṅgulimāla[163] illustrates this matter of the two dimensions of time and Eternity. Aṅgulimāla was a famous bandit. He was living in a great forest, somewhere in central India. Aṅgulimāla had a rather unpleasant habit. He used to catch travellers who were passing through the forest and chop off their fingers. He kept all the fingers and strung them together into a garland, which he wore round his neck. It was because of this in fact that he was called Aṅgulimāla, which means 'one who has a garland of fingers' (*aṅguli* is 'finger' and *māla* is 'garland').

When the story begins the Buddha was about to pass through the forest. The villagers, who knew about Aṅgulimāla, told the Buddha of the danger and tried to dissuade him from going. But of course he ignored their warnings and set off. That very day, as it happens, Aṅgulimāla had being getting a bit desperate. He apparently had ninety-eight fingers at this time and wanted to have a hundred. His old mother was living with him in the forest. She used to cook for him – a devoted old soul. And he had just decided to have her finger, because he was fed up with waiting any longer – maybe she used to nag him a bit too. He had resolved to take her finger, so that then he would only need one more to have a hundred. But as soon as he saw the Buddha coming he changed his mind. He thought, 'I can always come back and chop off her finger. I'll go and get a finger from this monk.'

We are told that it was a beautiful afternoon. There was a very peaceful atmosphere. The only sound was that of the birds singing in the trees. The Buddha was walking slowly, meditatively, along the little trail that wound through the forest. Aṅgulimāla's plan was to creep up on the Buddha from behind, spring on him, and chop off a finger before he could protest or struggle. So he emerged from the shadows of the forest and stealthily started pursuing the Buddha.

He was following the Buddha for quite a while when he noticed that a rather odd thing was happening. Though he seemed to be moving much more quickly than the Buddha, the distance between them was not decreasing. The Buddha was there in front of him walking slowly along. He was behind moving much more quickly, but getting no nearer to the Buddha. So he quickened his pace until he was running along. But again, the Buddha was just the same distance in front, still strolling along, slowly and mindfully. When Aṅgulimāla realized what was happening he broke out into a terrific perspiration, with fright and bewilderment. He decided to make one last effort, a last dash. He summoned up all his strength and sprinted along. But yet again he got no closer to the Buddha, and if anything the Buddha seemed to be walking even more slowly.

In desperation Aṅgulimāla called out to the Buddha, 'Stand still!' The Buddha turned round and said, 'I am standing still. It is you who are moving.' So Aṅgulimāla, who despite his fear had considerable presence of mind, said, 'You are supposed to be a monk, a *śramaṇa*, how can you tell a lie? You say that you are standing still, yet I can't catch up with you even though I am running as fast as I can. How can you say that you are standing still?' The Buddha said, 'I am standing still, because I am standing in nirvāṇa. You are moving, because you are going round and round in the saṁsāra.' This was the Buddha's reply. Aṅgulimāla of course became the Buddha's disciple.

Aṅgulimāla could not catch up with the Buddha because the Buddha was moving – or standing still, which is the same thing here – in a different dimension. Aṅgulimāla, representing time, could not catch up with the Buddha, representing Eternity. However long time goes on, it never comes to a point within time where it catches up with Eternity. Aṅgulimāla could be running now, still, after 2,500 years, but he would not have caught up with the Buddha: the distance between them would be the same now as it was then.

The Great Death

To return to our main topic, we have seen that the attainment of Enlightenment represents entry into a *new* dimension of being, not a prolongation of the old one, however refined. After his Enlightenment under the Bodhi tree, the Buddha is a different, even a new, person.

We tend unfortunately to think of the Buddha's Enlightenment in terms of our own experience of life. In the course of *our* lives, over so many years, we undergo various experiences, learn different things, go to different places, and meet different people, but underneath we remain recognizably the same person. Perhaps we are the same person *now* that we were twenty or thirty years ago when we were a child. Very often this is the case. We do not succeed in outgrowing the attitudes of our early childhood, and we often remain deeply, dramatically, and sadly, conditioned by our infantile past. Any changes that take place in us in the course of our lives are comparatively superficial. We even encounter Buddhism and take refuge in the Buddha, but the change is not very deep.

But the Buddha's experience of Enlightenment was not like that. It didn't represent just a little, peripheral change in him, a change only on the surface. It was something much deeper and much more dramatic than that. It was more like the change that takes place as between two lives, when you die to one life and are reborn in another, and there is a great gap in between. The Enlightenment experience is more like death. In fact in some Buddhist traditions Enlightenment is called the 'great death'. When you are Enlightened, everything of the past dies, is annihilated, and you are completely reborn.

In the case of the Buddha, Siddhartha dies. It is not that Siddhartha is changed, improved, patched up a bit. Siddhartha is finished. Siddhartha dies at the foot of the Bodhi tree and the Buddha is born. The Buddha comes into existence *only* after the death of Siddhartha. We say that the Buddha is 'born', but it is not actually even like that. Really at that moment when Siddhartha dies, the Buddha is seen as having been alive all the time. (By 'all the time' we really mean above and beyond time, out of time altogether.)

Another important reflection of Buddhist thought, and of metaphysical thought in the West, is that time and space are not – as we usually think they are – things in themselves. We think of space as a sort of box within which things move about; we think of time as a sort of tunnel along which things move. But they are not really like that. Time and space are really forms of our perception: we perceive things under the form of time and under the form of space. When we see, or experience, things under these forms, through these 'spectacles', through these dimensions, we speak of them as phenomena. These phenomena make up the world of relative, conditioned existence, or what Buddhists call 'saṁsāra'. But when we enter the dimension of Eternity, we go beyond time and space, and therefore we go beyond phenomena – which are only realities as seen under the forms of time and space. We go beyond saṁsāra and, in the Buddhist idiom, we enter nirvāṇa, or, in the Hindu idiom, we go from darkness to light, from the unreal to the real, from death to immortality.

Enlightenment is often described as awakening to the truth of things. It is seeing things as they really are, not as they appear – seeing things in their truth, free from any veils; seeing things with perfect objectivity, without being influenced by any psychological conditionings. It is also spoken of in terms of 'becoming one with things', becoming one with Reality. The Buddha, the one who has awoken to this truth, the one who as it were exists out of time in the dimension of Eternity, may be regarded, therefore, as Reality itself in human form. The form is human, but the 'substance' is Reality. This is what is meant by saying that the Buddha is an 'Enlightened human being'. There is a human form, but there is not the ordinary conditioned human mind. In the place of the conditioned human mind, with all its prejudices, preconceptions, and limitations, there is the experience or the awareness of Reality itself. Therefore, the Buddha symbolizes, or represents, Reality in human form.

The Pathless One

The Buddha is an altogether distinct, indeed unique, type of human being, and as such he cannot be classified or categorized. This is the moral of the story of the Buddha's encounter, shortly after his Enlightenment, with Upaka, the naked ascetic.[164] Upaka tried to categorize the Buddha as a *deva*, a *yakṣa*, a *gandharva*, even as a human being, but the Buddha repudiated all those categories and said that inasmuch as he had transcended all the psychological conditionings on account of which he might have been called a *deva*, or *yakṣa*, or *gandharva*, or human being, he was simply a Buddha – one free from all those conditionings.

Often people want to categorize you. In India, especially in southern India, one of the first questions asked – anywhere, by anyone – is 'What is your caste?' If they can't classify you according to caste they don't know how to treat you. They don't know whether they can take water from your hand or not, whether they can get to know you or not, whether you might marry their daughter or not. All these things are very important.

It is just the same in the West, although here we are not so direct. People try to worm the same sort of information out of you. They ask you what sort of job you've got – from that they may try to work out your income. They ask you where you live, where you were born, where you were educated. By taking these various sociological readings, they can gradually narrow down the field, until they've 'got' you, until they feel that you are neatly pigeonholed.

But you can't do that with a Buddha (you can't really do it with an ordinary human being, though you can try and even succeed to a great extent). When Upaka found that he couldn't pin the Buddha down, he did not know what to do. According to the account, he just shook his head, said, 'Well, it may be so,' and went away. He couldn't categorize the Buddha.

We find the same idea – that the Buddha cannot be categorized – expressed in the first verse of the *'Buddhavagga'* of the *Dhammapada*, where the Buddha says:

Whose conquest is not to be undone,
Whom not even a bit of those conquered passions follows,
That enlightened one whose sphere is endless,
By what path will you trace him – that pathless one?[165]

The Buddha doesn't go on any particular path; he is like a bird flying through the sky. You cannot trace a bird by following its path in the sky – it doesn't leave any track there. You can't trace the Buddha because he belongs to a different dimension, the transcendental dimension, the dimension of Eternity.

The same idea is expressed again in the *Sutta-nipāta*, where the Buddha says:

There is no measuring of man
Won to the goal, whereby they'd say
His measure's so: that's not for him;
When all conditions are removed,
All ways of telling are removed.[166]

When all psychological conditionings are removed in a person you have no way of accounting for that person, and this is what the Buddha is like. The same idea is expressed more abstractly in four of the list of 'Fourteen Inexpressibles'. These four positions are: whether the Buddha existed after death, or not, or both, or neither. Some of the ancient Indians were quite obsessed with the question. They used to go to the Buddha and say, 'Please tell us, when you die will you go on living, or not, or both, or neither?' The Buddha always used to repudiate all four positions. He would say, 'It is inappropriate, it is inapplicable, to say of a Buddha that after death he will continue to exist; it is also inappropriate to say that after death he will cease to exist; it is inappropriate to say that he will continue to exist *and* cease to exist; and it is inappropriate to say that he will neither continue to exist nor cease to exist.' He would go on to say, 'All these are inapplicable and inappropriate because even during his lifetime – even when he sits there in a physical body – the Buddha is beyond all your classifications: one cannot say anything about him.'

The Buddha is the person about whom one cannot say anything, because he doesn't have anything; he isn't anything, in a sense. This is why in the *Sutta-nipaṭa* again, there is an epithet for an Enlightened being, *ākiñcañña*,[167] which is usually translated as 'man of nought' – one who *has* nothing because he *is* nothing. You cannot say anything about such a person. That is very baffling for the human mind.

Many of the Buddha's Enlightened disciples felt that there was something very mysterious about the Buddha, something which even they – who were themselves Enlightened – could not understand or fathom. There is a story about Śāriputra in this connection which is typical.[168] Śāriputra was once in the presence of the Buddha and, out of his excess of faith and devotion, said, 'Lord,

I think you are the greatest of all the Enlightened Ones who have ever existed, or who will ever exist, or who exist now.' The Buddha was neither pleased nor displeased by that. He did not say, 'What a marvellous disciple you are. How wonderfully well you understand me.' He just asked a question, 'Śāriputra, have you known all the Buddhas of the past?' Śāriputra replied, 'No, Lord.' Then the Buddha said, 'Do you know all the Buddhas of the future?' Śāriputra acknowledged that he didn't. The Buddha asked, 'Do you know all the Buddhas that now are?' Again Śāriputra had to admit that he didn't. So the Buddha asked, 'Do you even know me?' Śāriputra said, 'No, Lord.' Then the Buddha said, 'That being the case, how is it that your words are so bold and so grand?' This shows that even the wisest of the disciples, Śāriputra, did not succeed in fully fathoming the Buddha.

Rūpakāya and Dharmakāya

After the death of the Buddha this feeling on the part of the disciples that the Buddha was unfathomable, that even though they were Enlightened, presumably just as he was Enlightened, they couldn't really fathom him at all, found expression in a list of 'Ten Powers'[169] and 'Eighteen Special Attributes' which they attributed to him to mark him off from all the other merely Emancipated and Enlightened disciples.

All this crystallized eventually into a very important distinction that was made with regard to the Buddha. That is the distinction between what came to be called his *rūpakāya*, his physical, phenomenal appearance, and his *dharmakāya*, his true form, his essential form. *Rūpakāya* literally means 'form body' and *dharmakāya* means 'body of Truth' or 'body of Reality'. *Rūpakāya* is the Buddha as existing in time; *dharmakāya* is the Buddha as existing out of time, in the dimension of Eternity. It is the latter, the *dharmakāya*, that is the real body. This is clear, for instance, from the Buddha's admonition to Vakkali. Vakkali was a monk who was very devoted to the Buddha. He was fascinated by the appearance and the personality of the Buddha, so much so that he would spend all his time just sitting and looking at the Buddha. He didn't want a teaching; he didn't have any questions to ask; he just wanted to look at the Buddha. One day the Buddha called him and said, 'Vakkali, this physical body is not me. If you want to see me, see the Dharma, see the *dharmakāya*, see my true form.'[170] The same point of view is found in two famous verses of the *Diamond Sūtra*, where the Buddha says to Subhuti:

Those who by my form [i.e. my physical appearance]
did see me,
And those who followed me by voice
Wrong the efforts they engaged in,
Me those people will not see.

From the Dharma should one see the Buddhas,
From the Dharma-bodies comes their guidance.
Yet Dharma's true nature cannot be discerned,
And no one can be conscious of it as an object.[171]

Most of us, like Vakkali, try to see the Buddha in the wrong way. It is not that we should ignore the *rūpakāya*, the physical body, the form body, but we should take it as a symbol of the *dharmakāya*, the true form and the true body – a symbol of the Buddha as he is in his ultimate essence, above and beyond time, in Eternity.

The 'Goal' of Nirvāṇa

Most of our problems, if not all of them, really boil down to the issue of happiness and unhappiness. What do we usually do when, for some reason or another, we feel unhappy? What we *don't* usually do is ask ourselves why we feel unhappy. If we do ask at all, we ask only superficially, and we give ourselves only a superficial answer – in terms of symptoms, or externals. What we usually do is try to escape from the feeling of being unhappy. We feel unhappy and simply ricochet – or try to ricochet – from that state into the opposite state of being happy. This usually means grasping at some object or experience which we believe will give us the happiness which we lack and seek. In other words, what we usually do is set up happiness as a goal and strive to achieve it.

We try to get away from our experience of unhappiness and try to reach the goal of happiness. But here, as you know very well, we nearly always fail. After all, our whole life through, in one way or another, we are in search of happiness – no one is in search of misery. Everyone sets up happiness as a goal, but everyone fails to reach it. There is no one who could possibly say that he is so happy that he couldn't imagine himself being even a little happier. Most people, if they are honest with themselves, have to admit that their life is one of more or less unease and dissatisfaction, punctuated with little flashes of happiness and joy, which make them temporarily forget, if not their actual misery, at least their discomfort and discontent.

All this brings us to a most important principle, which is that the setting up of goals in this way is really a substitute for awareness, or for self-knowledge. If we feel unhappy, instead of trying to understand why, we set up the goal of being happy, in order to escape from the unhappiness. This is automatic, or instinctive. There is no awareness or self-knowledge in it at all.

We should not try to escape from ourselves. We should begin by staying with ourselves as we are. We should try to understand, much more deeply than just intellectually, why we are what we are. If we are suffering, accept the suffering, and understand why we are suffering. Or, as the case may be, if we are happy, accept the happiness (don't feel guilty about it), and understand why we are happy. This understanding is not something merely intellectual; it is something which has to go very deep down indeed. For some people this penetration, or insight, will come in the course of meditation. Meditation is not just fixing the mind on an object, nor just revolving a certain idea in the mind. Meditation involves, among other things, getting down to the bottom of one's own mind and illuminating one's mind from the bottom upwards. In other words, it involves exposing one's motives, the deep-seated causes of one's mental states, the causes of both one's joy and one's sorrow. In this way, in awareness, real growth will take place.

Now, to address the subject of nirvāṇa, it is possible to describe nirvāṇa in various ways. One of the verses of the *Dhammapada*, for instance, reads *'nibbāṇaṁ paramaṁ sukhaṁ'*,[172] 'Nirvāṇa is the Supreme Bliss'. Suppose you are feeling unhappy; suppose you are going through a rather difficult period, with lots of upsets, and are feeling rather low. Suppose then that in that state you hear a lecture, in the course of which it is stated that nirvāṇa is the Supreme Bliss. What is your reaction? You think to yourself, 'Good, that's just what I want,' and you decide to make nirvāṇa your goal. But this, we may say, is the height of unawareness. This has nothing to do with Buddhism at all. You have just latched on to nirvāṇa (labelled as 'Supreme Bliss'), because it happens to fit in with your subjective needs and feelings at that particular time. This is happening constantly. We try to use nirvāṇa in a quite unaware, unconscious way for the resolution of problems which can actually be resolved only through awareness.

In the situation that I have outlined what you should do is begin by recognizing your unhappiness. Face up to the fact! Allow yourself to say 'I am unhappy,' or 'I am miserable,' even 'I am absolutely miserable.' Don't try to cover it up. Don't try to put on that usual smile to make everybody think you are on top of the world. Be cheerful with other people, certainly; don't get them down with your gloom. But at least don't disguise the fact of your unhappiness from yourself. Recognize yourself as an unhappy self – to begin with. Study this unhappy self. Live with it side by side. Don't try to be rid of it. Ask yourself, 'What is making me unhappy? What is the source of it?' Don't clutch at a way out of your misery. Don't too quickly or unconsciously try to set up a goal of non-misery, of happiness, even in the form of nirvāṇa. Try to see more and more clearly what it is in yourself that is upsetting you and making you miserable. If you can do that, you will be able to see that there is some possibility that gradually, eventually, nirvāṇa will be attained. Nirvāṇa, however, will certainly not be attained by using the idea of nirvāṇa – as 'Supreme Bliss' or in any other form – as an escape from unhappiness, without being aware of what the cause of that unhappiness is. It is the awareness, the self-knowledge, which is all important.

Perhaps at this stage we can indulge in a little paradox and say that the goal of Buddhism consists in being completely aware, at all levels, of why we want to reach a goal; or it consists in awareness of our need to reach a goal. Going a little further, we can say that nirvāṇa consists really in the complete awareness of why we want to reach nirvāṇa: if we understand fully and completely why we want to reach nirvāṇa, then we've reached nirvāṇa. We can even say that the unaware person is in need of a goal but, on account of his unawareness, is unable to formulate a (true) goal, whereas an aware person, on account of his awareness, *is* able to formulate a goal, but doesn't need it. That is really the position.

If I had given here a conventional account of nirvāṇa, stating that nirvāṇa is 'this' or 'that', you would have accepted or rejected this or that aspect of nirvāṇa in accordance with your own largely unconscious needs. If you feel an unconscious need for happiness, and I had said that nirvāṇa is Supreme Bliss, you would have latched on to that and settled down into it, without really realizing what you were doing. If, on the other hand, you are rather sensitive to your lack of knowledge and understanding, and I had said that nirvāṇa is a state of complete Illumination, again half-consciously you would have latched on to that. In the same way, if you feel that your life is constricted, that you have no freedom, if perhaps you are tied down to a job or a family, and I had mentioned that nirvāṇa is Emancipation, you would have thought, 'That is what I want.' Whatever I had said, you would have set up a goal in this half-conscious way, without trying to understand why you were unhappy, or ignorant, or tied down. You would have simply used nirvāṇa as a semi-conscious stop-gap, which would not, of course, have been very helpful.

Enlightenment

Buddhist tradition, of all schools, speaks of Enlightenment as comprising mainly three things. To begin with, Enlightenment is spoken of as a state of pure, clear – even radiant – Awareness. Some schools go so far as to say that in this state of awareness the subject–object duality is no longer experienced. There is no 'out there', no 'in here'. That distinction of subject and object is entirely transcended. There is only one continuous, pure, clear Awareness, extending as it were in all directions, pure and homogeneous. It is, moreover, an Awareness of things *as they really are*, which is, of course, not things in the sense of objects, but things as, so to speak, transcending the duality of subject and object.

Hence this pure, clear Awareness is also spoken of as an Awareness of Reality, and therefore also as a state of Knowledge. This Knowledge is not knowledge in the ordinary sense (the knowledge that functions within the framework of the subject–object duality). It is rather a state of direct, unmediated spiritual Vision that sees all things directly, clearly, vividly, and truly. It is a spiritual vision – even a transcendental vision – which is free from all delusion, all misconception, all wrong, crooked thinking, all vagueness, all obscurity, all mental conditioning, and all prejudice. First of all, then, Enlightenment is this state of pure, clear Awareness, this state of Knowledge or Vision.

Secondly, and no less importantly, Enlightenment is spoken of as a state of intense, profound, overflowing Love and Compassion. Sometimes this love is compared to the love of a mother for her only child. This comparison occurs, for instance, in a famous Buddhist text called the *Mettā Sutta*, the 'Discourse of Loving Kindness'.[173] In this discourse the Buddha says, 'Just as a mother protects her only son even at the cost of her own life, so should one develop a mind of all-embracing love towards all living beings.' This is the sort of attitude that we must cultivate. You notice that the Buddha does not just talk about all human beings, but all *living* beings: all that breathes, all that moves, all that is sentient. This is how the Enlightened mind feels. And that Love and Compassion consists, we are further told, in a heartfelt desire – a deep, burning desire – for their well-being and happiness: a desire that all beings should be set free from suffering, from all difficulties, that they should grow and develop, and that ultimately they should gain Enlightenment. Love and Compassion of this kind – infinite, overflowing, boundless, directed towards all living beings – is part of Enlightenment too.

Thirdly, Enlightenment consists in a state, or experience, of inexhaustible mental and spiritual Energy. This is very well exemplified by an incident in the life of the Buddha himself. As you may know, he gained Enlightenment at the age of thirty-five, and he continued teaching and communicating with others until the ripe old age of eighty, although his physical body eventually became frail. On one occasion he said 'My body is just like an old, broken-down cart, which has been repaired many times. But my mind is as vigorous as ever. Even if I had to be carried from place to place on a litter, if anyone came to me, I would still be able to teach him. My intellectual and spiritual vigour is undiminished, despite the enfeebled state of my body.'[174] So Energy is characteristic of the state of Enlightenment. We could say that the state of Enlightenment is one of tremendous Energy continually bubbling forth, one of absolute Spontaneity, one of uninterrupted Creativity. In a nutshell, we may say that the state of Enlightenment is a state of perfect, unconditioned Freedom from all subjective limitations.

This, then, is what is meant by Enlightenment, as it is understood in the Buddhist tradition – so far, at least, as Enlightenment can be described, so far as its different aspects can be tabulated in this way. What really happens is that knowledge passes into love and compassion, love and compassion into energy, energy into knowledge, and so on. We cannot really split any one aspect off from the others. Nonetheless, we are traditionally given this 'tabulated' account of Enlightenment, just to convey some hint of the experience, just to give some little idea, or feeling, of what it is like. If we want to have a better idea than this, we shall have to read perhaps some more extended, poetic account, preferably one found in the Buddhist scriptures; or we shall have to take up the practice of meditation, and try to get at least a glimpse of the state of Enlightenment as we meditate. So when Buddhism speaks of Enlightenment, of Buddhahood or nirvāṇa, this is what it means: it means a state of supreme Knowledge, Love and Compassion, and Energy.

Appendices

Further Reading

The Buddha

G. Bays (trans.), *The Voice of the Buddha (Lalitavistara)*, Dharma Publishing, USA

M. Carrithers, *The Buddha*, Oxford University Press, 1983

L.M. Joshi, *Discerning the Buddha*, Motilal Banarsidass, 1983

Bhikkhu Ñāṇamoli, *The Life of the Buddha*, Buddhist Publication Society, Kandy (Sri Lanka) 1978

Sangharakshita, *Who is the Buddha?*, Windhorse, Glasgow 1994

H.W. Schumann *The Historical Buddha*, Arkana, 1989

The Dharma

D.J. Kalupahana, *A History of Buddhist Philosophy*, University of Hawaii Press, 1992

Alex Kennedy (Dharmachari Subhuti), *The Buddhist Vision*, Rider, 1975

Sangharakshita, *The Meaning of Orthodoxy in Buddhism*, Windhorse, Glasgow 1986

Sangharakshita, *Mind – Reactive and Creative*, Windhorse, Glasgow 1989

Sangharakshita, *Vision and Transformation: A Guide to the Buddha's Noble Eightfold Path*, Windhorse, Glasgow 1990

The Sangha

H.B. Aronson, *Love and Sympathy in Theravada Buddhism*, Motilal Banarsidass, 1986

S. Dutt, *Early Buddhist Monachism*, Munshiram Manoharlal, 1984

C.S. Prebish, *Buddhist Monastic Discipline: The Sanskrit Pratimoksa Sutras of the Mahasamghikas and Mula-sarvastivadins*, Pennsylvania State Press, 1975

Sangharakshita, *Going For Refuge*, Windhorse, Glasgow 1986

Sangharakshita, *The History of My Going for Refuge*, Windhorse, Glasgow 1988

Sangharakshita, *Forty-Three Years Ago*, Windhorse, Glasgow 1993

Dharmachari Subhuti, *Buddhism for Today*, Windhorse, Glasgow 1988

Morality

D. Keown, *The Nature of Buddhist Ethics*, Macmillan, 1992

Sangharakshita, *The Ten Pillars of Buddhism*, Windhorse, Birmingham, 1996

Sangharakshita, 'Aspects of Buddhist Morality', in *The Priceless Jewel*, Windhorse, Glasgow 1993

Meditation

E. Conze (trans.), *Buddhist Meditation*, Harper and Row, 1956

Kamalashila, *Meditation: the Buddhist Way of Tranquillity and Insight*, Windhorse, Glasgow 1992

Nyānaponika Thera, *The Five Mental Hindrances*, Buddhist Publication Society, Kandy (Sri Lanka) 1978

Nyānaponika Thera, *The Four Sublime States*, Buddhist Publication Society, Kandy (Sri Lanka)

Nyānaponika Thera, *The Heart of Buddhist Meditation*, Rider, 1983

Paramananda, *Change Your Mind: A Practical Guide to Buddhist Meditation*, Windhorse, Birmingham 1996

P. Vajirañāna Mahathera, *Buddhist Meditation in Theory and Practice*, Buddhist Missionary Society, Kuala Lumpur 1975

Wisdom

Sangharakshita, *The Three Jewels*, Windhorse, Glasgow 1991

Sangharakshita, *A Survey of Buddhism* (7th edition), Windhorse, Glasgow 1993

Sangharakshita, *Wisdom Beyond Words*, Windhorse, Glasgow 1993

Śāntideva, *The Bodhicayāvatāra*, Kate Crosby and Andrew Skilton (trans.), Oxford University Press, 1996

Additional Reading

H. Bechert and R Gombrich, *The World of Buddhism*, Thames and Hudson, 1984

Bhadantacariya Buddhaghosa, *The Path of Purification (Visuddhimagga)*, Bhikkhu Ñānamoli (trans.), 2 vols, Shambhala, Boulder & London 1976

H. Dayal, *The Bodhisattva Doctrine in Buddhist Sanskrit*

Literature, Motilal Banarsidass, 1970
H.V. Guenther, *Philosophy and Psychology in the Abhidharma,* Motilal Banarsidass, (no date)
Peter Harvey, *An Introduction to Buddhism,* Cambridge University Press, 1990
Joanna Macy, *Mutual Causality in Buddhism and General Systems Theory*, SUNY, 1991
R.H. Robinson and W.L. Johnson, *The Buddhist Religion,* Wadsworth, 1982
Andrew Skilton, *A Concise History of Buddhism,* Windhorse, Birmingham 1994
Paul Williams, *Mahāyāna Buddhism,* Routledge, 1989
A.K. Warder, *Indian Buddhism,* Motilal Banarsidass, 1970

All the material in this book is taken from talks and lectures given by Sangharakshita. The lectures are available on audio cassette tape from Dharmachakra Tapes, P.O. Box 50, Cambridge, CB1 3BG

Notes

Introduction

1 See Sangharakshita, tape lecture no. 17: 'Is Religion Necessary?', Dharmachakra, London 1966.

2 I.B. Horner (trans.), *The Middle Length Sayings* (*Majjhima-Nikāya*), Pali Text Society, London 1967, Vol.I, 134–5.

3 Since this lecture was delivered in 1966, Sangharakshita has expounded the Dharma much more fully and consistently in evolutionary terms. Though 'the Higher Evolution' is not a traditional Buddhist term, the idea of spiritual development as an evolution of consciousness is consistent with and implicit in the Buddha's teaching.

The whole process of the development of life, from the primeval stirrings at its origins right up to the supremely developed consciousness of the Enlightened mind, can be seen as one long evolution, which can be divided into two distinct stages, the Lower Evolution and the Higher Evolution. The Lower Evolution denotes the process of development of life from its beginnings aeons back in prehistory up to the emergence of human life. The Higher Evolution begins from a certain level of self (or reflexive) consciousness and continues right up to Enlightenment itself. The Lower Evolution is what we have developed out of; the Higher Evolution covers what we can develop into, if we so wish.

It cannot be said that there is a definite point at which the Lower Evolution ends and the Higher Evolution begins. The junction of the two divisions is seen as a sort of broad band in which a certain degree of self-consciousness is developed, the kind of consciousness which enables man not only to be aware of the world around him but also to be aware that he is aware; with it, as the name implies, he reflects back and observes himself. This distinguishes him from animals which are only equipped with simple or sense consciousness.

The individual human being equipped with a sufficient degree of self-consciousness is able, if he wishes, to undertake the spiritual life, to embark on the process of the Higher Evolution, from the stage at which he finds himself, right up to Enlightenment itself. Thus, whereas the Lower Evolution is a biological and collective process, the Higher Evolution is an evolution of consciousness and can only be undertaken as a result of individual choice; progress can result only from individual effort. The Lower Evolution is covered by sciences such as physics, biology, and chemistry, and the Higher Evolution by psychology, philosophy, and religion.

For a detailed study of the Higher Evolution, see Sangharakshita's two series of tape lectures: *The Higher Evolution of Man* (nos. 75–82) and *Aspects of the Higher Evolution of the Individual* (nos. 83–90), Dharmachakra, London 1969 and 1970 respectively. Also see Robin Cooper (Ratnaprabha), *The Evolving Mind*, Windhorse, Birmingham 1996.

4 Shin Buddhism is one of the main groups of schools of Buddhism in Japan; it is a branch of the Indo-Chinese Mahāyāna tradition. In Shin, there is no effort to achieve the goal of Enlightenment; instead the devotee surrenders self to 'other power', that is to Amitābha, or Amida, the Buddha of Infinite Light. (For further details, see pp.53ff.) Such surrender leads to rebirth in Amitābha's Pure Land, Sukhāvatī (the 'Land of Bliss'). Shin devotees revere *The Larger and Smaller Sukhāvatī-vyūha Sūtras* and *The Amitāyur-dhyāna Sūtra*. See *Buddhist Mahāyāna Texts*, ed. E.B. Cowell and others, Dover Publications Inc., New York 1969.

5 Henri de Lubac, *Aspects of Buddhism*, G.R. Lamb (trans.), Sheed & Ward, London 1953.

6 For a full account of the importance of Going for Refuge, see pp.103ff; Sangharakshita, *The History of My Going for Refuge*, Windhorse, Glasgow 1988; and Sangharakshita, *Going for Refuge*, Windhorse, Glasgow 1986.

7 For a brief historical account of the spread of Buddhism, see Edward Conze, *A Short History of Buddhism*, Allen & Unwin, London 1982.

8 For a detailed account of the Pali Canon, the Chinese Tripiṭaka, and the Tibetan scriptures, see Sangharakshita, *The Eternal Legacy*, Tharpa, London 1985.

9 See Sangharakshita, *A Survey of Buddhism* (7th edition), Windhorse, Glasgow 1993, pp.355ff.

The Buddha

10 There are numerous accounts of the life of the Buddha. A very useful one, consisting mainly of passages from the Pali Canon stitched together by the author's own connecting threads, is *The Life of the Buddha*, trans. & arr. by Bhikkhu Ñāṇamoli, Buddhist Publication Society, Ceylon 1978. A poetic account of the life up to and including the Enlightenment is Aśvaghoṣa's *The Buddhacarita or Acts of the Buddha*, ed. E.H. Johnston, Oriental Books Reprint Corporation, New Delhi 1972. A more recent account is H. Saddhatissa's *The Life of the Buddha*, Mandala Books, Unwin Paperbacks, London 1976.

11 H.G. Wells, *An Outline of History*, Waverley Book Co. Ltd, London 1920, section xxvi.

12 See Aśvaghoṣa, op.cit., Canto iii; also *The Mahāvastu*, J.J. Jones (trans.), Luzac & Co. Ltd, London 1952, Vol. II, section 150.

13 I.B. Horner (trans.), *The Middle Length Sayings* (*Majjhima-Nikāya*) Vol. I, no.12: *Mahāsīhanāda-sutta*, Pali Text Society, London 1976.

14 F.L. Woodward (trans.), *Some Sayings of the Buddha*, The Buddhist Society, London 1974, pp.7–9; *Saṁyutta-Nikāya*, vv.421–3, Pali Text Society, London 1930.

15 *Aṅguttara-Nikāya* II, 37–9, quoted in *Buddhist Texts Through the Ages*, ed. E. Conze, I.B. Horner, etc., Harper & Row, New York 1954, pp. 104–5.

16 For an introduction to Jung's theory of the archetypes of the Collective Unconscious, see Jolande Jacobi, *The Psychology of C.G. Jung*, Routledge & Kegan Paul, London 1962; also, Frieda Fordham, *An Introduction to Jung's Psychology*, Penguin, London 1964.

17 A famous quotation from the Smaragdine Tablet, an ancient alchemical document ascribed to Hermes Trismegistus states the 'Hermetic correspondence' between higher and lower levels of reality: 'That which is above is like that which is below and that which is below is like that which is above, to accomplish the miracles of one thing.' For more information on Hermes Trismegistus and his work, see E.J. Holmyard, *Alchemy*, Penguin, Harmondsworth 1957.

18 See Note 10 above.

19 *Jātakas* (literally 'belonging to, or connected with, what has happened') and *Avadānas* (literally 'glorious or heroic deeds') are stories illustrating the workings of the law of karma, showing how the spiritual stature of the Buddha and his disciples is consequent upon their skilful actions in former lives. The *Jātakas* are devoted mainly to the previous lives of the Buddha, in which the Bodhisatta practises the Perfections. They incorporate much material from Indian folklore in the form of fables, fairy tales, and so on. In the canonical *Jātakas*, the Buddha is invariably a wise ruler or famous teacher; in the non-canonical stories, he is also depicted as an animal. The *Avadānas* deal mainly with the careers of the Buddha's disciples or famous Buddhist figures. See Sangharakshita, *The Eternal Legacy*, Tharpa, London 1985, pp.55–6.

20 Nāgārjuna, the author of *The Precious Garland*, flourished in the second century CE in India. He is credited with establishing the doctrinal basis of the Mahāyāna and in particular is regarded as the founder of the Mādhyamīka School. Legend has it that he descended to the depths of the ocean to receive the Perfection of Wisdom teaching from the king of the *nāgas*.

21 Padmasambhava was a great Indian teacher who was mainly responsible, in a short visit, for establishing Buddhism in Tibet in the eighth century CE. His life story is made up almost entirely of miraculous events, not least of which is his birth from a

great lotus flower. The highly symbolic but deeply stirring account of his life can be read in Yeshe Tsogyal's *The Life and Liberation of Padmasambhava*, Dharma Publishing, Emeryville, USA 1978.

22 Milarepa was a Tibetan Buddhist master of the eleventh century CE from whom the various Kagyu lineages are descended. He is famous for his asceticism, living on nettles in a cave in the snow-mountains and wearing only a thin cotton garment. His songs and the stories of the circumstances under which they were sung provide some of the best loved literature of Buddhist Tibet. Tibetan Buddhism in general and the Kagyus in particular stress the lineage stretching from disciple to guru back through many generations to such great figures as Milarepa and even to archetypal Buddhas like Vajrādhara. ṣGam.po.pa was one of Milarepa's principal disciples. Milarepa's story can be read in Lobsang P. Lhalungpa (trans.), *The Life of Milarepa*, Dutton, New York 1977. His songs are contained in Garma C.C. Chang (trans.), *The Hundred Thousand Songs of Milarepa*, Vols. I & II, Shambhala, Boulder & London 1977.

23 *Koṭi*: 'an extremely high numeral, representing approximately the figure of a hundred thousand'; *Pali English Dictionary*, ed. T.W. Rhys Davids & William Stede, Pali Text Society, London 1979.

24 See J.J. Jones (trans.), *Mahāvastu*, Luzac & Co. Ltd, London 1952, Vol. III, section 115.

25 The Tantras are the scriptures which pertain to the Vajrayāna, the third of the three *yānas* in the development of Buddhism in India. (Section 8 of *A Survey of Buddhism* gives a succinct account of these three phases.) The Vajrayāna eventually spread to Tibet and flourished there. Generally speaking, the Tantras were the last Buddhist discourses to be committed to writing; it is probable that even now many are only in oral, and not written, circulation. They are among the more esoteric Buddhist texts, concerned with spiritual practice rather than doctrinal principles.

See *The Eternal Legacy*, op. cit., ch.16; Sangharakshita, *A Survey of Buddhism* (7th edition), Windhorse, Glasgow 1993, pp.406–426; and Lama Anagarika Govinda, *The Foundations of Tibetan Mysticism*, Century, London 1987.

26 In Tantric Buddhism, the term *'yuganaddha'* (Sanskrit *yug* = 'yoke') denotes the unification of opposites in the experience of Enlightenment. It signifies the unification of intense bliss and very clear, penetrating Insight, or the inseparability of Wisdom (*prajñā*) and Compassion (*karuṇā*) as complementary aspects of the Enlightened mind.

27 The incident of the Buddha's teaching of the Abhidharma is referred to in 'The Expositor' of the Pali Canon; see *The Eternal Legacy*, op. cit., p.71. The descent to earth by means of a magnificent staircase is described in Rev. P. Bigandet's *The Life or Legend of Gaudama, the Buddha of the Burmese*, Delhi 1971, Vol. 1, p.225.

28 The Book of Genesis, Chapter 28.

29 Shamanism is the primitive religion of the Ural-Altaic peoples of Siberia, in which all the good and evil of life are thought to be brought about by spirits which can be influenced only by a Shaman, a witch-doctor or priest figure.

30 See *A Survey of Buddhism*, op. cit., p.50.

31 *'Vajra'* (Sanskrit) literally means 'diamond' or 'thunderbolt'. In Indian mythology, the *vajra* represents the natural phenomenon of lightning and is wielded by Indra, the king of the gods; it is similar to the thunderbolt wielded by Zeus, the king of the gods, in Greek mythology. The *vajra* is also like a diamond in that it can cut through anything but is itself indestructible. In the Tantric phase of Buddhism, known as the 'Vajrayāna', the *vajra* became a symbol for the nature of Reality, for *'śūnyatā'* (see Note 57 below). The practice of prefixing terms, names, places and so on by *vajra* (such as in *'vajracarya'*, *'vajracitta'*) represents the conscious attempt to recognize the transcendental aspect of all phenomena. The *vajra* is also extensively used in the rituals of the

Tantra and various figures in Tantric iconography – the two most famous being Vajrapāṇi and Vajrasattva – are represented wielding or holding the *vajra*.

For further information on the symbolism of the *vajra*, see Sangharakshita, tape lecture no.105: 'The Symbolism of the Sacred Thunderbolt or Diamond Sceptre of the Lamas', Dharmachakra, London 1972.

32 Sangharakshita, *The Three Jewels*, Windhorse, Glasgow 1991, Ch.IV deals briefly with this subject.

33 The incident of the Buddha's victory over Māra is mentioned in several texts, for example in the *Ariyapariyesana-sutta, The Middle Length Sayings* (I.B. Horner (trans.), *Majjhima-Nikāya*), Pali Text Society, London 1967, i. 167; T.W. Rhys Davids (trans.), *The Book of the Kindred Sayings* (*Saṁyutta-Nikāya*), Pali Text Society, London 1979, Pt. I, Ch. 4; *The Buddhacarita or Acts of the Buddha*, E.H. Johnston, Munshiram Manoharlal, New Delhi 1972, Canto xiii; G. Bays (trans.), *The Voice of the Buddha: the Beauty of Compassion* (*Lalita-vistara*), Dharma Publishing, Oakland 1983, Vol. II, Ch.21.

34 'Bodhisatta' (Sanskrit *Bodhisattva*) literally means 'Enlightenment Being'. The term Bodhisatta is used in the *Jātakas* (see Note 19 above) to refer to the Buddha in his previous lives. The term Bodhisattva occurs in all three *yānas* or traditions of Buddhism. The term has both denotative and connotative meanings. It denotes a being (*sattva*) totally orientated towards Enlightenment (*bodhi*), with the connotation that that Enlightenment is for the sake of all beings. This connotation was particularly stressed in the Mahāyāna, which is sometimes referred to as the *Bodhisattva-yāna*, especially as contrasted with the Hīnayāna and its ideal of the Arhant who, at least according to the Mahāyāna, sought Enlightenment for himself alone. This stressing of the altruistic and compassionate aspects of Buddhahood by the Mahāyāna seemingly developed in response to a perceived reductionism of the Hīnayāna schools, in particular its literalism, ethical formalism, and bias towards a purely conceptual approach to spiritual practice.

See Sangharakshita, *A Survey of Buddhism* (7th edition), Windhorse, Glasgow 1993, chapter 2.

35 See *The Voice of the Buddha: the Beauty of Compassion*, (*Lalita-vistara*), op. cit., pp.481–2.

36 In the Hīnayāna, the Perfections are the moral observances which the Buddha has practised and brought to perfection in the course of his thousands of lives as a Bodhisatta; they are an essential ingredient in his preparation for Buddhahood. In the Mahāyāna, the practising of the 'Six' or 'Ten Perfections' is the chief of four courses of conduct which the Bodhisattva has to follow in his spiritual career.

37 The word *'mudrā'* (Sanskrit) literally means 'gesture' or 'seal'. A *mudrā* is a symbolic gesture of the hands either performed in the course of a ritual or depicted iconographically in the statues and pictures of Buddhas, Bodhisattvas, or other eminent Buddhist figures. The *mudrā* signifies the expression, by the gesture of the hands, down to the finger tips – the furthest extension of one's physical being – of what has been inwardly realized and experienced, just as the sap rising up the trunk of a tree spreads through all the branches and eventually penetrates even the tiniest twig.

38 I.B. Horner (trans.), *The Book of the Discipline (Vinaya-Piṭaka)*, Vol. IV (*Mahā-vagga*), Pali Text Society, London 1982 (*Sacred Books of the Buddhists*, Vol.XIV), I, 5.

39 Ibid., I, 3.

40 For the position, names, and significance of the psychic centres, see diagrams and text in *Foundations of Tibetan Mysticism*, op. cit., pp.138–146. Traditionally, Buddhism is not concerned with the stimulation of the lower centres but rather with the three higher centres through which, in the course of meditation and other spiritual practices, the forces of the four lower centres are sublimated and transformed.

41 See books referred to in Note 16 above.

42 For more on *ḍākinīs* in general, see Note 51 and Note 140 below. Here, together with the guru and the *yidam*, the *ḍākinī* is one of the three esoteric Refuges which, in the Vajrayāna, correspond to the three exoteric Refuges of Buddha, Dharma, and Sangha. The guru, the spiritual teacher, is the embodiment of Buddhahood. The *yidam*, literally 'Oath-Bound One' (corresponding to the Indian *iṣṭa devatā* or 'chosen deity') is the Buddha or Bodhisattva figure one meditates on, thus representing the Dharma in one's actual experience. The *ḍākinī*, corresponding to the Sangha, is the spiritual companion, usually, though not necessarily, in the sense of a symbolic figure who inspires the devotee to further growth and development.

43 As distinct from the creative mind. See p.71.

44 The Five Mental Poisons are craving, hatred, distraction, conceit, and ignorance. (Jealousy is sometimes added.)

45 For detailed information on the term 'karma' (Pali *kamma*) see Lama Anagarika Govinda, *The Psychological Attitude of Early Buddhist Philosophy*, Rider, London 1961; Sangharakshita, *The Three Jewels*, Windhorse, Glasgow 1991, Chs. 10 and 12; and Sangharakshita, *Who is the Buddha?*, Windhorse, Glasgow 1994, pp.99–121.

46 The Wheel of Life is an important symbol in Tantric Buddhism. See pp.71ff.; also Alex Kennedy (Dharmachari Subhuti), *The Buddhist Vision*, Rider, London 1985.

47 See Sangharakshita, *The Drama of Cosmic Enlightenment*, Windhorse, Glasgow 1993, pp.143–167.

48 Scripture of the Lotus Blossom of the Fine Dharma (The Lotus *Sūtra*), translated from the Chinese by Leon Hurvitz, New York 1976; or Bunnō Katō etc, (trans.), *The Threefold Lotus Sūtra*, Weatherhill/Kosei, New York/Tokyo 1978.

49 The Pure Land is a realm of great beauty and delight where everything is conducive to spiritual progress. It is conceived by a Bodhisattva when he vows that when he gains supreme Enlightenment he will create a realm around him and that all those who supplicate him will be reborn there. The most well-known of these Pure Lands is Sukhāvatī, the Pure Land of the Buddha Amitābha. His realm is described in the *Sukhāvatī-vyūha Sūtras* (see Sangharakshita, *The Eternal Legacy*, Tharpa, London 1985, Ch. 11, for a survey of this literature); there is a lengthy and representative extract from one of the *Sukhāvatī-vyūha Sūtras* in *Buddhist Scriptures*, ed. E. Conze, Penguin, Harmondsworth 1959, pp.232ff. Some account of the theory of the Pure Land may be found in Sangharakshita, *The Inconceivable Emancipation*, Windhorse, Birmingham 1995, pp.25–42.

50 In all the spiritual traditions within Buddhism great importance is attached to what may be described as the heroic virtues, that is to say, courage, self-reliance, energy, initiative and so on. In the West we tend to think of the spiritual life primarily in terms of developing the more passive, so-called 'feminine' virtues: love, compassion, patience, sympathy, tolerance, gentleness. But the heroic virtues are no less important, and perhaps, in some ways, even more so.

51 The word '*ḍākinī*' is derived from a Sanskrit root meaning 'direction', 'space', 'sky'. The masculine form of the word is '*ḍāka*'. Rendered into Tibetan as '*khandroma*', it is usually translated as 'sky-walker' or 'walker in space'. Empty space represents absence of obstruction, freedom of movement. A *ḍākinī* is a being who enjoys such freedom. 'Sky' also represents mind in its Absolute aspect; the *ḍākinī* therefore represents that which moves about freely in the mind, the energies of the mind itself. In this sense the *ḍākinīs* symbolize powerful energies rising up from the depths of the mind. In Tantric Buddhism there are three orders of *ḍākinī*: (a) the *ḍākinī* as female Buddha form; (b) the *ḍākinī* as embodiment of one's own upsurging spiritual energies; (c) the *ḍākinī* as a spiritual companion. The third order represents the esoteric, Tantric form of the third of the Three Refuges, that is, the Sangha or Spiritual Community.

See Sangharakshita, tape lecture no.107: 'The

Symbolism of the Cremation Ground and the Celestial Maidens', Dharmachakra, London 1972.

52 Edward Conze (trans.), *The Perfection of Wisdom in Eight Thousand Lines and Its Verse Summary*, Four Seasons Foundation (Wheel Series 1), Bolinas 1973.

53 Saṁsāra (Pali and Sanskrit): literally 'faring on, a flow or stream (of becoming)'. In ancient Hindu texts it means to roam through or to pass through a succession of states. In Buddhist usage it came to mean the perpetual repetition of birth and death in the three worlds (see p.135) and the six realms of existence (see pp.75ff). Being the opposite of nirvāṇa, saṁsāra is, from the objective point of view, the conditioned as distinct from the Unconditioned, or the mundane as distinct from the transcendental; from the subjective point of view, it is bondage as distinct from Liberation: the purpose of the spiritual life is to escape from the bonds of saṁsāra into the perfect freedom of nirvāṇa. Saṁsāra and nirvāṇa can also be seen as two possible modes of being in one and the same Reality (see Sangharakshita, *A Survey of Buddhism* (7th edition), Windhorse, Glasgow 1993, Ch.1, section 14), saṁsāra being the reactive mode, nirvāṇa the irreversibly creative mode (see p.71). The Hīnayāna tended to speak in terms of two discrete states and of passing from one state into the other, from a real saṁsāra to a real nirvāṇa, whereas the Mahāyāna taught that saṁsāra and nirvāṇa are mere thought-constructions, that the discrimination between the two is, ultimately, an illusion, and that Liberation consists not in passing from one realm to another but in realizing the essential non-difference between them.

54 Tantra: literally 'something woven or elaborated'. In Buddhism a Tantra is a particular type of discourse or text distinct from the more commonly known 'sūtra'. 'Tantrism', 'the Tantra', and 'Tantrayāna' are alternative titles of the Vajrayāna or Diamond Way, the third of the three *'yānas'* of Buddhism (see Note 25 above) because it is the Vajrayāna which is intimately associated with the use of the Tantras.

For more detail on the Tantra, see *The Eternal Legacy*, op. cit., Ch. 16; *A Survey of Buddhism*, op. cit., pp.406–426; also Lama Anagarika Govinda, *The Foundations of Tibetan Mysticism*, Century, London 1987.

55 A reference to the Perfection of Wisdom teaching as expressed at the beginning of the *Heart Sūtra*: 'Here, O Śāriputra, form is emptiness and the very emptiness is form; emptiness does not differ from form, form does not differ from emptiness ...' Edward Conze (trans.), *Buddhist Wisdom Books*, Allen & Unwin, London 1958, p.81.

56 Skilful means (Sanskrit *upāya-kauśalya*), the most important of the four Perfections (*pāramitās*) practised by the Bodhisattva which are supplementary to the original six. See Note 81 below. The skilful means refers to the expedients he has recourse to in his efforts to help living beings.

The Dharma

57 i.e. *śūnyatā'* (Pali *suññatā*), usually translated 'empty' or 'emptiness'. The Enlightened mind is 'void' in the sense that it is void of unchanging substance or selfhood. The Mahāyāna teaching on *śūnyatā* is central and its profundity is expounded in the Perfection of Wisdom Sūtras (see Note 52 and Note 55 above). Baldly stated, the *śūnyatā* teaching emphasized that all *'dharmas'* (the basic 'irreducible' constituents of Reality according to the Hīnayāna) are 'empty', that is all phenomena whatsoever, both persons and things, are devoid of any enduring substance or independent selfhood; they arise in dependence on conditions and cannot be described as either truly existent or non-existent. Applied to the human personality, this becomes the doctrine of *anātman* or 'no-self' (see p.181).

See Sangharakshita: *A Survey of Buddhism* op. cit., pp.293ff. and 335ff; *The Three Jewels*, Windhorse, Glasgow 1991, Ch. 11; tape lecture no.47: 'The

Nature of Existence: Right Understanding', Dharmachakra, London 1968.

58 See Agehananda Bharati, *The Tantric Tradition*, Rider & Co, London 1965, Ch. 5 'On Mantra'.

59 For some examples of wrong views, see p.80.

60 I.B. Horner (trans.), *The Book of the Discipline* (Vinaya-Piṭaka), Vol. IV (*Mahā-vagga*), Pali Text Society, London 1982, 23, 3–5.

61 *Tathāgata* is one of the titles of the Buddha, perhaps even more common in all scriptures than the term 'Buddha'. It is understood variously as the 'Thus Gone One' (i.e. gone to nirvāṇa) or the 'Thus Come One' (i.e. come to the world in Compassion).

62 For more on the wish-fulfilling tree, see Alex Kennedy (Dharmachari Subhuti), *The Buddhist Vision*, Rider, London 1985, pp.131–2.

63 Edward Conze, *Thirty Years of Buddhist Studies, Selected Essays*, Bruno Cassirer Ltd, Oxford 1967, pp.185ff.

64 Edward Conze (trans.), *Buddhist Wisdom Books*, Allen & Unwin, London 1970.

65 See p.128.

66 The Eightfold Path is the fourth Noble Truth: the path which leads to the end of suffering, the eight stages or limbs being: Right View (or Vision), Right Resolve, Right Speech, Right Action, Right Livelihood, Right Effort, Right Mindfulness, Right Meditation. Sangharakshita favours the word 'perfect' instead of 'right' and translates the second stage as 'Perfect Emotion'.

See Sangharakshita, *Vision and Transformation: A Guide to the Buddha's Noble Eightfold Path*, Windhorse, Glasgow 1990.

67 See Note 3 above.

68 In the Roman Catholic Church, an indulgence is a remission of the temporal punishment for sin which the soul has to undergo in this life or in purgatory, even though the sin has been forgiven and absolved in the sacrament of Confession. There are both plenary and partial indulgences and the remission is usually earned by good works or the recital of certain prayers. In the famous theses which he nailed to the door of the church at Wittenberg in 1517, Martin Luther, the leader of the Protestant Reformation, attacked, amongst other things, the abuse of selling indulgences to obtain funds for church building and restoration work.

69 A reference to the four sessions of the Second Vatican Council, held in Rome from 1962 to 1965. The lecture from which this section is an edited extract was delivered in 1966. (The First Vatican Council started in 1869 and was discontinued in 1870 but never finally dissolved.)

70 The 'Five *Skandhas*' are the 'Five Aggregates' or 'Heaps' which constitute the individual human being and are represented by the later *nidāna 'nāma-rūpa'* (see p.83); all the elements of the psycho-physical organism belong to one or other of the *skandhas*. The five are *rūpa* (form), *vedanā* (feeling), *saṁjñā* (perception or recognition), *saṁskāras* (volitions) and *vijñāna* (consciousness).

For an interesting short account of the *skandhas*, see Alex Kennedy (Dharmachari Subhuti), *The Buddhist Vision*, Rider, London 1985, pp.97–100.

71 There are two English versions of the text: (a) *The Tibetan Book of the Dead or the After-Death Experiences on the Bardo Plane*, ed. W.Y. Evans-Wentz, Oxford University Press, London 1960; (b) Francesca Fremantle and Chögyam Trungpa (trans.), *The Tibetan Book of the Dead: The Great Liberation Through Hearing in the Bardo*, Shambhala, Boulder & London 1975.

72 This is explained on p.85.

73 See p.130.

74 See Martin Willson, *Rebirth and the Western Buddhist*, Wisdom, London 1986.

75 F.L. Woodward (trans.), *The Minor Anthologies of the Pali Canon, Part II: Udāna, Verses of Uplift and Itivuttaka, As It Was Said*, Pali Text Society, London 1985, X, pp.8–11.

76 It was the custom of the Buddha and his disciples, as it was of many other wanderers at the time, to obtain their food by begging on daily almsrounds in the towns and villages.

77 All twelve are explained in the following section.

78 See Sangharakshita, *A Survey of Buddhism* op. cit., pp.312ff; also *The Three Jewels*, Windhorse, Glasgow 1991, pp.111–112.

79 See p.103.

80 See Note 66 above.

81 For a list of the 'Six Perfections', see p.41. The remaining four, later added to the six to make up the 'Ten Perfections' are: Skilful Means (*upāya-kauśalya*), Vow (*praṇidhāna*), Power or Strength (*bala*), and Knowledge (*jñāna*).

See Sangharakshita, *A Survey of Buddhism* op. cit., pp.461–489.

82 See Note 3 above.

83 For a detailed explanation of the vitally important distinction between *samādhi* in the sense of concentration of mind in meditation and *samādhi* in the sense of establishment of the whole being in Enlightenment, see Sangharakshita, *Vision and Transformation*, Windhorse, Glasgow 1990, Ch.8.

84 i.e. Transcendental. In most contexts, Sangharakshita distinguishes clearly between the spiritual and the transcendental; in this instance, the term definitely denotes the transcendental.

85 See p.100.

86 See also pp.177ff.

87 For a brief discussion of this difficult term, see *A Survey of Buddhism*, op. cit., pp.278ff.

88 See Sangharakshita, *The Meaning of Conversion in Buddhism*, Windhorse, Birmingham 1994, pp.63–76.

89 F.L. Woodward (trans.), *Udāna: Verses of Uplift, The Minor Anthologies of the Pali Canon*, Part II, Oxford University Press, London 1948, V, v. p.67.

The Sangha

90 For a detailed treatment, see Sangharakshita, *The Three Jewels*, Windhorse, Glasgow 1991, Part III.

91 For more information, see Sangharakshita, *The Meaning of Conversion in Buddhism*, Windhorse, Birmingham 1994, pp.29–49.

92 Sangharakshita goes into the breaking of the first three Fetters in *The Taste of Freedom*, Windhorse, Glasgow 1990.

93 See the passage on rebirth, p.83.

94 In Memoriam, Part xcvi, stanza 3.

95 In the parable the Buddha speaks of the Dharma as the raft which ferries us across from this shore, the shore of saṁsāra, to the other shore, the shore of nirvāṇa. I.B. Horner (trans.), *The Middle Length Sayings (Majjhima-Nikāya)*, Pali Text Society, London 1967, Vol. I, pp.134–5.

96 The Pure abodes are 'a group of celestial sub-planes located at the summit of the world of pure form (q.v.). They are five in number'. *The Three Jewels*, op. cit., p.162.

97 See p.135.

The *rūpaloka*, 'world of pure form' and the *arūpaloka*, literally 'the formless world' are traditionally the two highest worlds of the 'threefold world system' or the mundane universe according to Buddhist cosmology, the third and lowest world being the *kāmaloka* or 'world of sense desire'. Each of the three worlds is divided into a number of levels or realms. The four levels of the *rūpaloka* correspond to the four *rūpa dhyānas* or levels of higher consciousness, and the four levels of the *arūpaloka* to the four *arūpa dhyānas*. (See p.166.)

The *rūpaloka* is also known as the world of archetypal form, a world which is experienced at a subtle level beyond that of sense experience, perceived more directly through the mind, and containing subtle forms which are imbued with clarity and radiance, which embody emotionally and even spiritually significant qualities. In the experience of the *arūpaloka*, the consciousness is of such a high degree of refinement that the objective pole of the experience is correspondingly refined and subtilized. Both the *rūpa-* and *arūpalokas* are experienced as the result of skilful actions, but the experience of both is temporary and mundane, in the sense that Insight, the goal of the path, is still to be achieved.

98 As the first step on his search for the truth, the Buddha himself adopted the life of the homeless wanderer, known as *parivrājaka* (Pali *paribbājaka*), literally 'one who has gone forth', i.e. from life at home. The Buddha and his disciples were one of many such groups of wanderers in north-east India at that time.

See *The Three Jewels*, op. cit., pp.205–6.

99 For a discussion of the term *'prātimokṣa'* (literally, according to some scholars, 'binding', 'obligatory', 'obligation') see Sangharakshita, *The Ten Pillars of Buddhism*, Windhorse, Birmingham 1996, pp.40ff.

100 For a detailed study of the importance of Going for Refuge, see Sangharakshita, *The History of My Going For Refuge*, Windhorse, Glasgow 1988; also an earlier pamphlet, *Going for Refuge*, Windhorse, Glasgow 1986.

101 One of the first books to draw the attention of the English speaking world to Buddhism was Sir Edwin Arnold's *The Light of Asia* published in 1879. The scholar Max Muller helped introduce Buddhist scriptures to the West and in 1881 co-founded the Pali Text Society.

102 The application of the basic ethical principles of Buddhism to the whole area of 'gainful employment' or working for a living is known as Right Livelihood. The essential principle underlying this is that such livelihood, in order to be ethical, must be non-violent, non-exploitative, and, as far as possible, related to the spiritual goal.

For a detailed discussion of the subject, see Sangharakshita, *Vision and Transformation*, Windhorse, Glasgow 1990, Ch.5.

103 For the explanation of these terms, see pp.128ff. The sixth stage or limb of the Eightfold Path consists in preventing and eradicating the unskilful and cultivating and maintaining the skilful.

See Sangharakshita, *Vision and Transformation*, Windhorse, Glasgow 1990, Ch.6.

104 In Buddhism, there is no personal creator God; it is a non-theistic religion.

105 The relationship between guru and disciple is explored in Sangharakshita's tape lecture no.90: 'Is a Guru Necessary?', Dharmachakra, London 1970.

106 Vinaya, Mahāvagga, VIII. 26, F.L. Woodward (trans.), *Some Sayings of the Buddha*, Buddhist Society, London, 1973, p.84.

107 In his *Metaphysics of Morals*, Kant states: '... so act as to treat humanity, whether in thine own person or in that of another, in every case as an end, never only as a means.' Quoted in Will Durant's *Outlines of Philosophy: Plato to Russell*, Ernest Benn Ltd, London 1962, p.245.

108 The kalyana mitra is, literally, the 'good, even beautiful, friend', usually rendered as 'spiritual friend'. Traditionally a kalyana mitra is a spiritual teacher with whom one has a close personal relationship. The Bodhisattva is the kalyana mitra *par excellence*. This friendship is 'vertical' in that it is between people of different degrees of spiritual development. Buddhism also recognizes the importance of 'horizontal' friendship between spiritual peers and within the FWBO the term 'kalyana mitrata' can refer to spiritual friendship in both the horizontal and vertical senses. Within the FWBO spiritual friendship, of either type, is seen as of vital importance. Friendship is integral to the spiritual life.

109 Vinaya, Mahāvagga, VIII. 26, F. L. Woodward (trans.), *Some Sayings of the Buddha*, Buddhist Society, London, 1973, p.85.

110 Sangharakshita uses the term 'group' to denote the ways in which we identify ourselves on the basis of economic, social, political, psychological, sexual, family, and other conditionings.

111 See Note 98 above.

112 For a definition of 'unskilful', see p.128.

Introduction to Part 2

113 This talk is published in full in Sangharakshita, *The Taste of Freedom*, Windhorse, Glasgow 1990.

114 'T'ien-t'ai' (Japanese 'Tendai') means literally 'great heaven' and is the name of the mountain in south China where the master Chih-i (531–597 CE) lived and taught and established a centre which became the sort of headquarters of the whole movement. He was mainly known as a lecturer. The T'ien-t'ai was many-sided, an almost encyclopaedic movement; its work, especially under the influence of Chih-i, was an attempt to systematize the whole Buddhist tradition as known at that time in China. It was an eclectic school, with no sectarian emphasis. In a seminar (unpublished) which he conducted on the text *Dhyāna For Beginners* (see Note 115 below), a collection of Chih-i's lectures, Sangharakshita draws a parallel between the T'ien-t'ai and the FWBO, with respect to the eclectic approach of the two movements.

For more on the T'ien-t'ai, see Sir Charles Eliot's *Buddhism and Hinduism: An Historical Sketch*, Routledge & Kegan Paul, London 1954, Vol. III, pp.310ff; also Junjiro Takakusu, *The Essentials of Buddhist Philosophy*, Motilal Banarsidass, India 1978, Ch.IX.

115 Mentioned at the beginning of the preface to '*Dhyāna For Beginners*', in *A Buddhist Bible*, ed. Dwight Goddard, Beacon Press, Boston 1966, p.437.

116 *The Table Talk and Omniana of Samuel Taylor Coleridge*, ed. T. Ashe, George Bell & Sons, London 1905.

117 See Goethe's *Criticisms, Reflections, and Maxims*, trans. W. B. Rönnfeldt, The Scott Library, London 1982.

118 See Sangharakshita, *A Survey of Buddhism* op. cit., pp.163ff.

119 See Sangharakshita, 'Aspects of Buddhist Morality', in *The Priceless Jewel*, Windhorse, Glasgow 1993

120 See Sangharakshita, *Vision and Transformation*, Windhorse, Glasgow 1990, Ch. 8. Also Sangharakshita, *Human Enlightenment*, Windhorse, Glasgow 1987, pp.36ff.

121 Wisdom is the last in the list of the Six Perfections which the Bodhisattva practises; yet it is the first of the Perfections in the sense that the other five are truly Perfections only by virtue of the development of the Perfection of Wisdom, *prajñā pāramitā* (literally 'the Wisdom which has gone beyond'). *Prajñā* is from the Sanskrit root 'to know'. *Prajñā* is knowledge *par excellence*, knowledge of Reality. The word for Reality here is *'śūnyatā'*.

122 The *sahasrāra-padma*, the thousand-petalled lotus, is the highest of the seven psychic centres and is situated above the crown of the head. Buddhism is concerned mainly with the three higher psychic centres in relation to spiritual practice. The implication here is that the thousand-petalled lotus only comes into bloom with the development of Insight. (See Note 40 above.)

For more about the psychic centres and their relation to practice, see Lama Anagarika Govinda, *The Foundations of Tibetan Mysticism*, Century, London 1987, pp.143ff.

Morality

123 Exodus, chapters 19, 20, 33, 34.

124 Genesis, 2, xvii.

125 Genesis, 3.

126 Though it does have more specific meanings, *'agape'* is the word used in the Greek New Testament to denote man's love for his neighbour, translated in the Authorized Version as 'charity'. *'Eros'* of course denotes erotic love.

127 This is an unpublished translation by Sangharakshita. Another version of this verse is 'As a bee taking honey from flowers, without hurt to bloom or scent, so let the sage seek his food from house to house'. W.D.C. Wagiswara & K.J. Saunders (trans.), *The Dhammapada*, John Murray, London 1920, section 4, verse 6.

128 A chart of the three worlds with all the different levels and classes of being can be found in Randy Kloetzli's *Buddhist Cosmology*, Motilal Banarsidass, Delhi 1983.

129 See p.101

130 J.R.R. Tolkien, *The Lord of the Rings*, George Allen & Unwin, London 1969.

131 Sangharakshita (trans.), *The Dhammapada*, section 8, verse 1, (unpublished).

132 See also Sangharakshita, *Vision and Transformation*, Windhorse, Glasgow 1990, Ch.3.

133 *The Dhammapada*, op. cit.

134 German-born Buddhist teacher and writer, Lama Anagarika Govinda (1899–1985) was the author of *The Way of the White Clouds* and *Foundations of Tibetan Mysticism* and the founder of the Buddhist movement, Arya Maitreya Mandala.

135 See pp.155ff; also Sangharakshita, *A Survey of Buddhism* op. cit., pp.173ff; and Sangharakshita, *Vision and Transformation*, Windhorse, Glasgow 1990, Ch.7.

Meditation

136 Meditation, Systematic and Practical C.M. Chen, published privately, 1980, p.121.

137 See pp.88ff.

138 The five progressive *śūnyatā* meditations are as follows: (a) meditating on *śūnyatā* as the absence of real selfhood; (b) meditating on conditioned *dharmas* as being devoid of the characteristics of the Unconditioned; (c) Meditating on the Unconditioned as being empty of the characteristics of the conditioned; (d) meditating on the emptiness of all discriminations, especially that between 'conditioned' and 'Unconditioned'; (e) meditating on the emptiness of Emptiness. The Hīnayāna schools restricted themselves to the first three, while the Mahāyāna used all five. The most highly developed practitioners of the Vajrayāna made special efforts to realize the fifth level within a single lifetime.

139 For more on *śamathā* and *vipaśyanā*, see '*Dhyana For Beginners*' in *A Buddhist Bible*, op. cit., in which the terms are translated as 'Stopping' and 'Realizing'.

140 '*Dāka*' (masculine form) and '*ḍākinī*' (feminine form) are derived from a Sanskrit root meaning 'direction', 'space', 'sky'. The *ḍākas* and *ḍākinīs* are 'sky-walkers' or 'walkers in space'. Empty space represents absence of obstruction, freedom of movement. The *ḍākas* and *ḍākinīs* enjoy such freedom. Sky represents mind in its Absolute sense: so the *ḍākas* and *ḍākinīs* represent that which moves about freely in the mind: the energies of the mind itself. In this sense they represent powerful energies rising up from the depths of the mind. There are many forms of *ḍākas* and *ḍākinīs* (especially the latter) depicted in the iconography of the Vajrayāna.

'*Dharmapāla*' means literally 'guardian or protector of the Dharma'. In Tibetan scroll paintings of mandalas, figures of *dharmapālas*, invariably depicted huge in stature and of wrathful aspect, guard the gates of the sacred circle at the cardinal points and prevent the invasion of hostile energies. Performing the same function, gigantic *dharmapāla* figures can also be found in temple precincts just outside the entrance.

141 See Note 71 above.

142 See pp.117ff.

143 From 'Burnt Norton', the first section of T.S. Eliot's *The Four Quartets*, *Collected Poems*, Faber & Faber, London 1963.

144 Rabindranath Tagore (trans.), *Gitanjali (Song Offerings)*, MacMillan Paperback, London 1986, no.95, p.87.

145 Wilhelm Reich (1897–1957), a Viennese psychologist who, in treating patients, concentrated on their overall character structure rather than on individual symptoms. Works include T. Wolfe (trans.), *The Function of the Orgasm* (1927), Noonday, New York 1961, pp.114ff; and Theodore P. Wolfe (trans.), *Character Analysis* (1945), Vision, 1958, in which he expounded his theory that patients build up what he calls 'character armour' as a defence against discovering their own underlying neuroses.

146 The story is told in Geshe Wangyal's *The Door of Liberation*, Lotsawa, California 1978.

147 Part of the story referred to above.

148 Edmund Burke has a saying to this effect, but it could be that he borrowed it from Montaigne, who said: 'In the midst of compassion, we feel within us a kind of bitter-sweet pricking of malicious delight in the misfortunes of others.' (*Essays*, Book 3, Ch.1).

149 Marion L. Matics, *Entering the Path of Enlightenment*, Allen & Unwin, London 1970, p.67.

150 T.W. and C.A.F. Rhys Davids (trans.), *Dialogues of the Buddha* (*Dīgha-Nikāya*), (series: 'Sacred Books of the Buddhists') Pali Text Society, London 1971, II,82.

151 For information on the significance of the stupa in Buddhism, see Sangharakshita, *The Drama of Cosmic Enlightenment*, Windhorse, Glasgow 1993, pp.143–167.

152 See Note 25 above.

Wisdom

153 *'Tathatā'*, literally, 'Suchness'.

154 I.B. Horner (trans.), *The Middle Length Sayings* (*Majjhima-Nikāya*), Pali Text Society, London 1967, Vol. I, sutta no.26.

155 See F.L. Woodward (trans.), *The Book of the Kindred Sayings* (*Saṁyutta-Nikāya*), Pali Text Society, London 1930, Part V, pp.421–3.

156 In *Metamorphoses* (book 5), Ovid says the sirens had feathers and feet of birds but human features. They lived on an island near Scylla and Charybdis; their beautiful song lured sailors to the jagged shores of their island and to certain death. There is a famous sirens episode in Homer's *Odyssey* (book 12).

157 Edward Conze, *Buddhism: Its Essence and Development*, Harper & Row, New York 1959, pp.46–8.

158 See also Note 34 above.

159 For more on the Bodhisattva Ideal and the Bodhicitta, see Sangharakshita, *A Survey of Buddhism* op. cit., pp.431ff.

160 passim, in his translation of sGamp.po.pa's *The Jewel Ornament of Liberation*, Shambhala, Boston & London 1971.

161 A metrical text, entitled *Bodhicitta-varaṇa*, verse 2. See *Master of Wisdom, Writings of the Buddhist Master Nāgārjuna*, Dharma Publishing, 1986, p.33.

162 Edward Conze (trans.), *Buddhist Wisdom Books*, Allen & Unwin, London 1958, pp.77–8.

163 *Majjhima-nikāya*, Sutta no.86; the story is reproduced in Bhikkhu Ñāṇamoli's *The Life of the Buddha*, Buddhist Publication Society, Ceylon 1978, pp.134ff.

164 This is an incident in the *'Ariya-pariyesana-sutta'*, I.B. Horner (trans.), *The Middle Length Sayings* (*Majjhima-Nikāya*), Pali Text Society, London 1967, Vol. I, 170–1, p.214.

165 *The Dhammapada*, section *Buddhavagga*, 'The Enlightened One', verse 179.

166 E.M. Hare (trans.), *Woven Cadences of the Early Buddhists*, Oxford University Press, London 1947, Ch. 5, 'The Way to the Beyond', stanza 1076.

167 Ibid., Ch. 1, 'The Chapter of the Snake', stanza 176.

168 *Mahā-parinibbāṇā Suttanta*, T. W. Rhys Davids (trans.), *Dialogues of the Buddha (Digha-Nikāya)*, Pali Text Society, London 1977 (*Sacred Books of the Buddhists*), Part II, 82.

169 The Ten Powers are enumerated in the *Mahā-sīhanāda-sutta* of the *Majjhima-Nikāya*. See Sangharakshita, *A Survey of Buddhism* op. cit., p.78.

170 F.L. Woodward (trans.), *The Books of the Kindred Sayings* (*Saṁyutta-Nikāya*), Pali Text Society, 1925, Vol. III, 120, p.103. Also quoted in F.L. Woodward (trans.), *Some Sayings of the Buddha*, The Buddhist Society, Oxford University Press, London 1973, pp.85–6.

171 Edward Conze (trans.), *Buddhist Wisdom Books*, Allen & Unwin, London 1958, p.63.

172 *The Dhammapada*, section on 'Happiness' (*Sukhavagga*), verse 204.

173 F.L. Woodward (trans.), *Some Sayings of the Buddha*, The Buddhist Society, Oxford University Press,

London 1974, pp.44–5.

174 The Buddha refers to his aged body as a worn-out cart in the *Mahā-parinibbāṇā Suttanta, Dīgha-Nikāya*, ii, 99; quoted in *Some Sayings of the Buddha*, op. cit., p.227.

Index

Page numbers in **bold** indicate primary entries, those in *italics* refer to illustrations. Entries under Buddha, Dharma, Sangha, morality, meditation, and wisdom deal primarily with material found *outside* the sections dedicated to those subjects. Terms in italics are Sanskrit unless otherwise stated.

T

Y

Z

The Windhorse symbolizes the energy of the enlightened mind carrying the Three Jewels – the Buddha, the Dharma, and the Sangha – to all sentient beings.

Buddhism is one of the fastest growing spiritual traditions in the Western world. Throughout its 2,500-year history, it has always succeeded in adapting its mode of expression to suit whatever culture it has encountered.

Windhorse Publications aims to continue this tradition as Buddhism comes to the West. Today's Westerners are heirs to the entire Buddhist tradition, free to draw instruction and inspiration from all the many schools and branches. Windhorse publishes works by authors who not only understand the Buddhist tradition but are also familiar with Western culture and the Western mind.

For orders and catalogues contact:

WINDHORSE PUBLICATIONS
UNIT 1-316
THE CUSTARD FACTORY
GIBB STREET
BIRMINGHAM
B9 4AA UK

WINDHORSE PUBLICATIONS INC
14 HEARTWOOD CIRCLE
NEWMARKET
NEW HAMPSHIRE
NH 03857
USA

Windhorse Publications is an arm of the Friends of the Western Buddhist Order, which has more than sixty centres on four continents. Through these centres, members of the Western Buddhist Order offer regular programmes of events for the general public and for more experienced students. These include meditation classes, public talks, study on Buddhist themes and texts, and 'bodywork' classes such as t'ai chi, yoga, and massage. The FWBO also runs several retreat centres and the Karuna Trust, a fundraising charity that supports social welfare projects in the slums and villages of India.

Many FWBO centres have residential spiritual communities and ethical businesses associated with them. Arts activities are encouraged too, as is the development of strong bonds of friendship between people who share the same ideals. In this way the FWBO is developing a unique approach to Buddhism, not simply as a set of techniques, less still as an exotic cultural interest, but as a creatively directed way of life for people living in the modern world.

If you would like more information about the FWBO please write to:

LONDON BUDDHIST CENTRE
51 ROMAN ROAD
LONDON
E2 0HU
UK

ARYALOKA
HEARTWOOD CIRCLE
NEWMARKET
NEW HAMPSHIRE
NH 03857 USA

Also from Windhorse

SANGHARAKSHITA

A SURVEY OF BUDDHISM: ITS DOCTRINES AND METHODS THROUGH THE AGES

Now in its seventh edition, *A Survey of Buddhism* continues to provide an indispensable study of the entire field of Buddhist thought and practice. Covering all the major doctrines and traditions, both in relation to Buddhism as a whole and to the spiritual life of the individual Buddhist, Sangharakshita places their development in historical context. This is an objective but sympathetic appraisal of Buddhism's many forms that clearly demonstrates the underlying unity of all its schools.

'It would be difficult to find a single book in which the history and development of Buddhist thought has been described as vividly and clearly as in this survey.... For all those who wish to "know the heart, the essence of Buddhism as an integrated whole", there can be no better guide than this book.' *Lama Anagarika Govinda*

'I recommend Sangharakshita's book as the best survey of Buddhism.' *Dr Edward Conze*

544 pages
ISBN 0 904766 65 9
£12.99, $24.95

ANDREW SKILTON

A CONCISE HISTORY OF BUDDHISM

How and when did the many schools and sub-sects of Buddhism emerge? How do the ardent devotion of the Pure Land schools, the magical ritual of the Tantra, or the paradoxical negations of the Perfection of Wisdom literature, relate to the direct, down to earth teachings of Gautama the 'historical' Buddha? Did Buddhism modify the cultures to which it was introduced, or did they modify Buddhism?

Here is a narrative that describes and correlates the diverse manifestations of Buddhism – in its homeland of India, and in its spread across Asia, from Mongolia to Sri Lanka, from Japan to the Middle East. Drawing on the latest historical and literary research, Andrew Skilton explains the basic concepts of Buddhism from all periods of its development, and places them in a historical framework.

272 pages, with maps and extensive bibliography
ISBN 0 904766 66 7
£9.99/$19.95

SANGHARAKSHITA

THE THREE JEWELS: AN INTRODUCTION TO BUDDHISM

The Three Jewels are living symbols, supreme objects of commitment and devotion in the life of every Buddhist.

To understand the Three Jewels – the Buddha, the Dharma (the Path), and the Sangha (the spiritual community) – is to understand the central ideals and principles of Buddhism. To have some insight into them is to touch its very heart.

Although subtitled 'An Introduction to Buddhism', the depth of scholarship of this concise account means that it will be of interest to those who already have some knowledge of Buddhism but would like a clearer overview of the tradition, as well as to the newcomer seeking a thorough introduction.

290 pages
ISBN 0 904766 49 7
£8.95/$18.00

VESSANTARA

MEETING THE BUDDHAS: A GUIDE TO BUDDHAS, BODHISATTVAS, AND TANTRIC DEITIES

Sitting poised and serene upon fragrant lotus blooms, they offer smiles of infinite tenderness, immeasurable wisdom. Bellowing formidable roars of angry triumph from the heart of blazing infernos, they dance on the naked corpses of their enemies.

Who are these beings – the Buddhas, Bodhisattvas, and Protectors, the 'angry demons' and 'benign deities' – of the Buddhist Tantric tradition? Are they products of an alien, even disturbed, imagination? Or are they, perhaps, real? What have they got to do with Buddhism? And what have they got to do with us?

In this vivid informed account, an experienced Western Buddhist guides us into the heart of this magical realm and introduces us to the miraculous beings who dwell there.

368 pages, with text illustrations and colour plates
ISBN 0 904766 53 5
£13.99/$24.00